Tunisian Civil Society

Investigating the political transition after the 2011 Tunisian revolution, this book explores whether civil society is fulfilling its democratic functions. Examining the existence of a civil political culture, that is identified through the presence of the six criteria of Freedom, Equality, Pluralism, Tolerance, Trust, and Transparency.

The innovation of the volume lies in its critiques of the "transitology" literature, its illustration of the drawbacks of culturalist and Orientalist narratives of Arab politics, and the complexity it notes with respect to civil society and its varied roles, especially that civil society is not always an unconditionally "good" or democratic force. Using a combination of survey, interview, and observation research approaches, these chapters engage with the development of democratic political culture and democratic knowledge in civil society organisations (CSOs) by understanding how CSOs interact with the state, other CSOs, and their members.

Presenting both critical theoretical arguments and extensive empirical evidence to demonstrate why Tunisia is such an important case, this book will be of interest to students and researchers interested in political culture, civil society, and Middle East and North African studies.

Alexander P. Martin is a lecturer in International Relations and Politics at the University of Lincoln and a Visiting Research Fellow at Durham University. He previously worked for the University of Tunis, the American University of Beirut, and the University of Exeter. He holds a PhD in Politics from Durham University.

Routledge Studies in Middle Eastern Democratization and Government

Edited by: Larbi Sadiki, *Qatar University*

This series examines new ways of understanding democratization and government in the Middle East. The varied and uneven processes of change, occurring in the Middle Eastern region, can no longer be read and interpreted solely through the prism of Euro-American transitology. Seeking to frame critical parameters in light of these new horizons, this series instigates reinterpretations of democracy and propagates formerly 'subaltern,' narratives of democratization. Reinvigorating discussion on how Arab and Middle Eastern peoples and societies seek good government, *Routledge Studies in Middle Eastern Democratization and Government* provides tests and contests of old and new assumptions.

22 **Clientelism and Patronage in the Middle East and North Africa**
   Networks of Dependency
   Edited by Laura Ruiz de Elvira, Christoph H. Schwarz and Irene Weipert-Fenner

23 **Hamas and Palestine**
   The Contested Road to Statehood
   Martin Kear

24 **The Palestinian Authority in the West Bank**
   The Theatrics of Woeful Statecraft
   Michelle Pace and Somdeep Sen

25 **The Failure of Democracy in Iraq**
   Religion, Ideology and Sectarianism
   Hamid Alkifaey

26 **Tunisian Civil Society**
   Political Culture and Democratic Function Since 2011
   Alexander P. Martin

For more information about this series, please visit: www.routledge.com/middleeaststudies/series/RSMEDG

Tunisian Civil Society
Political Culture and Democratic Function Since 2011

Alexander P. Martin

LONDON AND NEW YORK

First published 2020
by Routledge
2 Park Square, Milton Park, Abingdon, Oxon OX14 4RN

and by Routledge
52 Vanderbilt Avenue, New York, NY 10017

Routledge is an imprint of the Taylor & Francis Group, an informa business

© 2020 Alexander P. Martin

The right of Alexander P. Martin to be identified as author of this work has been asserted by him in accordance with sections 77 and 78 of the Copyright, Designs and Patents Act 1988.

All rights reserved. No part of this book may be reprinted or reproduced or utilised in any form or by any electronic, mechanical, or other means, now known or hereafter invented, including photocopying and recording, or in any information storage or retrieval system, without permission in writing from the publishers.

Trademark notice: Product or corporate names may be trademarks or registered trademarks, and are used only for identification and explanation without intent to infringe.

British Library Cataloguing-in-Publication Data
A catalogue record for this book is available from the British Library

Library of Congress Cataloging-in-Publication Data
A catalog record for this book has been requested

ISBN: 978-0-367-14915-4 (hbk)
ISBN: 978-0-429-05390-0 (ebk)

Typeset in Times New Roman
by Wearset Ltd, Boldon, Tyne and Wear

For Hanèn, *enti hayati*

Contents

List of illustrations		viii
List of abbreviations		ix
	Introduction	1
1	'Civil' civil society: the buttress of democratisation	7
2	Tunisia's history of civil society activism: 1574–2010	28
3	Civil society activism from revolution to transition	48
4	Surveying Tunisian CSO members' attitudes	77
5	Interviews with CSO leaders	93
6	Inside a CSO: an ethnographic study	120
	Conclusion	140
	Epilogue	148
	Appendix	152
	Bibliography	173
	Index	187

Illustrations

Map

1	Political map of Tunisia	6

Figures

1.1	The theoretical background of the research design	26
4.1	Survey results index scores	81

Tables

4.1	Survey results summary table	79
4.2	Population percentage by region	80
4.3	Survey results by pooled region	81
4.4	T-test results: 'Gender vs Tolerance Index'	83
4.5	Survey question 30: results table	85
4.6	ANOVA test result: 'Region vs Trust Index'	86
A.1.1	Attitude survey results	152
A.1.2	Completed interviews	167
A.1.3	Additional data verification interviews	172

Abbreviations

ATFD	Tunisian Association of Democratic Women
CPC	Civil political culture
CSO	Civil society organisation
JID	Young Tunisian Democrats
LTDH	Tunisian League for Human Rights
LPR	Leagues for the Protection of the Revolution
MENA	Middle East and North Africa
MEPI	U.S.–Middle East Partnership Initiative
NCA	National Constituent Assembly
NDP	Neo-Destour Party
NGOs	Non-governmental organisations
ONAT	Tunisian Lawyers Association
RCD	Constitutional Democratic Rally
UGTT	General Union of Tunisian Workers
UTICA	Tunisian Confederation of Industry, Trade and Handicrafts

Introduction

The 2011 Tunisian revolution of "Freedom and Dignity", the first in the wave of Arab uprisings across the Middle East and North Africa (MENA) region, was unexpected given the apparent political stability and economic prosperity of Zine El-Abidine Ben Ali's dictatorship. The revolution brought an end to 24 years of corrupt leadership by Ben Ali, his mafia-like family, and the majority of the ruling elite who were removed from their positions of power and privilege. Despite halted economic progress, rising unemployment rates, political assassinations, and episodes of political deadlock in the years since 2011, democratisation progress in this small North African state has been hailed as a success in its path towards removing authoritarian, one-party state governance. The political transition has brought Tunisia closer to becoming a democratic country than the other Arab states that experienced uprisings: Egypt, Libya, Syria, Bahrain, and Yemen. Although comparisons between these Arab Uprising states can be made, they are, however, limiting because each country has experienced different aftermaths to their revolutions. Furthermore, in addition to the specific dynamics of each country, each had undergone different colonial and post-independence experiences before the uprisings. Furthermore, simply labelling Tunisia as a success ignores the pressing need for further political reforms and the continuity of authoritarian structures, power relations, and practices.

This book focuses on understanding the factors that are unique to Tunisian civil society and Tunisian political culture and how they have influenced Tunisia's post-revolutionary transition. This book uses an understanding of civil society as playing a democratising function through Oppositional-Resistance and Liberal-Associative roles, both of which rely on the existence of a civil political culture (CPC).

Research questions and aims

This book addresses the gaps in the current literature regarding the contribution of CPC in enabling civil society organisations (CSOs) to positively influence the political transition from authoritarianism to democratic governance. Therefore, this book asks "Have Tunisian civil society organisations exhibited a civil political culture, and how has this influenced their ability to fulfil a democratic

2 *Introduction*

function through the post-2011 transition?" Three sub-questions that emerged from the primary research question are:

1   Has civil society in Tunisia exhibited political civility through the democratic transition?
2   How has political civility in CSOs supported the democratic transition?
3   How does this inform the theoretical understanding of civil society's position in democratic transition?

The historical chapters provide the structural factors which determine the context in which civil society operates. Civil society under authoritarianism was shaped by the lack of space provided by the state, while the post-authoritarian era demonstrates that civil society filled the opened public space. The fieldwork research chapters examine the discourses and practices of the Tunisian CSOs which occupy the public space and searches for evidence of the elements of CPC.

Argument summary

This book demonstrates that in a post-authoritarian context, Tunisian civil society has performed a democratising function, and checked state authority but has also been allowed to flourish through the state's provision of an enabling legal framework that protects freedom of association. This research project provides evidence that CPC, the political culture required for democratic consolidation, is emerging amongst CSOs in Tunisia.

Why civil society and political culture?

The assumption that civil society is synonymous with democracy and a pro-democratic vehicle is partly derived from the third wave of democratisation where anti-government movements, driven principally by civil society, facilitated political transformations from dictatorial to democratic systems. This assumption is reinforced by the hypothesis that a diverse and vibrant civil society encourages democratic practice and political participation. However, it should not be assumed that a civil society inherently supports democracy learning or embeds a political culture that supports democracy. Political transitions can fail or become derailed leaving states with features of both dictatorial and democratic governance. Civil society can only play an effective democratising role, which has been attributed to it, if its actors and organisations adopt and practise CPC.

CSOs are formed for different reasons but their existence is often linked to the belief that the state is in some way insufficient and requires organised citizenry to draw attention to, address, or confront an issue (Lewis and Wallace, 2000). Therefore, they often seek to inform and influence public policy or exert influence on political decisions. Their work is often related to a particular domain whereby a common interest is pursued. However, CSOs represent different ideologies and vary in their focus which often leads to a lack of homogeneity within any civil society.

CSOs may be non-state, non-economic, non-commercial, and non-governmental entities but since they are actors with the capacity to influence the political transition, their practices and discourses should also be analysed and critiqued. CSOs' actions could be detrimental to democratic transition and therefore should not be exempt from criticism.

Tunisia is a state with a tradition of anti-authoritarian civil society activism and civil society actors indeed played an important role in fighting against a dictatorial state during the revolution and transition. However, the role civil society actors need to play in building post-revolutionary democratic governance and supporting a democratic state require CSOs to both operate with and assist the development of a political culture that supports democracy and CPC.

Methodology

This book aims to understand CSO political culture from three different directions to gain a multi-layered understanding of the complexities of the political culture of a civil society in a political transition from authoritarianism to an emerging democracy. Therefore, it aims to address the research question by seeking to understand the internal operation of CSOs through observing behaviour, CSOs' relationships with other CSOs and the state, and attitudes and values of CSO members.

This book applies Stephen Welch's (2013) theory of political culture, which recognises that political culture manifests as both discourse and practice. To understand civil society's discourse and practice, Welch's theory is developed into a methodology of three research methods, drawn from both positivist and interpretivist approaches of social science research. The role of civil society in the Tunisian transition is assessed in relation to its counterpart – the state. A triangulation of methods – a quantitative attitude survey, structured interviews, and ethnographic participant-observation – examines inter-CSO relations, how CSOs interact with the state, and the internal CSO dynamics, in addition to CSO institutional culture. This approach enables the assessment of the discourse and practice of CSO members' political culture. Furthermore, the methodological advances in this study offer insight into further political culture research.

This book demonstrates that political culture research can be conducted in the MENA region, without committing orientalism, if the enquiry focuses on both discourses and practices and if the research is conducted/performed with methodological rigour.

Book contribution

As an application of civil society theory to a post-authoritarian MENA context, this book also contributes to empirical studies of MENA CSOs. The Tunisian transition towards democracy demonstrates that civil society in Tunisia had previously been shaped by the authoritarian regime. This book diverges from the culturalist argument that MENA civil society is shaped by Middle Eastern or Arab culture, or the consequent assumption that this renders MENA civil society undemocratic. In doing so, it argues that civil society can significantly contribute to democratic consolidation if CSOs are provided with sufficient public space and if their practices and discourse exhibit a CPC. This book also argues that prerequisites of democracy existed in Tunisia and that the country's progress towards democracy is partly due to its history of constitutionalism, political institutionalism, and civil society activism. This has meant Tunisia's pre-existing culture of consensus and political moderacy has aided the transition.

Book structure

Chapter 1 establishes that the concept of civil society has evolved to hold a pro-democracy meaning, therefore it can influence democratic transition on the condition that a political culture of civility is exhibited. MENA civil society is not inherently different, but it has been described differently from Western civil society because it emerged in the contexts of colonialism and authoritarianism. Therefore, MENA civil society has not been able to influence democratic transition because it existed under authoritarianism and was heavily restricted. It also identifies the six criteria of CPC (Freedom, Equality, Pluralism, Tolerance, Trust, and Transparency), as derived from civil society, democratisation, and political culture literature. They respectively define the methodology and methods required to study Tunisian CSOs and to assess the extent to which their political culture is civil. This methodology was developed through the application of Welch's theory of political culture, MENA literature on the use of political culture, and a critical assessment of other studies in political culture. This chapter posits the hypothesis that, if Tunisian CSOs demonstrate civility, then they can perform their democratic functions of maintaining freedom and equality which prevent despotism.

Chapters 2 and 3 offer a historical overview of Tunisian political history with a focus on the function of civil society. Chapter 2 uses literature on Tunisian history which demonstrates that Tunisian civil society was limited and restrained under colonialism and authoritarianism. Chapter 3 uses news reports, press releases, international non-governmental organisation reports, and academic work published since 2011, to emphasise the vital role that civil society has played in Tunisia's transition and that Tunisia is no longer under authoritarian conditions. Chapters 2 and 3 provide historical and contextual background to the research period and illustrate the relationships between the Tunisian state and civil society.

Chapters 4, 5, and 6 each present the results of the data collected from the three methods: an online attitude survey, structured interviews, and ethnographic participant-observation respectively. These results are based on ten months of fieldwork research, conducted by the researcher while living in Tunisia (2013–2014). They represent the methodological contribution of the thesis; that a multi-layered, micro-interpretivist approach is optimal to researching a political culture. Through analysis of CSOs' relationships with the state, other CSOs and their own members, these three chapters present evidence that the six criteria of CPC are interconnected and are developing at different rates in Tunisian CSOs.

All interviewees agreed to be quoted directly for Alexander P. Martin's PhD thesis, titled *Have Tunisian civil society organisations exhibited the civil political culture required to fulfil a democratic function through the post-2011 transition?* submitted to Durham University in 2016, on which this publication is based.

6 *Introduction*

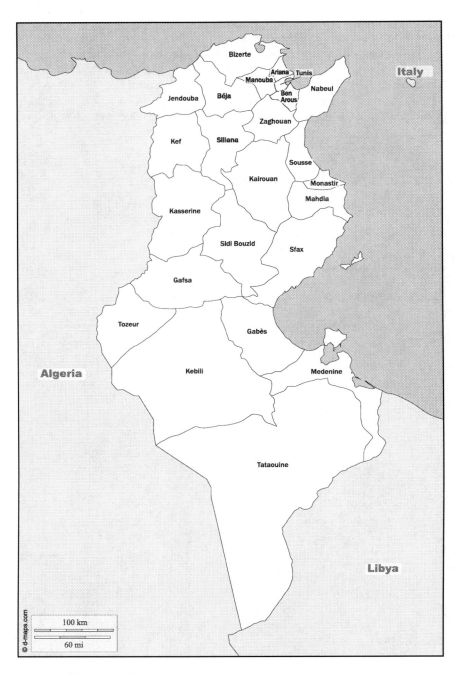

Map 1 Political map of Tunisia

1 'Civil' civil society
The buttress of democratisation

Introduction

The 2011 Tunisian revolution of "Freedom and Dignity", the first in the wave of uprisings commonly known as the Arab Spring across the Middle East and North Africa (MENA) region, was unexpected given the apparent political stability and economic prosperity of Zine El-Abidine Ben Ali's dictatorship. The revolution brought an end to 24 years of corrupt leadership by Ben Ali, his mafia-like family, and the majority of the ruling elite who were removed from their positions of power and privilege. The political transition has brought Tunisia closer to becoming a democratic country than the other Arab states that experienced uprisings: Egypt, Libya, Syria, Bahrain, and Yemen. Although comparisons between these Arab Uprising states can be made, they are, however, limiting because each country has experienced different aftermaths to their revolutions.

Studies of politics and political culture in a MENA context have been inhibited by the presence of authoritarian governments which restricted the possibility of applying, on-the-ground, micro-interpretivist research methods. Prior to the Arab Uprisings, the study of civil society in MENA was conducted in the context of authoritarian governments and dictatorial regimes, where only Israel and Lebanon could be considered exceptions. Within this context, Tunisia's transition away from authoritarian government provides the unique opportunity of advancing a revised approach to the study of political culture. This is accomplished in this book through the triangulation of research methods to implement Welch's theory of political culture (2013) while including direct observation of discourse and practice in the examination and assessment of Tunisian civil society's political culture.

Through its establishment of six essential criteria for civil political culture (CPC), this book examines the civility of Tunisia's civil society and reveals the vital role played by civil society throughout a democratic transition. Through an exploration of Tunisian civil society's traits and evolution, which began prior to colonialism, survived through French occupation, and then became a vital part of nationalist struggle, this book provides insight into the structures that contributed to civil society's important role in supporting the country's democratic transition.

The revolution liberated Tunisian civil society by enabling the proliferation of civil society organisations (CSOs) that have performed an active role in guiding the transition and ensured democratic, non-authoritarian outcomes were achieved. However, this book argues that it was not simply the increased space for CSO activity or the state of their activities that enabled them to play this role. It demonstrates that a CPC has been a requirement for civil society, enabling it to effectively assist a transition, fulfil a democratic function, and complete a democratic consolidation.

What is civil society?

Civil society originated in Aristotle's work when he used the term *koinōnía politike* to describe a portion of society which is separate from government but consists of a community of citizens with shared interests (Davis, 1996). Despite its Western genealogy, the term is directly translated, *muj'tema al-madani*, and widely used in both the Tunisian context and the study of Middle Eastern societies (Norton, 1995). As this book will explore, civil society is not inherently civil and democratisation theory's uncritical assumption that civil society activity inevitably leads to democracy is speculative.

Civil society is a non-governmental entity as the elements do not seek to hold office in public administration, election to a parliamentary body, or require authority granted by an electorate. Rather than seeking political power, it seeks power to influence the political decision-making processes, thus regulating the state.

As Held summarises, "Civil society constitutes those areas of social life – the domestic world, the economic sphere, cultural activities and political interaction – which are organised by private or voluntary arrangements between individuals and groups outside the direct control of the state" (1993: 6). It can loosely be defined in three categories; institutions (e.g. legal system, citizenship, family), organisations (e.g. non-governmental organisations, NGOs), and individuals (e.g. membership, organising events). Media, however, falls under several categories since it has institutional, in addition to organisational and individualistic, characteristics.

The complexity of the concept means several perspectives of what civil society is exist. However, Walzer's definition is suitably encompassing and avoids abstract characterisation; "Civil society is the sphere of un-coerced human association between the individual and the state, in which people undertake collective action for normative and substantive purposes, relatively independent of government and the market" (1998: 123–124).

Scholte adds another dimension to this definition by arguing that "pure" civil activities "involve no quest for public office and no pursuit of pecuniary gain" (2002: 283), thus excluding political parties, firms, and commercial mass media. Considering this viewpoint, Scholte notes that civil society is present when rules that govern society are influenced by voluntary associations and lists the actors as:

> academic institutions, business forums, clan and kinship circles, consumer advocates, development cooperation initiatives, environmental movements,

ethnic lobbies, faith-based associations, human rights promoters, labour unions, local community groups, peace movements, philanthropic foundations, professional bodies, relief organisations, think tanks, women's networks, and youth associations.

(2002: 283)

McLaverty (2002) analyses scholars Hall, Perez-Diaz, and Gellner who have defined civil society through expressing the importance of its normative aspects. Hall (1995) and Gellner (1996) focus on factors such as opposition to despotism, the role of controlling the state through acting as a counterbalance, volunteerism, and modular members of autonomous groups. Perez-Diaz lists the socio-political institutions that civil society includes; "rule of law, limited and accountable public authority, economic markets, social pluralism and public sphere" (1998: 211). Seligman expands the ethical-normative component by arguing the "ethical ideal of the social order that if not overcomes, at least harmonises the conflicting demands of individual interest and social good" (1992: x).

These works suggest that independence from the state and legal protection by the state are required for civil society to act as an opposition to a despotic state. In an ideal and non-co-opted form, civil society is defined by its independence from the state, enabling it to challenge government policy but acting within the rule of law and not in order to seek power. Chapter 2, which examines the history of Tunisian civil society, explores the processes of civil society co-option by the pre-revolution Tunisian authoritarian government as one way of controlling and shrinking civil society space.

Furthermore, these works raise issues of the normative and the ethical perspectives which assume that because a civil society is non-power seeking entity that engages civic or philanthropic purposes, it is an inherently "good" force. This perspective that civil society is pre-disposed to being good and acting with altruistic virtue is naive. Through an in-depth inquiry into the role played by civil society in Tunisia's democratic transition, this book establishes that civil society needs to exhibit CPC in order to be a force for 'good' in the establishment and support for democratic structures and procedures.

Anheier determines civil society to be "a collective of institutions, organisations, and individuals located among the family, the state and the market, in which people associate voluntarily to advance common interests. It functions primarily as a check on state power" (2001).

To summarise, in an ideal and non-co-opted form, civil society is defined by its independence from the state, enabling it to challenge government policy but acting within the rule of law and not in order to seek power.

Civil society's relationship with democracy – what are the connections?

If writers like Keane consider that "a pluralist and self-organising civil society independent of the state is an indispensable condition of democracy" (1988: 51), what is the connection between the function of civil society and democracy? How does civil society contribute to democracy? And why might civil society action lead to building and strengthening democracy?

The connections between civil society and democracy are based on the historical roles that civil society has played. It's the functions that civil society performs which have meant it has developed a relationship with democracy.

In a rudimentary sense, civil society can act as a voice of the people and a social, political, and economic barometer. This voice can therefore influence the state but through mobilisation of actors and organisations, and without a mandate to represent an electoral district. Civil society can be citizen-led force that helps to represent the interests of private citizens and maintain a balanced relationship between the state and non-state actors. This, however, is based on the condition that it is an entity which is removed or has a degree of separation and is granted autonomy from the state government. A co-opted, government controlled civil society, however, inevitably has a more limited democratic function and cannot act as "a permanent thorn in the side of political power" (Keane, 1988: 15).

In the twentieth century, as democracy became the increasingly favoured method of government, civil society became more closely associated with being a pro-democratic vehicle that facilitated a balanced relationship between the state and non-state actors. This contrasts to sixteenth-century English political thought of understanding civil society as being part of the state (Scholte, 2002: 283). The enlightenment period's contribution to civil society's connection to democracy draws on works from Locke, Hegel (Stillman, 1980), and de Tocqueville who saw that it can act as a check on the state's political and economic power. This is what I determine to be the 'Liberal-Associative' function of civil society: one that seeks to prevent despotism and act as an obstacle to unlimited state power. By preventing elected despotism and protecting the freedom of citizens, it prevents democracy from being sabotaged by an overbearing state.

In addition to the Liberal-Associative approach civil society can play an 'Oppositional-Resistance' role. This understanding is rooted in the works of revisionist, cultural Marxist Antonio Gramsci, and focuses on challenging the state and seeking to prevent its hegemony, in both ideation and physical forms. Gramsci's definition of the non-state or private sphere consisted of all organisations and institutions outside the process of production and the state's authority. Although Gramsci saw civil society as the intellectual battleground between the capital and labour classes, he also recognised it was the "sphere of all the popular-democratic struggles" (Simon, 1982: 69).

Both Liberal-Associative and Oppositional-Resistance strands can have the capacity for a democratising effect through preventing state dominance. While Liberal-Association civil society offers a supportive, yet watchful, stance towards liberal government, Oppositional-Resistance civil society is equally necessary for the democratising role by acting as a more vigorous check on state authority while posing a greater challenge to state hegemony.

Civil society and democratic transition

Civil society can serve different purposes depending on the political situation. Subsequently, civil society in an established democracy behaves differently from one that operates under authoritarian conditions. This section addresses literature that recognises the important role that civil society plays in order for democratic transition, and later democratic consolidation, to take place. It concludes by suggesting that civil society can contribute to democratic transition and consolidation if certain preconditions are met.

As the third wave of democratisation occurred in Latin America and Eastern Europe, driven principally by civil society forces, a common assumption began formulating in the 1990s that civil society was synonymous with democracy. This was based on the postulation that a diverse and vibrant civil society may encourage democratic practice and political participation (see Cohen and Arato, 1992; Putnam, 1993; Carothers, 1999).

Without using the term civil society, French aristocrat Alexis de Tocqueville was "the first to attribute the importance of associationalism and self-organisation for democracy" (Kaldor, 2003: 19). A neo-Tocquevillian position was established in the works of a series of democratisation scholars such as Putnam, Fukuyama, and Diamond. It reflected the linkage of civil society to democracy and became a key element of the post-Cold War zeitgeist (Ishkanian, 2007: 58). Putnam argued that civil society is crucial to "making democracy work" and that "Democratic government is strengthened, not weakened, when it faces a vigorous civil society" (1993: 182). This is because civil society holds the state to account and enables society to reach agreement on values and norms. Furthermore, as Entelis notes:

> without a well-developed civil society, it is difficult, if not impossible, to have an atmosphere supportive of democracy. A society that does not have free individuals and group expression in non-political matters is not likely to make an exception for political ones.
>
> (1996: 47)

Scholars in the field of transitology maintain this view; that an active, functioning civil society is necessary for democratic transition. However, transitology tends to argue that the role of civil society is necessary for democratic consolidation, the latter stages of transition, rather than recognising that civil society can initiate political change or steer a country through a transition. This book's exploration of Tunisian civil society's democratic function and role leading to and in the initial stages of the revolution and democratisation process challenge this transitology assumption. Tunisian civil society history and evolution, coupled with a conducive post-revolution legal framework, have enabled it to play a positive democratising role.

Classic transitology can be traced back to Rustow's 1970 work which stated that no particular social and economic preconditions are required in order for reforms towards democracy to be enacted. The experience of the Latin American states' political transitions from authoritarianism to democratisation in the 1980s further inspired the concept of transitology which became a sub-field of the democratisation literature. Transitology looks to explain and create a framework for the conditions required for democratic government, structures, norms, and values to become embedded in society after dictatorships have been removed. These works use empirical data to challenge previously made assumptions on democratisation; O'Donnell (1973, 1988) questions Lipset's (1959) assumption that democracy only comes from modern urbanised, educated, and mass media consuming industrial societies, and Dahl's (1971) assumption that higher social-economic development increases the possibility of democracy, by pointing to high and low levels of modernisation in South American states, yet a lack of democratisation. Also, contrary to the assumption that religion is an obstacle to democratisation, Karl (1990) acknowledges the role of the Catholic Church as another form of opposition to authoritarianism.

Regarding civil society, O'Donnell and Schmitter (1986) recognise mass mobilisation and the "resurrection of civil society" as being crucial to the democratic transition process; however, as a later stage in transition, rather than from the start of a transition process. This book diverges from this perspective by arguing that in the Tunisian case, civil society has been central to the transition process. Doorenspleet supports the position that civil society is an agent of transition by identifying cases of Argentina, Chile, Spain, Peru, the Philippines, and South Korea that show the positive role of civil society in liberalisation and creating disunity amongst ruling elites, in addition to noting that literature on the collapse of the communist regimes in Eastern Europe and democratisation in Latin America attribute the influential role of civil society (2005: 5). Furthermore, Doorenspleet argues that civil society promotes democratic transition since:

> Civil society can alter the balance of power between state and society, by organising opposition against the state, by mobilising the citizens of the state in opposition against the present non-democratic regime and providing information, which may inspire citizens to protest against the regime.
>
> (2005: 6)

Transitology largely champions civil society as "the antithesis of the totalitarian conception of the state as the single institution possessing legitimate authority" therefore defined by being "not central but dispersed; not hierarchically or vertically organised, but horizontally structured (or indeed completely unstructured); not official but private and voluntary. It was not despotic or controlling or part of the power structure" (Armstrong et al., 2011: 4). This is not to say that transitions and the process of democratic consolidation are always a success. Regarding the countries described as 'transitional', and therefore trying to achieve democracy, there have been successes, moderate successes, and failures. However, most countries fall into what Carothers (2002) describes as "Grey Zone", where the state has both democratic features and democratic deficits. Within the Grey Zone there is vast diversity and Carothers creates a series of terms for these qualified democracies, "including semi-democracy, formal democracy, electoral democracy, façade democracy, pseudo-democracy, weak democracy, partial democracy, illiberal democracy, and virtual democracy" (Collier and Levitsky, 1997: 430–451).

The works of de Tocqueville, in addition to J.S. Mill, argue that "many social benefits flow from membership of voluntary organisations in the community" (Newton, 2001: 202). Newton principally agrees but is more sceptical in his belief that empirical evidence to support the claim that CSOs generate trust between citizens is lacking. Instead, he argues that "the relationship between social and political trust and democracy is more complex and indirect than appears to be the case at first" (2001: 202). In spite of highlighting these differences, Newton agrees that civil society is a boon for democracy. His work identifies that they are said to teach trust, social understanding, empathy, the art of compromise, and cooperation, in addition to breeding and enforcing reciprocity (2001: 206). Regarding the relationship between civil society and democracy, Newton makes a positive correlation;

> Poorly developed civil societies are unlikely to sustain developed democracies. As social capital is created in civil society so it is easier to create political capital as well, but the link between the social and the political is not necessarily close in any given case, though it is generally found in most nations.
> (2001: 212)

In contrast to the literature that suggests active civil society is required for democracy, works that are more critical of civil society have been produced that argue civil society itself is not guaranteed to be sufficient and the assumption that a strong civil society ensures democracy is misleading. Berman (1997) uses the case of Weimar Germany to describe how, in certain conditions, a civil society that is *too* strong and influential can undermine democracy and subvert, rather than solidify, democratic and liberal values. However, this unique case is an anomaly. Equally, there is no certainty that democracy guarantees a strong civil society. Carothers points to how Japan, France, and Spain have stable democratic governments and weak civic associations (1999: 23).

Despite the recognition of these exceptions and critical perspectives, the positive impact of civil society on democratisation is frequently acknowledged. Scholte discusses the democratising possibility civil society offers and how democratic deficits can be reduced through civil society activism (2002: 281). Also, in contrast, this work expresses caution that civil society has the potential to both detract from and add to democracy: "civil society is not inherently a force for democracy any more than the public sector or the market" (Scholte, 2002: 299).

Should we assume that civil society is "a way to enhance public participation, consultation, transparency and accountability" (Scholte, 2002: 293) without understanding how this might happen?

The above-mentioned works provide a nuanced understanding and varied perspectives of the role and functions of civil society in autocratic and democratising environments. However, this literature's empirical basis remains contextually limited to the West, Eastern Europe, and Latin America. Very few scholarly works, especially prior to the 2011 uprisings, have been conducted to conceptualise civil society or democratisation in a MENA context. In addition, as this chapter will later explain, the application of these perspectives to a MENA context is often challenged by a predominant culturalist approach to the study of politics in the region. This book seeks to highlight this gap in MENA literature and, through the triangulation of research methods, aims to produce a context-sensitive tool to examining civil society and political culture within a democratising MENA context.

Scholte looks at six potential contributions that civil society might offer to the process of democratisation. First, civil society gives a voice to stakeholders by opening political space which can enable organisations to inform governance agencies. This also empowers civil society members, leading to greater participatory democracy. Second, since democracy requires an "informed citizenry", civil society can fulfil the role of educator. Third, democracy also requires "vigorous, uninhibited discussion of diverse views" (2002: 293), therefore civil society can help to fuel debate by facilitating discussion opportunities and creating openings for dissent. Fourth, civil society enacts regulatory frameworks so that institutions are subject to public scrutiny. Fifth, "Increasing the public accountability of the regulatory agencies concerned" (2002: 294), has a democratic accountability function. Finally, the aforementioned five points combined help with creating legitimacy. When citizens respect the legitimacy of the government they, therefore, acknowledge its right to govern and their duty to obey. Furthermore, legitimate government tends to be more effective, more productive, and less violent than illegitimate rule. Civil society working with regulatory bodies can "give stakeholders a voice, improve public education, promote debate, raise transparency and increase accountability" (2002: 294). Also, the space created by civil society allows dissent to be expressed at what is deemed illegitimate. However, this book argues that the legal status of civil society, determined by the state, plays a major role in developing and shaping the public space. This consequently determines the type of civil society that is permitted to exist.

Noting that democracy may also be damaged by civil society, Scholte qualifies that civil society can only fulfil the role described above if it improves its own practices (2002: 296). A voice must be given to all stakeholders and all must have equal access and opportunity to participate. If not, "civil society can reproduce or even enlarge inequalities" (2002: 296). In some cases, the cultural base of CSOs is too narrow as they consist of Western-styled, Western-funded NGOs that are led by Western elites. Regarding education, civil society can fail to educate if behind the scenes lobbying takes precedent or CSOs misinform the public. Debate can be stifled if civil society members are co-opted, or they stop fuelling debate. Also, if civil society's discourse is co-opted, it can be recast by official institutions. In agreement with Anheier (2001), Scholte also recognises that civil society is not an intrinsically virtuous space; rather that "it includes destructive elements ... who seek to deny the democratic rights of others" (2002: 296). First, through practices like lobbying, democratically legitimate processes can actually be undermined by CSOs. Second, professionals in civil society can become convinced their views are correct to the detriment of the masses they consequently ignore. Finally, CSOs may themselves operate in non-transparent way. Scholte concludes that if civil society is to be a force for democracy, it needs to demonstrate its own democratic credentials. Also noting the importance of civil society's own practices but without arguing that civil society either helps or hinders democracy, McLaverty concludes that those who think that civil society is the best way of enhancing democracy may be mistaken. He argues "CSOs may represent important democratic initiatives; in reality, they often fall short in democratic principles" (2002: 314). This clearly emphasises the importance of civil society possessing and exhibiting democratic values.

The role of civil society in democratic transition

De Tocqueville, Keane, Entelis, Putnam, Fukuyama, Diamond, and others in the transitology field argue that a vibrant civil society can lead to democracy. However, the works of Berman, Carothers, Scholte, and McLaverty recognise that civil society is not intrinsically a force for democratisation. Therefore, critical analysis of a civil society is essential for assessing whether it is performing the democratic function it is presumed to perform. The latter group of scholars' critical stance towards civil society's democratising potential poses fundamental observations regarding the importance of CPC within civil society.

Transitology is a useful framework for understanding transitions from authoritarianism to democracy. However, the lack of recognition it gives to civil society's potential in a political transition means it is a flawed paradigm. Classic transitology literature identifies three stages in the process of transition: an *opening* of the authoritarian regime, a *breakthrough* to democracy where a democratic government comes to power via elections, and, last, the long-term process of *consolidation* where democratic habits become entrenched, the state institutions are reformed, and civil society is established and strengthened. This book, however, disagrees with the prescriptive sequencing of transition transitology described whereby civil society's contribution is only possible during the democratic consolidation phase. This book demonstrates that civil society can play a vital role throughout a transition, as was the case in Tunisia.

In a post-authoritarian context, where a democratic transition is occurring, civil society can play various roles to aid this process. This book examines the seminal democratising role played by Tunisian CSOs in the earliest stages of transition after the revolution, such as anti-corruption watchdogs, pro-democracy associations, and political mediator CSOs. The presence and role of these actors proved essential as a platform for opposition needs to be established to ensure authoritarianism does not return. As democratisation and consolidation occur, the role of civil society develops to include interest groups, human rights organisations, professional associations, development and social services NGOs, and political reform movements. However, the development of these CSOs would be unique to the various contextual needs of each case.

Diamond (1999) argues that civil society advances democracy in two ways; by helping generate a transition from authoritarian rule to elected democracy and by consolidating democracy. This book focuses on Tunisian civil society's role in both of these stages. Diamond's work highlights the importance of the public in the third wave of democratisation drawing on O'Donnell and Schmitter's (1986) analysis of citizenship revival and civil society resurrection, which occurs when weaknesses in authoritarian rule appear, and Collier and Mahoney's (1997) work on protests and strikes destabilising authoritarianism. Diamond forms a comprehensive thirteen point list of how civil society assists democratic development, which draws on both Gramscian and Tocquevillian conceptions of civil society (1999: 239–250). Two points are of particular note from his thirteen-point assessment. First, civil society can play a role in checking, monitoring, and restraining the exercise of state power by holding it accountable. This function helps avoid corruption and adds legitimacy to new governments by demonstrating their accountability, transparency, and responsiveness to the public (1999: 239–240). Second, civil society can stimulate and increase political participation, which "strengthens the legitimacy and the institutionalisation of democratic government, which are essential for consolidation" (1999: 242).

Civil society and democracy learning

Civil society can facilitate learning of democracy. Helping the population understand the practices and procedures of democracy is an important aspect of transition in which CSOs can partake. De Tocqueville regarded associations as schools of democracy and the associational model of civil society, that scholars such as himself and Putnam advocate, affirms that civil society can assist a state in transition by endorsing the norms and values of political civility. This occurs within associations by imparting "habits of co-operation, solidarity and public-spiritedness" on its members (Putnam, 1993: 89–90). In the context of Tunisia's revolution, civil society has the potential to help citizens acquire 'democratic knowledge' (Sadiki, 2015). If it can play an instructional or didactic role in educating, enculturating, and socialising the populace into democratic practices, Tunisian civil society can synthesise local and global knowledge production to support the development of good governance.

Due to the lack of MENA examples where civil society has successfully influenced a democratic transition, cases from Latin America, Eastern Europe, and East Asia are considered. Friedman and Hochstetler identify that civil society in Brazil continues to influence the intermittent transition. Cooperation between Brazilian state actors and CSOs to create regular consultation and participation through institutionalised interactions in councils has helped transform a military dictatorship into either a cooperative or a deliberative democracy. Yet it is social movements that play a vital, Gramscian 'confrontation with state' style role in reaction to "incomplete democratisation and the impact of economic transformation" (2002: 37). Referring to the levels of political influence and organisational capabilities, Ekiert and Kubik argue that "the post-communist experience as a whole, however, attests to the positive and important role that civil society can play in democracy's consolidation" (2014: 53). They cite Polish unions' and farmers' groups' ability to defeat or delay proposed economic and social reforms as evidence.

> In the Philippines, South Korea and Thailand, without the participation of the masses or civil society, democratisation would not have been achieved. Although their role was only supportive, it lent popular weight to the democratic transition and helped deepen democracy.
> (Bunbongkarn, 2004: 137)

Bunbongkarn asserts that civil society contributes to democratic consolidation, first, by creating political pressure on the government to implement reform. Thailand is an example of pressure from a developed business sector and urban middle class on the military leadership whereas the Philippines drew on their pre-existing democratic consciousness in response to electoral irregularity. Second, organisations and groups must commit to democracy. In doing so they can propagate democratic principles and ideas that lead to ensuring that both political elites and the majority of the people believe democracy is the best form of government (2004: 34, 141). South Korean civil society became increasingly critical of the authoritarian government. These efforts "empowered the people, making them more assertive in the political arena" (Bunbongkarn, 2004: 142).

In order to identify the objective of a transition, Linz and Stepan describe the process of democratic transition as complete when,

> sufficient agreements have been reached about political procedures to produce an elected government, when government comes to power that is the direct result of a free and popular vote, when this government de facto has the authority to generate new policies, and when the executive, legislative and judicial power generated by the new democracy does not have to share power with bodies de jure.
> (1996a: 3)

Of the five areas that Linz and Stepan (1996a: 7–13) describe as requirements for "consolidated democracy", three of these interconnected and mutually reinforcing conditions mention the role of civil society. First, conditions for the development of a free and lively civil society must exist. Second, civil society should not make way for "political society" during democratic consolidation. Instead, civil society should continue to be a field for alternative viewpoints and to monitor the government's progress in transition. Third, that the rule of law, which protects and embeds civil and political society in a spirit of constitutionalism, is required. Linz and Stepan see these three as "virtually definitional prerequisites of a consolidated democracy" (1996a: 10). The other two, "democracy as the form of governance" and an "economic society" do not directly address civil society but they argue that democracy is an interacting system and these five conditions support one another.

This establishes the prerequisites of a consolidated democracy. However, this book argues that the preconditions of state must be considered when assessing a democratic transition. A state's history, including its civil society traditions, is relevant when considering its chances of successful democratic transition. Although transitology does not have a single party line, there are certain works in the field that hold a no preconditions assumption: that any country can achieve democracy and that the underlying conditions in the so-called transitional countries will not be major factors in either the onset or the outcome of the transition process. This book does not subscribe to this perspective view. Instead, this book illustrates the relevance and significance of Tunisia's unique civil society evolution which predated French colonisation in shaping its positive influence on the revolution and subsequent democratic transition. Also, these works include the secondary assumption that the required level of 'state-building' to make a coherent, functioning state is not an obstacle to democratic transitions (Carothers, 2002). The list of countries from the third wave of democratisation that have not transitioned to democracy but remain in the Grey Zone between dictatorship and democracy is testament to the naivety of the transitology paradigm and demonstrates that states which lack necessary preconditions are significantly disadvantaged when attempting to make a successful transition.

A state faced with the triple transition of state-building, market reforms, and democratisation, according to Jankauskas and Gudžinskas (2008) is more likely to end up in the Grey Zone. They argue the importance of preconditions and that a functioning state is a prerequisite to democratic transition, and therefore state-building should take priority. This suggests that transitology was only related to a specific set of countries at a specific time or that the Latin American experiences are non-transferrable to other world regions. Chapter 2 illustrates this point by identifying the significance of the historical development of Tunisia's civil society. The assumptions that preconditions to democratisation are irrelevant demonstrate the weaknesses of the transitology paradigm. This book demonstrates that Tunisia had the preconditions necessary to transition from dictatorship to democracy due to its pre-existing constitutional and civil society history which meant that extensive state-building was not required. This is further evidence that the paradigm "has outlived its usefulness" and a "better lens" is required (Carothers, 2002: 6).

As such, this book applies an alternative lens to examining the processes of civil society democratic learning in the Tunisian democratising environment, based on an understanding of democratisation as "involving a didactic process, and the inherently constructivist production of democratic learning" (Sadiki, 2015: 709). By examining and measuring the extent to which Tunisian civil society has engaged in a process of democratic learning, this book supports Sadiki's call for understanding democratic knowledge production in newly democratising settings as a bottom-up didactic process, rather than "people being at the receiving end of democracy, when passively packaged through all kinds of ready-made moulds" (2015: 709).

Diamond asserts that "civil society can, and typically must, play a central role in building and consolidating democracy" (1999: 259–260) but adds that the deconstruction of any patron–client relationship with the government is crucial as it would prevent civil society from functioning independently and effectively. A level of cooperation with the state government is required. Civil society can remain 'in opposition to the state', but if this relationship is over-confrontational or civil society overwhelms the state with demands, which can be the case after long periods of authoritarianism, it becomes a counterproductive force to democratisation.

Furthermore, this chapter has established that civil society is not an inherent force for any 'good'. The existence of civil society actors and organisations' activities should not be viewed as automatically assisting democratic transition. It has the potential to be corrupted and manipulated from above and within. Therefore, a critical examination of civil society that assesses the extent to which its culture is democratic and questions if and how democratic knowledge is being acquired in these Tunisian 'schools of democracy' is required for assessing progress. If dynamic, collaborative, reflexive (internal), and cross-cultural (external) learning is essential in democratic knowledge acquisition (Sadiki, 2015: 709), understanding the political culture of Tunisian civil society is equally important.

The political culture of democracy: beyond institutions and procedures

Democracy is not merely an institutional, bureaucratic, or procedural process. It is also a political culture (see Tan and Whalen-Bridge, 2008) and, as Ayubi describes, "a cultural and intellectual tradition" (1995: 397). Almond defines political culture as a "particular pattern of orientations to political action" in which "every political system is embedded" (1956: 396). As a field of political enquiry, political culture has diverse origins and was influenced by various disciplines such as European sociology, social psychology, and psycho-anthropology. However, Almond credits the development of the attitude survey as the "catalytic agent" in the conceptualisation of political culture (1989: 10–16). Political culture is, collectively, traditions of society, spirit of public institutions, passions, and collective reasons of citizens, and style and operating codes of its leaders. Therefore, they are not just random but products of an historical experience. For an individual, political culture provides controlling guidelines for effective political behaviour, therefore ideals and operating norms. "A political culture is the product of both the collective history of a political system and the life histories of individuals who currently make up the system" (Pye and Verba, 1965: 8).

Furthermore, rather than a static concept, political culture is fluid and changeable. Beliefs and attitudes, in addition to norms and behaviours, within a country can change, dependent on the political events and developments that country experiences. Traditions, history, and governmental policies may accelerate or reduce the rate of change, but political culture is ever changing.

What is the political culture of democracy?

The political culture of democracy, the political culture required to make democracy work, is also referred to as political civility. Political civility is vital for both installing democracy and ensuring the functioning of a democratic system. Indeed, it was Almond and Verba's 1963 work which argued that civic culture "is the type of political culture most conducive to stable democracy" (Welch, 1993: 15).

But what is political civility and what are the defining features of this political culture? To begin with, non-violence is a primary requirement of political civility. State organisation, centralisation, and monopolisation of 'legitimate' violence is key to this non-violent definition (Volpi, 2011: 828). In turn, the state is expected to guarantee a 'non-violent' space for discourse and behaviour. This is, of course, an ideal that is based on the assumption that the state is solely responsible for providing a space for these interactions to take place.

Non-violence sets the bar for political civility rather low. Therefore, my research has developed this term and recognises the following six criteria: *Freedom*, *Equality*, *Pluralism*, *Tolerance*, *Trust*, and *Transparency*. Principally based on themes stemming from de Tocqueville's *Democracy in America* (2003) and Almond and Verba's *The Civic Culture* (1989), this set of criteria is derived from the existing literature on civil society, political culture, political civility, and democratisation. Together, they are the components and characteristics of political civility.

- Rousseau (1998) discusses the importance of citizens retaining freedom through a social contract and de Tocqueville understood that freedom of citizens, via civil society, counterbalances state power. Habermas' conception of democracy and a strong civil society requires freedom *from* domination (in Flyvbjerg, 1998: 219). For civil society activity, freedom is the liberty of not being at risk from state censorship or persecution, the freedom to join any association and to leave without the risk of persecution, and that freedom must also be legally enshrined and defended by the state.
- Equality is based on the de Tocqueville emphasis on the importance of "equality of conditions" to the existence of democracy. It refers to permission for all citizens to participate, in the understanding that, with the exception of inciting violence, all voices and opinions are equally valid. If certain voices in a political system or a civil society are suppressed or considered unacceptable, then equality is not given to the population and the culture cannot be considered to exhibit civility.
- Pluralism is derived from the Weberian concept of the multi-dimensionality of power and refers to the presence of a range of voices expressing a range of opinions. De Tocqueville's work also saw the plurality of numerous associational groups as a means to prevent majoritarian democracy from becoming

tyrannical. Gramsci denotes the value of pluralism in civil society as a means to challenge the ideational hegemony of the state. Diamond describes pluralism as a feature of civil society as "no organisation that is civil can claim to represent all the interests of its members" (1999: 231–233).
- Tolerance is "the willingness of individuals to accept disparate views and social attitudes; to accept the profoundly important idea that there is no right answer" (Norton, 1995: 12) or "a mutual accommodation of differences in everyday dealings" (Volpi, 2011: 835).
- Trust is recognised as a "democratic character" by Almond and Verba (1963) who add that a functioning democracy depends on sufficient public trust in democratic institutions and procedures. However, trust is also a "main component of social capital, and social capital is a necessary condition of social integration, economic efficiency, and democratic stability" (Newton, 2001: 202). Therefore, trust at civil society level is relevant to supporting democracy and, according to de Tocqueville and J.S. Mill (1859), developing trust through participation in voluntary associations is a major benefit of civil society action.
- Transparency, pertaining to the notions of openness and accountability within government, is imperative to civility. If Almond and Verba argue that the democratic citizen is expected to be actively involved in politics and to make informed, rational political decisions (1963: 31), then transparency within political processes is required. Diamond asserts that "transparency is a precondition for accountability and reform" (1999: 240). Furthermore, the lack of transparency can lead to hindering accountability and oversight, therefore increasing the risks for corruption which "undermines democratic capacities of associations within civil society by generalising suspicion and eroding trust and reciprocity" (Warren, 2004: 329). Although civil society may seek transparency from the state, Scholte (2002) discusses the importance of transparency from the perspective of civil society's practices as a means of exhibiting its democratic credentials.

The interplay between these six criteria would vary in each political system as it would be implausible to expect any one political culture to simultaneously express all attributes to a complete degree. Although they represent normatively ideal attributes for a CPC, evidence of all six would be required to consider a political culture as civil.

Is a civil society civil?

As culture is a fundamental aspect of democracy, it is "hard to ignore culture" when seeking to understand conditions that foster democracy and a supportive civil society (Hudson, 1995: 71). If a civil society needs to exhibit civility in order to be a force for supporting and strengthening democratisation, an approach for assessing civility and determining its level must be employed. Furthermore, determining whether a civil society is operating with civility is also vital for this assessment.

This book measures the civility of the Tunisian civil society's political culture with the aim of assessing its ability to fulfil a democratic function, especially during the democratic transition. This leads to the question of what approach to studying civil society and political culture should be employed? More specifically, which methods are most suitable or relevant to mitigate the gap in the theoretical underpinning of the study of politics and democracy both in the wider MENA region context and the unique Tunisian post-revolution and democratic transition context?

The starting point is a dualistic conceptualisation of political culture. Stephen Welch's theory of political culture (2013) presents a dualistic understanding of the phenomenon, which manifests both in people's discourse and in their practices. In other words, not only what people say, or only what they do, but the combination of both is significant to assessing the extent of their political civility. The development of the attitude survey may well have been the "catalytic agent in the conceptualization of political culture" (Almond, 1989: 15) but assessing political culture through only a singular research method does not account for potential discrepancies between what people say and what people do. Therefore, the application of research methods that both collect contemporary discourse and directly observe practice are required in order to fully comprehend a political culture. One perspective without the other is not sufficient and a political culture simply cannot be fully assessed without the use of methods that capture both discourse and practice.

Political culture studies conducted in the MENA region

The habit of using cultural attributes to describe and explain political situations has been a regressive and intellectually weak, albeit predominant, feature of Middle Eastern studies. Works that use supposed Middle Eastern cultural traits, such as fatalism, primordial chauvinism, or herd instinct as explanations for contemporary political contexts fail to recognise Western-imposed political structures and Western support for authoritarian regimes motivated by Western economic interests and demands for natural resources.

Instead, these culturalist works have relied on the use of history, tradition, or religion as explanatory variables for political culture, thus resorting to generalisations about the region, its people, and their belief systems to understand and frame political realities. Von Grunebaum (1962), Lewis (1990, 2003), Gellner (1981), Vatikiotis (1987), and Huntington (1991) all frame Islam to highlight the region's aversion to democracy. Berque (1985), Hourani (1991), and Patai (1973) use Arab peoples as their explanatory variable through stereotyping and looking at the Bedouin substructure of the Arab personality, shame, honour, and the Islamic component of the Arab identity. Kedourie concluded that Arab culture is non-democratic and "democracy is quite alien to the mind-set of Islam" (1994: 1) while Pryce-Jones blames Islam, tribalism, shame, and honour culture for the lack of democracy, even stating "an Arab democrat is not even an idealisation but a contradiction in terms" (1989: 406).

I reject this culturalism approach to studying political culture because its reductionism, unrepresentativeness, and static conceptualisation of culture leads studies that employ this approach to commit Orientalism. Said's influential work, *Orientalism* (1978), criticises the culturalist approach by highlighting the false assumptions and prejudices that Western writers express against "the Orient" as they depict Arab or Muslim peoples as inferior, irrational, illogical, sexualised, and violent. These works conversely portray the West as intellectually and culturally superior. This book does not present a full analysis of Said's work but seeks to identify and account for the methodological and ethical problems Said highlights of reducing studies of MENA, such as relations to democracy, to cultural explanations and further presenting said culture as a static entity. Said did not state that Westerners should not work on MENA issues, as he rejects the argument that "only a black can write about a black, a Muslim about Muslims" (1978: 322). However, he argues that the Middle East is more complicated and cannot be summarised, studied, or understood from a distance.

To conduct political culture research in the MENA region that avoids Orientalist tendencies, direct observation of discourse and practice must take place. It cannot be conducted from a distance (macro), but must be 'on the ground' (micro) and must be dualistic to account for the nature of the phenomenon being studied. Therefore, to avoid conducting research that may essentialise the Tunisian civil society's political culture being studied, this book's research design combines both positivist and micro-interpretivist approaches.

A positivist approach employs hypothesis-testing methods of inquiry that are rigorous, objective, and scientific. Rather than reject political culture as a tool for analysing the MENA region based on the weakness of the culturalist approach, use of a natural science inspired approach to political culture research ensures that "the political culture baby" does not need to be thrown out with the "Orientalist bathwater" (Hudson, 1995: 65). A positivist method, such as the opinion survey I designed for this research, however, will only be able to capture the discourse side of political culture.

To understand and assess practice, an interpretivist method that observes behaviours, is required. Interpretivism does not implement a quantitative, "scientific" approach to research, but looks at understanding and interpreting social actions. It focuses on specificities rather than general patterns or trends. In recognising the potential disparity between discourse and its manifestations in practice, Welch (2013) advocates the importance of observation to understanding behaviour in the duality of political culture based on the premise that patterns of behaviour are not always the same as what people say about their patterns of behaviour. As White adds, political culture is "the attitudinal and behavioural matrix within which the political system is located" (1979: 1).

It is important to recognise the variation between micro and macro approaches of interpretivism as this distinction is key when conducting political culture research in the MENA region. The important distinction is the scale at which the interpretivist approach is conducted. Culturalism is a macro-interpretivism approach as it interprets culture through the use of historical synopsis or generalisation. As stated,

I reject the use of culturalism. It is a defective form of interpretivism as it does not consider detail, views culture statically, and essentialises those it seeks to understand. Said's critique opposes this 'synoptic' culturalism and macro-interpretivism, which exposes studies that use these approaches to the risk of committing Orientalism. Micro-interpretivist approaches and methods reduce this risk by conducting contemporary research that recognises fluidity within culture.

A political culture study requires some contextual analysis and understanding of the historical institutional and political background to acknowledge structures that have influenced the political culture being examined. This structuralist approach to examining a political context is less reductive than the flawed macro-interpretivism/culturalism approach.

As established, the macro-interpretivist, culturalist approach, which makes assertions such as 'the culture in state Y is X because the people from state Y are or have historically been that way', is reductive. A structuralist approach, however, focuses on structural determinants such as political regime, political economy, and institutional legacies (see Brynen et al., 2012), rather than looking for something 'cultural' that is undemocratic, and therefore by default wrong, in the political culture.

Establishing how a political culture has been influenced by a political system does not negate the need to conduct an 'on-the-ground political' culture study. A study still requires context, so analysis of structural issues should provide a deeper understanding of the institutional context. However, it does not capture how political and democratic discourses are evolving or being implemented into practice.

In the case of pre-revolution Tunisia, a political culture with minor aspects of political civility existed as there was some political pluralism, thanks to minor and 'loyal' opposition parties plus the General Union of Tunisian Workers (*Union Générale Tunisienne du Travail*, UGTT) 'checking' authoritarian control. Yet the legacy of authoritarianism also influenced the political culture as state intolerance for opposition encouraged social intolerance for difference and non-conformity.

In the context of studying political culture in the MENA region, the structuralist approach engages with the ways in which the political structures of authoritarian governance constrain citizens; although 'subjects' is a more accurate description of the population. Rather than making generalisations towards Islam and Arab or Bedouin practices as explanations for the lack of democracy in the states of the region, a culturalist examination provides a historical and non-Orientalist approach to studying political culture. Notably, the presence of authoritarian governance has prevented political culture research on MENA from using on-the-ground, micro-interpretivist research methods, thus contributing to the reproduction and predominance of macro-interpretivist cultural studies of MENA scholarship.

Within this regional context, the post-2011 political opening in Tunisia provided an opportunity for on-the-ground micro-interpretivist research, thus rendering the Tunisian case study unique. After the revolution, the authoritarian governance apparatus was scaled back and the Directorate of State Security was suspended, thus disbanding the old regimes' strongest means of coercion, the political police (Bouguerra, 2014). In addition to Decree-Law 88 (adopted in 2011) which established freedom of association, fieldwork-led, micro-interpretivist political culture research could be conducted without risk of arrest for researchers or interviewees and respondents. A similar study could not be recreated in a state with a more active and oppressive security apparatus and without legal protection for freedom of expression.

Methodology

Does Tunisian civil society possess and exhibit the criteria of CPC? This section addresses how I constructed a methodology to answer this research question that avoids orientalist analysis and is more sophisticated and multifaceted than research that uses one method.

- This is because political culture manifests as discourse and practice and therefore needs to be captured with two or more different methods.
- It uses CPC's six criteria as variables to investigate.
- It disaggregates culture to avoid essentialising assessments of a 'national' political culture.

First, culturalism and macro-interpretivism are defective forms of interpretivism that feature essentialist, static, large-scale analysis that makes generalisations and derogations of the subjects. Following the 2011 revolution, Tunisia presented the unique opportunity to adopt a micro-interpretivist research approach with a structuralist contextual analysis to assess a political culture in a MENA state that is transitioning away from authoritarianism without the risk of committing orientalism or jeopardising the safety of interviewees.

Second, as a political culture is a dualistic phenomenon that manifests as discourse and practice, this research was designed through the triangulation of different but suitable and complementary methods to capture both what people say and what people do.

Third, political civility, or CPC, is used as the model or ideal type of political culture that is supportive of democratic processes and institutions. As established, political civility comprises the six attributes; Freedom, Equality, Pluralism, Tolerance, Trust, and Transparency, and each criterion can be assessed through direct observation of discourse and practice. In order to understand the degree of political civility of Tunisia's civil society, this book examines evidence revealing the presence or absence of these criteria in Tunisian civil society's political culture.

Fourth, this research avoids recourse to historical, traditional, or religious explanations by disaggregating national culture and focusing on the sub-culture of civil society members. Rather than using Hofstede's (1991) causal approach to understanding a national culture, I implement Hudson's (1995), White's (1979), and McSweeney's (2002) recommendations to disaggregate political

26 "Civil" civil society

culture and focus on examining the political culture of CSOs, due to their potential to influence democratic transitions.

Overall, I developed a mixed methods approach that uses positivist and interpretivist ontologies. This applies McSweeney's and Hudson's separate recommendations to conduct methodologically multifaceted political culture studies. This also utilises Welch's (2013) political culture theory and provides the optimum approach for studying political culture.

The use of exclusively either positivist or interpretivist methods is insufficient for capturing discourse and practice and also for identifying the six attributes of CPC. Therefore, I used three separate research methods. Each method is employed as a window into understanding various aspects of the political culture of Tunisian civil society. Therefore, this triangulated methodological approach to a political culture study addresses the research question from three different directions in order to gain a multi-layered understanding of the complexities of the political culture of a civil society in a political transition from authoritarianism to an emerging democracy.

For the positivist approach, I created and disseminated an attitude survey. This method has been the standard since Almond and Verba (1963) formalised political culture research and is suitable for obtaining information on attitudes and values. But despite Eckstein's claim that "Almond and Verba got the concept exactly right" (1996: 473), attitude surveys, on their own, are insufficient for understanding the practice side of political culture.

When the results from ethnographic observation work are juxtaposed with quantitative data from opinion surveys, they complement each other. Therefore, to understand what people 'do' rather than only what they 'say', I deployed ethnographic participant-observation to witness the internal operation of a Tunisian CSO and the behaviour of its members, with a view to further uncovering the criteria of CPC. I also interviewed the CSO members to verify my observations.

For a third research method, I conducted interviews with a broad range of CSO representatives. I designed structured interviews because it ontologically sits between positivism and interpretivism. The structured and repeated line of questioning ensures the resulting data was systematic and easily comparable to facilitate rigorous analysis, bearing in mind the impact of my interpretation and interaction with the interviewees on the data collection process. Figure 1.1 charts the research design.

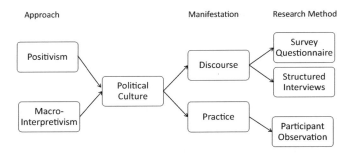

Figure 1.1 The theoretical background of the research design.

The research project is fundamentally shaped by the dualistic understanding of political culture that marries approaches of positivism and interpretivism and seeks to understand and measure discourse and practice manifestations through the application of three different research methods. The use of three methods creates a balanced assessment drawn from inquired, observed, and subject self-assessed understandings of civil society's political culture to identify different levels of political culture. It is also shaped by the theoretically rooted understanding of civil society as possessing the potential to perform a democratic function.

2 Tunisia's history of civil society activism
1574–2010

Ottoman semi-autonomous rule

Before France colonised the country under the auspices of a protectorate in 1881, Tunisia was a semi-autonomous Ottoman province governed by a succession of Beys.[1] In 1574, the Ottoman naval fleet defeated the Spanish supported Hafsid monarchy and created the Ottoman province of Tunis. By 1591, the Ottoman sultanate decentralised control of the North African provinces and granted them 'Regency' status; independence with the exception of providing the empire with military forces. After an administrative power struggle, the official rank of Bey became the supreme authority of the province where the Muradid and the following the Husainid dynasties ruled Tunis (Moalla, 2004).

During this 'Ottoman' period, until the decline of Beylical power due to European encroachment, a civil relationship existed between the Bey and society. The Bey's government was primarily concerned with its provinces collecting revenue and "many of the Beys proved to be capable administrators and reformers, and Tunisia developed a strong tradition of central control and functioning government" (Murphy, 2001: 19). On the condition that taxes were paid, the Bey governed society in a laissez-faire manner and the state did not interfere with religious and commercial affairs of the main actors in this period: guilds, tribal leaders, the bourgeoisie, and the *Ulama*.[2] Requiring a functioning economy, however, the Bey could not afford to ignore the interests of the guilds. Granted independence, guilds "made and enforced rules that governed who could practice particular trades, quality of their work, prices, and taxes" (Alexander, 2010: 13). Furthermore, "Tribal leaders traded tax collecting and peacekeeping duties for autonomy" (Alexander, 2010: 13). Joffe recognises that North African states' pre-colonial experience impacted the development of state and society relations, particularly between the state and the urban bourgeoisie whose vested economic and political interests were "reflected in their close interrelationship with central authority" (2009: 931). Although they could not challenge the state's power, the Tunisian *Ulama* were able to 'check' the Bey did not abuse power.

The Tunisian context challenges the notion that the Orient is "all state and no society" as it did not reflect a complete "absence of the autonomous individual exercising conscience and rejecting arbitrary intervention by the state" (Turner, 1994: 34). The plurality of socio-political actors in this period filled the space between state, market, and family, and therefore constituted a civil society. This emerging civil society was cooperative, since its autonomy was ensured by a non-meddlesome state, but also limited the Bey from acting as an absolute ruler. Murphy argues that "the institutionalism of the political system which has existed since Ottoman days" has had a lasting impact which even managed to restrain President Ben Ali's hold on power (1997: 120). Stepan adds that medieval and Ottoman Tunisia had cultural roots of tolerance and openness in its liberal and rights-friendly political system (2012: 97) which would have impacted the conduct of civil society.

European colonialism and the struggle for independence

The colonial period enabled civil society to absorb many of the values of republicanism, constitutionalism, and aspects of liberalism. However, Tunisian civil society's autonomy was weakened under French control. In response to the injustice of colonial administration, civil society changed its main function from an 'economic focus', as seen in the Ottoman era, to an Oppositional-Resistance, anti-establishment function that resisted, and later sought to replace, the French order's hegemony during the nationalist struggle for independence. In this era, newly established political parties, the Destour and later Neo-Destour (ND), acted as Oppositional-Resistance civil society. Additionally, the construct of Tunisian Ethnic Arab nationalism was espoused to support and legitimise the call for self-determination. This was, however, not connected to the Pan Arab nationalism that was growing in popularity during the early and mid-twentieth century.

After the Tunisian state was declared bankrupt in 1869, France stepped in as 'Protector' of its extensive investment on 12 May 1881 with the signing of the Treaty of Bardo. The 1883 protectorate treaty, the al-Marsa convention, created a 'façade of independence' that gave France ultimate power in Tunisia, allowing the bureaucratic administration of the local state to be retained, strengthened, and extended (Anderson, 1986: 9). Through centralising power, land reforms, and privatisation, while strengthening existing central state institutions, the French undermined and severely weakened the autonomy of local political authorities and economic institutions without destroying them (Alexander, 2010: 21). The Bey remained but only as a figurehead ruler in a state where French authority was supreme. As Perkins describes, "Ali Bey continued to reign, but he no longer ruled" (2014: 45).

Resentment towards the colonial power grew as inequalities with the French became more evident (Alexander, 2010). As the income and influence of the traditional elite and bourgeoisie came under greater threat, it gave rise to Tunisia's nationalist movement; initially led by the Young Tunisians, then later the Destour and the ND parties. Anderson (1986) notes how these three stages of the movement engaged and mobilised the Mamluk aristocracy, the Bourgeoisie, and the hinterlands respectively to become a national-level campaign.

Civil society activism worked against the French Protectorate in the form of an independence struggle. Political parties, trade unions, and influential figures orchestrated boycotts and strikes, wrote critical journals, and courted foreign dignitaries for international support. The movement's absence of violent means represents a degree of civility; with the major exception being the 1938 Neo-Destour party (NDP) instigated riots in response to the arrest of its party leaders (Perkins, 2014: 107). Civil society activism in an independence struggle is in line with the Gramscian Oppositional-Resistance understanding of civil society. The independence struggle reveals that an ideational hegemony was not held over the population as increasing numbers of individuals and groups resisted French control. The social groupings of Tunisian civil society were able to confront the coercive apparatus or repressive institutions of the state. The independence struggle sought to challenge the dominance of the state, or in this case, colonial power (Ransome, 1992: 138–141) and has gone on to represent resistance within an authoritarian regime (Foley and Edwards, 1996: 40).

The nationalist struggle was initiated by the Young Tunisian movement. However, this movement lacked mass appeal as the members were almost exclusively hailing from the wealthier *baldiyya*[3] families. This weakened the movement as their social status "distanced them from the bulk of the population and prevented them from embracing changes that would negatively affect their class interests" (Perkins, 2014: 76).

From 1907 onwards, the Young Tunisians published a newspaper, *Le Tunisien*, a means of expression and to gain sympathisers to their cause. It became an important nationalist newspaper despite being printed in French. Meanwhile, their Alumni Association of Sadiki College encouraged greater educational reform that better equipped students for professional life (Perkins, 2014: 75).

Although the Young Tunisians were not responsible for instigating the 1911 riots, which were a response to French land confiscation of the Jellaz cemetery, this act of civil disobedience led to a clampdown on Young Tunisian activity. They were still able to organise a transportation boycott in the capital in 1912, but the French reacted by exiling their leaders Ali Bach Hamba, Abdelaziz Thâalbi, and Hassan Guellaty to Medinine, a city over 400 km south of the capital. Despite this bringing an end to the Young Tunisians, these actions unified society against the French officials (Perkins, 2014: 77). The Young Tunisian movement's impact remained limited, however, as it did not question the legitimacy of the protectorate or demand independence (Anderson, 1986: 160).

Activists from *Baldiyya* families were not the only Tunisians resisting the colonial presence. The 1915–1916 al-Hana uprisings, misleadingly referred to as a revolution, caused problems for the French as members of the Tunisian Udarna tribe of the Tataouine region coordinated with Libyan tribesmen to raid colonial outposts (Khalil, 2014: 49). These attacks, however, did not spread throughout the country (Ziadeh, 1962: 89). Guerrilla raids are certainly not actions of 'civil' civil society organisations (CSOs), but they highlight a widespread frustration towards French interference.

Conditions in post-First World War Tunisia had a negative economic impact on all Tunisians. French imports rose, which affected Tunisian producers and businessmen, while taxes were increased to cover the cost of new infrastructure and transport projects necessary for France's colonial economic exploitation objectives. Employment of French nationals in the administration rose at the expense of Tunisian nationals. Two awful harvests in 1919 and 1920 led to famine and disease. The Tunisian young men who fought for France in the war were especially dissatisfied with the economic situation that faced them on their return home (Perkins, 2014: 81).

The frustration culminated in 1920 with the establishment of the Destour[4] party. As the party's name suggests, its revolutionary goals were the restoration of the 1861 Constitution and the liberation of Tunisia from French control.

The party had a wider appeal and was more inclusive than the Young Tunisian movement but could not fully integrate Union and Communist perspectives. Executive positions in the party were taken by Sadiki College graduates from *Sahelian*[5] background, while *Zitouna*[6] University graduates, who had also adopted an anti-French stance, formed the lower and medium cadres of the party (Micaud, 1974: 93). Destour leaders showed some support for strikes organised by the *Confédération Générale des Travailleurs Tunisiens*[7] (CGTT) but saw union tactics of demonstrations and strikes as "vulgar and dangerously provocative" which weakened their alliance (Perkins, 2014: 91). The *Parti Communiste Tunisien* (PCT) also had uneasy relations with Destourians which hampered the latter's chances of creating alliances with leftists in Paris.

Although the nationalist movement was divided, the Resident General recognised the threat it posed to French authority. In 1926 he banned political criticism, criminalised various political activities, and restricted the press. The Tunisian monarch Amir Bey supported the Destourians, but his successor Mohammed Bey saw greater cooperation with the French as more prudent for Tunisia's interests. Ziadeh (1962) compliments the Destourian movement's approach and tactics in the national struggle as its activities, organisation, and ability to cause disruption laid important groundwork for its successors, the ND. Its divergence of opinions reflected the existence of the civil political culture (CPC) criterion of plurality. However, disagreements between its leaders over 'methods and means' of resistance, further internal disputes, and Abdelaziz Thâalbi's departure for Italy, weakened the national movement (Ziadeh, 1962: 121).

The rise of the NDP

Following a split from the Destour at a party conference, the NDP was established in 1934. Learning from the elitist approach of its predecessors, the NDP sought to gain support from all walks of life in Tunisia and encouraged nationwide participation. Presenting itself as the party of the whole nation, the NDP attracted "all elements of the population" (Anderson, 1986: 175) which if nothing else was united by their exploitation by colonialism.

Membership not only included upper-middle class urbanites and *Zitouna* graduates but attracted merchants, artisans, businessmen, and landowners who thought the NDP was more likely to further their interests. The *Union Tunisien de l'Artisant et du Commerce* (UTAC) backed the NDP which importantly represented support from the business community (Perkins, 2014: 121). The NDP engaged youth and forged ties with youth organisations that saw the Destour as a failure but it simultaneously also managed not to isolate *Sadiki* or *Khalduniyya*[8] alumni. In order to maintain nationwide appeal and to ensure the populations of the hinterlands were not neglected, the NDP adopted a decentralised organisation structure. Practically, this saw the creation of NDP 'cells' in all districts of major cities in addition to rural areas.

The party had a clear leadership structure and the charismatic Habib Bourguiba, a former Destourian from the Sahel, emerged as the leader of the new party. He advocated for "elites regaining contact with the masses" (Anderson, 1986: 168) which added to his popular appeal.

As a Sorbonne University law and political science graduate, Bourguiba was heavily influenced by French ideas, notably secularism. However, as a skilled politician he managed to combine the defence of the nation with the defence of Islam by portraying the French as "meddling with Islam" (Perkins, 2014: 95–97). His ideological inclusivity had limits as he was not able to reconcile with communist perspectives. He argued the PCT's imported ideology was at odds with Tunisia's traditional values (Perkins, 2014: 115).

Zitouna University graduates formed an important part of the ND movement and mosques became safe meeting places. The nationalist struggle became intertwined with defending the faithful as "Islam provided both a simple way to distinguish the vast majority of Tunisians from their European rulers and a legitimisation of the struggle to which the party urged the people" (Anderson, 1986: 175). The NDP also adopted less traditional protest methods and employed aggressive oppositional tactics that defied the protectorate such as refusing to pay taxes, boycotting French goods, and refusing to appear for military service (see Perkins, 2014: 100–101; Anderson, 1986).

The national movement remained quiet during the Second World War but the UGTT, established in 1946 separately from the French-run CGTT, took a leading role in opposing French rule by organising a general strike. The UGTT remained focused on nationalist goals but rejected overtures from the World Federation of Trade Unions and remained at odds with the communist Franco-Tunisian *Union des Syndicats des Travailleurs Tunisien* (USTT). The national movement also received monarchical support from Lamin Bey, who would also be the last Bey of Tunisia, as he used his limited political power to aid the national movement by preventing the UGTT from being dissolved and publicly aligned himself with the NDP (Perkins, 2014: 123).

During the 1950s relations between the NDP and UGTT remained close as UGTT leader Farhat Hached led the struggle for independence while nationalist movement leaders were detained or fled abroad. Despite the leadership struggle within the NDP, between Secretary-General Salah ben Yusuf and Bourguiba, both managed to remain united to the goal of independence. In addition to the NDP bridging societal differences and the use of Islam as a unifying factor, Sadiki (2002) attributes the rise of Tunisian "ethnonationalism", nationalism based on a common ethnicity, as a reaction to French colonialism.

Identity was, prior to colonialism, predominantly based on tribal or regional background. It was colonisation that created an 'us vs them' or 'Tunisian vs French' dichotomy. This helped to instil a 'Tunisianess' and "marked the onset of state-orientated ethnic nationalism", which included the liberal notion of national identity and the commonality of race, history, and language (Sadiki, 2008: 115–116). These notions were not dissimilar to the identity-building process other Middle East and North African (MENA) nations fighting a colonial background faced (see Pratt, 2007). Furthermore, the Tunisian singularity, the one-people narrative, had profound implications for the future of Tunisian politics and society since a focus on consensus restrained the development of pluralism, critical opposition, and alternative opinions as they could be considered un-Tunisian.

The nationalist regime in the post-independence era

During the post-independence period of authoritarianism, civil society existed within the constraints of an inclusive government system. President Bourguiba modified civil society into a co-opted and corporatised set of associations. This enabled the notion of citizenship to develop but prevented organisations from developing a democratic function as opposition was included within the system or suppressed.

Unlike Algeria's bloody war with France, Tunisian independence was negotiated in 1956. This represented a degree of civility as the national movement established behavioural norms of non-violent approaches in addressing dispute. Emancipation from France could have created 'citizens' in Tunisia, but "Colonial hegemony was replaced with an indigenous hegemony" (Sadiki, 2008: 118). The French colonial legacy meant that at the time independence was achieved, Tunisia was "an established bureaucratic state" (Salamé, 1994: 16–17). In addition to their wide support base, this enabled the NDP to gain comprehensive control over the state. The NDP's formal structure was modelled on that of the French Social party where "their executive committee were freely elected at annual branch assemblies" (Micaud, 1974: 84) making it both democratic and centralised. From this point in history, the NDP can no longer be considered a civil society actor as it became the state.

Civil society can be articulated, in the Gramscian sense, as opposition to a regime, but Henry argues that because it is "shaped by laws, regulations, and historical legacies of conflict and co-operation with authorities" (1999: 12–13) it is the state that facilities the existence or oversees the repression of civil society. In Tunisia's 'First Republic', newly appointed President Bourguiba's approach to civil society was somewhat destructive. Under Bourguiba's rule, discourse and policies of 'national unity' by the NDP soon became the modus operandi.

This may have been a necessary unifying strategy during the national movement and to create cohesion during the uncertainty of the immediate post-independent era, but it became an entrenched strategy which lacked tolerance of alternative views.

Despite pluralistic tendencies at the beginning of his rule, Bourguiba forcefully created a system that revolved around him and his party. This was a ruler buoyed by the prestige of successfully negotiating Tunisia's independence and famously quipped "Le systeme? C'est moi le systeme."

The 'national organisations' (NOs), such as the UGTT and the *Union Generale de l'Agriculture Tunisienne* (UGAT) which acted as intermediaries between state and society and during the struggle for independence, saw their autonomy constrained. Henry (1965) discusses how all NOs were eventually quietened and co-opted to become arms of the NDP. Even the powerful UGTT and the outspoken *Union Générale des Étudiants de Tunisie* (UGET) found themselves politically weakened and under the control of the single-party state. *L'Union Tunisienne de l'Industrie, du Commerce et de l'Artisanat* (UTICA) and *l'Union Nationale des Agricultures Tunisine* (UNAT), major economic associations, were political creations of the NDP. Although the UGTT could claim some independence, it remained close to the state because its leaders were also ND members which enabled the Union to be instrumentalised for political purposes. Henry notes that the vibrant civil society that existed at independence was redesigned by the one-party government "into administrative hierarchies paralleling those of the government" (Henry, 1999: 17). Civil society could not be considered independent as it was brought into national associational life. This incorporatism prevented the development of oppositional voices and the distinction between state and the non-state, and between political and civil societies, became less apparent. Therefore, national associational life was constrained by the single-party state rule.

Despite allowing a small degree of freedom, the NDP "subordinated professional interests to the national interest, they helped to maintain Tunisia's cohesion; but party control sapped their vitality and tended to divorce them from their members" (Henry, 1965: 159). The divisive institutions which were united in the struggle for independence were largely banned or co-opted as a mass movement turned into an authoritarian party.

After independence, the single-party state's national agenda made opposing the NDP akin to acting as an enemy of the state. After cohesion between the party and organisations in the struggle for liberation, NOs became a threat to the NDP. "After independence, the national organisations threatened to become free-wheeling pressure groups, rivalling the supremacy of the party" (Henry, 1965: 160). By turning NOs into branches of the one-party state, the NDP removed the vibrancy and autonomy from Tunisian civil society. NOs acted as arms of the party as "party control seemed to be exercised at all levels" (Henry, 1965: 164–165). Party members were also trade unionists and the merry-go-round of organisation leaders played to Bourguiba's advantage. Furthermore, the political positions of the UGTT were similar to those of the government. "Ben Salah and

Ahmed Tlili as trade unionists both identified themselves with national rather than class interests" (Henry, 1965: 162). This undermined the credibility of the UGTT because when a trade union no longer prioritises working class interest, or even harmonises the interests of labour and management, it fails to effectively represent its members (Clarke and Pringle, 2008: 85).

Even student organisations were co-opted. The leftist views from the UGET were suppressed as leading members were arrested and public rallies were overrun by the NDP Youth organisation. Therefore, realising the restrictions on their organisation, students began using UGET as a launch pad for a career in politics. UGET became closer to a state institution instead of a movement. "In politics, there was little feeling of participation because the party's small ruling clique dominated political life" (Henry, 1965: 180). The constitutional state, akin to Locke and Kant's model, did not exist in Tunisia, instead a clientelistic ruling culture was the reality (Krichen, 1992: 119–120).

Pluralism was constrained but what about other criteria of CPC? Equality, namely women's rights, improved in this era, albeit as a tactic to ensure national unity and loyalty to the state.

The emancipation of women, via the 1956 Personal Status Code, led to greater freedom and equality, such as equal divorce rights for both women and men. Bourguiba endeavoured to

> portray himself not as sweeping aside Islam, as had [Turkish leader Mustapha Kemal] Ataturk, but rather as reinterpreting it through *ijtihad*,[9] or independent reasoning – a process esteemed by 19th and 20th century Islamic reformers as well as Bourguiba, for whom the rationalism instilled by his French education ranked among the most noble of human qualities.
> (Perkins, 2014: 140–141)

For the sake of progress and sovereignty of the Tunisian people, women occupied a central position in the nation-building process because Bourguiba believed that social reform was closely related to the emancipation of women (Voorhoeve, 2012). *L'Union Musulmane des Femmes de Tunisie* had been founded in 1936 but was a conservative organisation and would not have effectively served the government's modernising programme. In order to educate women and run health programmes, Bourguiba established the *Union Nationale des Femmes Tunisiennes* (UNFT). "Neo-Destour officials knew that providing girls with a modern education would influence the social values they would impart to their families when they became wives and mothers" (Perkins, 2014: 143).

By the 1980s, in response to the Islamist resurgence, the Bourguiba government developed a less secular discourse on family law and women's rights. In addition, it "sought to strike a balance between often contradictory demands from different groups in society, such as the Islamists and the women's rights organizations" (Sonneveld, 2015: 5). This suggests that Bourguiba's approach to citizenship and secular society aimed to reduce the Islamic traditions and create loyalty to Tunisia rather than the patriarchy of fathers and husbands.

Empowering women politically and in the workplace was a way to solidify Tunisian national identity on a broader base. Furthermore, this was a utilitarian move, in the sense of reinforcing the ethnoreligious national identity. The Personal Status Code was considered a forceful reform by the *Ulama* and conservatives who opposed this form of Quranic reinterpretation (Touati and Zlitni, 2014: 164), but, in comparison to Ataturk's reform programme, the Tunisian approach was more restrained.

In order to reduce the appeal of leftist politics, the NDP renamed itself *Le Parti socialiste destourien* (PSD) in 1964 and enacted state-led economic development programmes. By the early 1970s, this socialist experiment had proven largely unsuccessful. Instead, Tunisia embarked on an economic liberalisation programme to encourage private investment and export-led development. It also saw the creation of the breakaway *Mouvement des démocrates socialistes* (MDS) party but did not lead to further democratisation or a plurality of parties. The switch from socialism to economic liberalism increased economic disparity while Bourguiba's "preferences for authoritarian personalised rule ultimately undermined corporatist structures" and left the party incapable of addressing the conflicting interests of the NOs (Murphy, 1999: 78–79).

These worsening economic conditions and political disagreement led to an opening in public sphere dialogue. University campuses became fields of ideological conflict between the leftists and Islamists who struggled to become the mantle of opposition to Bourguiba. Both groups shared an oppositional stance and sought to challenge the corporatist vision in the late 1970s early 1980s. This division of opposition, however, became a greater opportunity for the Islamist 'camp'. Bourguiba considered the leftist perspective a greater threat to his rule and the UGTT became the major opposition force. As the communist criticism of the new economic policies became increasingly vocal on university campuses, Bourguiba allowed the establishment of the Association for the Preservation of the Quran because "a culturally oriented Islamist organisation could provide a useful counter to his critics on the left" (Alexander, 2000: 470).

In this window of opportunity in the 1970s, Rashid Ghannouchi masterminded the creation of the *Mouvement de La Tendance Islamique* (MTI). This later became the Ennahda Movement.

Despite their growing criticism of Habib Bourguiba's authoritarianism in the mid-1970s, the Islamists initially refrained from engaging with class-related issues, lacked access to worker networks, mostly ignored the labour movement, and said nothing about economic liberalisation (*infitah*). In the early 1980s, Islamist rhetoric became more sensitive to labour issues, but "the movement still did not develop an explicit union strategy" (Alexander, 2000: 466–467).

A change of strategy occurred for Islamists when, borrowing from Iranian leader Ayatollah Khomeini's ability to reframe leftist themes in explicitly Islamic terms, Ghannouchi "published a tract that defended workers' rights and extolled the Islamic virtues of trade unions" (Alexander, 2000: 471–472) and MTI created a more populist message.

Ben Ali's false liberalisation: the National Pact and the destruction of Islamists

After Zine El-Abidine Ben Ali replaced Habib Bourguiba in a bloodless 'medical' coup, the brief political opening in a phase of pseudo-democratisation facilitated a growth of CSOs. However, the oppositional role these organisations sought to play was suppressed after the regime cracked down on political Islamist opposition. Attempts to pressure the state to implement democracy ceased and authoritarian government structures prevented civil society from performing a democratic function. Any form of opposition or attempts to speak out against Ben Ali's dictatorship, from civil society or public and political spheres, was met with arrest, police harassment, or exile.

President Bourguiba's failed economic policies were key to his demise. Tunisia was not an exception to the liberalisation trend across the MENA region from the 1980s onwards, as ineffective and failed economic policies forced governments to make reforms. Foreign aid was received by pro-democracy and human rights groups yet governments failed to grant any real autonomy to civil society. While the rest of the world seemed to be liberalising, Arab state leaders made promises of liberty and democracy as a tactic to improve the flimsy state of their legitimacy amongst the population in the face of progressively worsening economic conditions. These 'top-down' reforms did not, however, provide the essential basis for the growth and development of a civil society. Instead, they were measures to increase government control masked in the rhetoric of liberalisation. Instead, the liberalisation phase fragmented civil society and the reforms strengthened central power (Anderson, 2006: 195). For example, non-governmental organisations (NGOs) were established by political and economic elites "in order to feel the people's pulse and manipulate interests" (Schlumberger, 2004: 374). Also, CSOs were legally created then had "a web of bureaucratic practices and legal codes" imposed upon them, which allowed the state to closely monitor their activities, thus increasing central state control (Wiktorowicz, 2000: 43).

During the late 1970s and early 1980s, Tunisia witnessed the beginnings of a new plurality in the civic associations. UGTT leader Habib Ashour "turned trade unionism into a fairly dynamic and autonomous, and at times, confrontationalist, branch of civil society" (Sadiki, 2008: 119). One of the MENA region's first human rights organisations, *la Ligue Tunisienne des droits de l'homme* (LTDH), was founded in 1977 (Hawthorne, 2004: 8). A non-state Islamic organisation, the origins of the MTI, was established (Hermassi, 1991) and student groups were allowed to operate as political organisations (Belkhodja, 1998: 249).

Yet, in the political sphere, no opposition party gained the required 5 per cent of the vote in the 1981 parliamentary election in order to be legalised. This enabled the PSD–UGTT 'National Front' coalition to maintain its hegemony. Furthermore, the trade union movement, that was already a political heavyweight in its own right, remained part of the "corporatist system" (Waltz, 1995: 50). Tunisia's civil society seemed to be developing in this period (Alexander, 1997) but Bourguiba's preoccupation with national unity and his patrimonial manner of rule meant that his "brand of nationalism left no room for any free space for non-governmental or non-party actors" (Moore, 1988: 178).

Islamist groups managed to carve out some space in this largely closed arena. The rise of the Ennahda Movement saw the emergence of the *Union Générale Tunisienne des Etudiants* (UGTE) student union as an opposition to the leftist UGET. Antagonism between the two student unions resulted in violent clashes across Tunisian universities.

> By the mid-1980s, Islamists had established themselves as the best organised and most influential force on the university scene. This willingness to engage in a prolonged, often violent, campaign against the left on campus makes it difficult to believe that ideology is what kept them away from the unions.
>
> (Alexander, 2000: 466–467)

These disagreements continued until Tunisia's Second Republic was established by a bloodless coup on 7 November 1987 in which Interior Minister Zine El-Abidine Ben Ali seized the presidency from the erratic and senile Bourguiba. Official doctors declared the President was medically unfit to rule and Ben Ali took control.

Despite hopes that Ben Ali's rule would lead to greater political and social liberalisation, this would ultimately prove to be a façade of reform.

Suggestions of democratic opening and promises to implement democratic political reforms (Alexander, 1997) did not materialise. It was singularity, national unity, and collective interest that remained the themes of the Tunisian elite. Ben Ali implemented reforms that were "cast in a language that suggested a deeper commitment to democracy" (Alexander, 2010: 54). In addition, tangible gestures towards pluralism were made, for example, Islamists were released from prison and joined in the national debate while opposition parties were legalised.

The opening of the civic space allowed for a proliferation of associations. Political liberalism moved to implement new freedoms for the press as "press department rules were relaxed and television and radio stations were instructed to be more objective in their coverage and to concentrate less on PSD affairs" (Murphy, 1999: 168).

However, the co-option tactics of the Bourguiba era continued. Current and former members of the LTDH, an internationally recognised, 3000-member organisation, Hamouda Ben Slama, Saadedine Zmerli, and Mohamed Charfi found themselves co-opted and included in Ben Ali's new cabinet, which "clearly illustrated Ben Ali's incorporative intentions" (Murphy, 1999: 168). Some became part of the regime while others were suppressed. LTDH Secretary-General Khemais Chemari was arrested in 1987 for ensuring jailed MTI leaders received suitable treatment (Perkins, 1997: 100).

The rise of women's organisations also seemed to demonstrate an opportunity for Liberal-Associative civil society groups to operate. But these organisations also found themselves within the regime's web of control and were incorporated into the party system. *L'Association des Femmes Tunisiennes pour la Recherche sur le Développement* (AFTURD) was government organised but independent women's organisations also appeared, such as *L'Association Tunisienne des Femmes Democrates* (ATFD), established in 1989. ATFD and LTDH, established in 1977, were two exceptions that both managed to retain a degree of political independence yet were confronted with the operational difficulties from suppression and arrest to infiltration and manipulation from party loyalists (Alexander, 2010: 65). The false liberalisation limited their ability to operate.

The National Pact and the removal of Islamist political challenge

In September 1988, Ben Ali invited key political and civil society actors to reach a national consensus known as the National Pact. The 16 invited organisations were legal opposition parties, trade unions, NOs, and representatives of the MTI. They discussed their commitment to liberal reform and created a document that appeared to be a pathway towards reform. Instead, it was the corporatist state model reasserting its control by including dissenting voices within the system and a tactic to weaken any forms of opposition.

At a political level, Ben Ali intended the National Pact to "foster a formal national political consensus in the period leading up to the first election of the post-Bourguiba era" (Perkins, 1997: 133). Opposition figures and intellectuals joined the re-named ruling party, the *Rassemblement Constitutionnel Démocratique* (RCD) and accepted positions in the new government with the intention of implementing the reforms they demanded (Belhassen, 1988). MTI representatives also followed these steps. To obtain legal status and obey the law which prohibited party names from containing religious references, "in early 1989, MTI renamed itself *Hizb Ennahda* (the Renaissance Party) to comply with Ben Ali's stated position that no single group should monopolize the claim to be Islamic since all Tunisians were Muslim" (Esposito and Piscatori, 1991: 431).

This political liberalisation was not, however, a step towards democracy but a strategy to gather information and identify opposition. By listening to their grievances and making appropriate changes, Ben Ali removed the opposition movement's potency. The RCD learnt how to rule more effectively and co-opted opposition into government through appointing their most influential leaders.

The National Pact discussion also had major implications for civil society. After an opening for potential change, Tunisia's Second Republic remained an authoritarian state; manipulating the fear of Islamism and terrorism to weaken civil society influence and close the space in which they operated. The National Pact "reinvigorated the role of national organisations as partners with the state, rather than potential and sometimes actual combatants" (Murphy, 1999: 173). As part of the state, the NOs were legally permitted to operate. However, they were co-opted into the system meaning they lacked true separation and independence. A subordinate UGTT was required for Ben Ali's economic reforms to be implemented. By 1993, a younger and more technocratic minded leadership had replaced the older and confrontational members and the UGTT was left "weak and internally divided" (Murphy, 1999: 187–192). An alternative students' union, the Islamist-inspired UGTE, was established to compete with and divide UGET members. UGTE created more independent bodies that could think independently and challenge national associations. The regime would later be forced to co-opt these too.

The lack of violence by civil society, in most cases, points to some evidence of civility, but freedom, equality, and pluralism were constrained by the nationalist struggle first, and later, by corporatist state structures. Leftist opposition views were incorporated into the one-party state while dissidents were suppressed. Regime imposed secularism remained a key criteria of citizenship to combat the threat of Islamism. Repressive security state apparatus and violent secret police methods created a general ambience of mistrust, in both the regime and others in society (Hibou, 2006: 187).

This chapter concludes that prior to the 2011 revolution, Tunisia had a pre-existing history and tradition of civil society that operated in various and limited forms under colonial and authoritarian rule and that Tunisian civil society was shaped and characterised by the systems of government under which it operated. Therefore, in a post-authoritarian context, Tunisian civil society can be re-evaluated. It is appropriate to apply civil society and political civility literature and to ask new questions about the quality of Tunisian democratic practices.

CSOs could still exist and operate in the Ben Ali era but only when at least partially co-opted by the regime. Opposition organisations, those not established by the regime, had little impact and suffered from high risk of arrest. Therefore, since they were forced to participate and operate within the parameters of the regime, there were overlaps in personalities between political parties and CSOs. For example, the LTDH members in Ben Ali's cabinet meant that the RCD claimed to include opposition and voices. By allowing grievances to be aired within the regime, the potency of opposition voices was reduced.

CSOs became progressively controlled by the regime when they relied on the government for funding to cover the operational costs or undermined when the government established associations to compete with existing ones, e.g. *Le comité supérieur des droits de l'Homme et des libertés fondamentales* against the LTDH.

> Ben Ali's effort to break the connection between elite and popular politics has also created a profound strategic malaise for the organizations that long constituted the bedrock of associational life. As elsewhere in the region, the struggle for meaningful autonomy from state control has dominated the lives of workers' and students' unions, human rights groups, women's groups and Islamist organizations in post-independence Tunisia. At the same time, though, these organizations have always understood that the line between state and civil society is blurry at best. For more than 30 years, establishing alliances with individuals and factions of the governing elite

and playing on tensions within party and state bureaucracies was a fundamental part of these organizations' strategies for influencing government policy. The dissolution of these ties, the end of opposition politics as it operated for so long, has left Tunisia's traditionally vigorous civil society adrift.

(Alexander, 1997)

While political parties based on religion remained illegal, they were permitted a limited existence in civil society. The role of religion was recognised in the UGTE, the student organisation that had close relations with MTI, which was legalised in September 1988. Also, a new cabinet position, Secretary of State for Religious Affairs, was created in November (Murphy, 1999: 179). "Hoping to encourage Islamist moderation, Ben 'Ali promised MTI/Ennahda leaders that he would legalise their party if they would keep peace at the universities and give him time to consolidate his position" (Alexander, 2000: 474).

Ben Ali indeed consolidated his position as President when he won a landslide electoral victory in 1989 with 99.2 per cent of the vote. In the parliamentary elections, Ennahda gained 152 per cent of the vote, outperforming the secular opposition parties. However, thanks to "the electoral parliamentary formula – based on a single round to be won by a simple majority of votes" (Martínez Fuentes, 2010: 526) the RCD dominated the chamber of deputies and held all 141 seats. Ennahda represented the only genuine threat to the RCD and Ben Ali reneged on his promise to legalise the Islamist party. This prompted the party's more militant elements, especially students, to argue that "the government's refusal [was] proof that trading moderation for legalisation would never pay off" (Alexander, 2000: 476). A protest and repression exchange followed until Ennahda was depleted and its leaders imprisoned or exiled.

Faced with growing apathy at the lack of opportunity in the unfair election process and government harassment of Ennahda, the movement's spokesman, Ali Laarayedh, accused the government of being incapable of dialogue but argued that Ennahda should, "continue the fight because there is no longer any means of reaching an agreement with the government. Through demonstrations in the street, we fight for our rights and the country's" (Marouki, 1990: 33). As a response, Ennahda became more militant through increased protests and lifting its ban on violence (Soudan and Gharbi, 1991). Ben Ali countered Ennahda with suppression when 200 Islamic activists were arrested in December 1990 (Alexander, 2010: 60). On 17 February 1991, three Islamic activists attacked the RCD office. The government claimed it was an assassination attempt on Ben Ali. In response, government oppression dramatically increased and between 1990 and 1992 over 8000 allegedly dangerous or threatening Islamists were arrested (Waltz, 1995: 72).

Ben Ali further strengthened his position by using the Algerian Civil War and Islamic terrorist attacks against France in the 1990s to emphasise the Islamist threat and shift to a hard-line policy towards Islamic activists (Esposito and Piscatori, 1991: 432). As a pro-Western Arab leader he used the situation to strengthen his hold on power by crushing Islamic opposition at home, and continuing authoritarian measures, knowing he had the complete backing of Europe. The Algerian case allowed Ben Ali to argue that "democracy needed to be introduced gradually or Tunisia would follow Algeria's descent into instability and violence" (Wood, 2002: 97).

As compensation for severe violations of political and civil rights, women's rights were enhanced under Ben Ali. Also, some pressure on Islamists was relieved, such as the loosening of the ban on university students wearing the veil (Sonneveld, 2015: 5). However, "Islamist opposition, which expressed the frustrations of masses either unrepresented by secular parties or suppressed within the national organisations, was not to be tolerated at all" (Murphy, 1999: 79). The Islamist UGTE was also suspended in 1991 under the accusation of stockpiling weapons (Khlifi, 2013). After the Islamist threat was crushed, the voice of the legal opposition was also limited.

Ben Ali had defeated his opposition through co-option, coercion, and electoral manipulation while offering tokens of liberty to a restricted civil society.

Human rights and Western support

Now that Islamist associations posed no immediate threat to Ben Ali's hegemony, he sought to control human rights and lawyers organisations. These organisations were permitted to exist as it helped support this illusion that Tunisia was democratic. He did so by implementing a new Law of Associations in 1992 to restrict membership and activities. This included clauses whereby LTDH members could not hold office in other associations or political parties. Therefore, the overlap between party and CSO personalities ended and LTDH lost active leaders. Former LTDH leader Moncef Marzouki responded by establishing the *Comite National pour la Defence des Prisonniers d'Opinion* (CNDPO) but while the government allowed this organisation to exist, it also monitored its membership and activities. The regime denied the existence of political prisoners or torture cases, instead seeking to highlight the improvements in human rights and political freedom which they had implemented.

Ben Ali, paradoxically, postured as a human rights supporter while simultaneously quashing genuine activists (Murphy, 1999: 205–207). Mohammed Moada, leader of the legal MDS party, was sentenced to 11 years in jail for an open letter that called for a gradual move towards a pluralist culture and democratic choice. Marzouki was arrested for running as a presidential candidate in the 1994 election, and the Tunisian press was suffocated as journalists were routinely harassed. An additional example of Tunisian state oppression was the case of Judge Mukhtar Yahyaoui. He wrote an open letter to President Ben Ali on 6 June 2001[10] which criticised the oppressive control over the judicial system. The regime responded by dismissing him from the body of magistrates and confiscating his property (Marzouk, 2015).

Ben Ali also managed to escape criticism from Western governments due to their trade and security cooperation with Tunisia. Wood (2002) acknowledges how Tunisia's poor human rights record was constantly overlooked by the French government despite the French and international press highlighting the problem. The 'special relationship' between France and Tunisia, underpinned by their mutually profitable trade association, added to Ben Ali's confidence that he was somehow untouchable. In addition, Ben Ali's speed at denouncing the 9/11 terrorist attacks on American soil and his pledge of support for the United States' response ensured international pressure on his regime would be alleviated.

Perhaps Ben Ali would have become less repressive as French and international pressure to liberalise intensified in the late 1990s but the 9/11 attack helped Ben Ali galvanise French and European Union support for Tunisia as an anti-terrorism, pro-Western Arab regime. Furthermore, the 'War on Terror' international climate allowed authoritarianism to increase. The structures supporting authoritarianism were not only deeply rooted but capable of adaptation to modern conditions thus keeping ahead of the developing societal forces. While civil society was benefiting from new information technologies, regimes could also use these instruments to their own advantage to enhance surveillance capabilities. This is evident in Tunisia as by December 2001, FBI involvement in Maghrebi counter-terrorism significantly improved the Tunisian security services (Wood, 2002). Human rights activists were often imprisoned as part of this increased oppression. In particular, prior to a United Nations-sponsored world summit on information in November 2005, there was an increase in state repression focused against leading human rights activists (Rishmawi, 2007).

Freedom of information and transparency were also limited. On a social-welfare level, the government stepped in to reduce the need for welfare provision for CSOs. The National Solidarity Fund or *Fonds de Solidarité Nationale* (FNS), also known as 'Caisse 26–26' (26–26 Fund) and *21–21* Fund, established to help the poor and needy, aimed to reduce inequality and prevent "the rise of NGOs that could utilise charity as a springboard for political recruitment" (Sadiki, 2008: 127). However, the non-existence of freedom of information acts and the lack of transparency meant that how these funds were spent or to where they were transferred remained unknown (Henry, 2012: 668). Indeed, open-governance was non-existent and authoritarian rule was hardly encouraging the practice of transparency. A World Bank report cites the "lack of transparency and rampant abuse by cronies" in Tunisia's economy as major factors behind the anger that caused the revolution (2014: 27).

Economic corruption had increased during the 1970s when the state implemented a privatisation programme to replace state-led economic development. Data from the privatisation process was either inaccurately reported or not published. Under Ben Ali's rule, levels of crony-capitalism and mafia-style family control of businesses became rampant as rules were manipulated to serve the interests of those connected to Ben Ali's family.

> Members of the ruling family – as the parents, brothers, sisters and allies of Ben Ali and his wife, Leila Trabelsi, are known – have been the main beneficiaries of the privatisation of public companies, dubious bank loans and

the flourishing black market. Several have one foot in the public sector and the other in the private. They use their position for personal gain, acting as brokers.

(Labidi, 2006)

To illustrate the stranglehold the ruling family held over the economy, of the 220 businesses owned by family members, the World Bank determined that while these firms accounted for only 3 per cent of economic output, they controlled 21 per cent of net private sector profits (World Bank, 2014). Corruption was facilitated by the lack of adequate participation, transparency, and accountability in the management of public affairs. Hibou (2011) describes how corporatism, paternalism, and corruption permeated all levels of Tunisian society which left transparency absent.

Civil society before the revolution

Prior to the 2011 revolution, Tunisian civil society activity was heavily regulated and limited due to the authoritarian tendencies of the regime. Of the few that functioned, even fewer escaped the regime's corporatist civil society mechanisms. Civil society mostly consisted of many service provision NGOs and fewer labour unions and professional associations. The limited number of prodemocracy groups had a precarious legal status and they were continuously harassed by the state. The Islamic associations were closely controlled by the government. "This is due to Tunisia's history of state-enforced secularism, which intensified in the late 1980s and 1990s with the government's attempts to eradicate an incipient Islamic opposition movement, Al Nahda, and any other independent Islamic activity" (Hawthorne, 2004: 8–9).

CSOs were only able to perform a Liberal-Associative or Oppositional-Resistance function because they were constrained by the risk of their organisation being closed and members arrested. The majoritarian view (Alexander, 2010: 120) prevented debates and dissent was not tolerated.

The government operated under a "with us or against us" policy, the same approach that had been prevalent since Bourguiba's disagreements with any internal opposition, such as supporters of ND Secretary-General Salah Ben Youssef. The decade-long Algerian civil war helped ingrain the idea that political Islam would threaten economic prosperity; therefore, the RCD's secular governance and liberal economic approach was the only acceptable option for stability and prosperity. Worker grievances were addressed in the UGTT, which was also largely co-opted by the regime. This left opposing or criticising the government akin to an act of treason. CSO activities which were in any way against the majority view received no media coverage as the media was also forced to self-censor in fear of repression.

The 'false liberalisation' that Ben Ali applied was not unique to Tunisia. It was in fact consistent with the analysis of civil society in liberalised autocracies throughout the MENA region. As Brumberg noted at the time, CSOs have not been able "to pierce the armour of liberalised autocracies" (2002: 63).

Chapter conclusion

The analysis of the four historical phases outlined in this chapter cannot, however, sufficiently account for the existence of CPC within the civil society. Despite organisations' commitment to survive by working with the regime or to challenge the regime from the periphery of the legal constraints, in addition to their use of non-violent approaches, it cannot entirely explain how organisations operated or what values and beliefs their members held.

A civil society, which prevented despotic government tendencies of the Bey, existed prior to French colonialism. French rule then further centralised power and largely dismantled pre-existing civic traditions by weakening local political and economic institutions. As the nationalist movement against the French developed under the Young Tunisians, Destour, and ND, each party respectively learned from their predecessor and progressively engaged greater sections of society. Resistance to colonialism created Tunisian identity based on ethno-nationalism (Sadiki, 2008) and links across society encouraged homogenisation.

The ethno-nationalism of Bourguiba's and Ben Ali's authoritarian rule created an exclusive 'us vs them' dichotomy, which was coupled with the incorporation of dissenting opinions within the ruling party structures and the suppression of Islamic identities. These government policies may account for an intolerance of difference in the post-independence era. To some extent, the nationalism struggle encouraged peaceful cooperation. However, the post-independence leadership's suppression of opposition succeeded in inhibiting the development of socio-political pluralism or tolerance towards alternative visions, as the national associations became increasingly state controlled.

Civil society may have been co-opted and constrained. However, the political openings during the 1978 strike, riots in the early 1980s, the small window of opportunity after Ben Ali came to power in 1987, and the involvement in the 1988 National Pact contributed to maintaining the tradition of an active civil society. Indeed, civil society was able to exhort influence on government and had a role in effecting change. The extensive networks of the UGTT, for example, demonstrated an oppositional-resistance capacity through its large membership base and the ability to call a general strike.

Albeit under the conditions of authoritarianism, Tunisia has a history of "elected parliaments and opposition politics, a smattering of nongovernmental Islamic societies, professional associations, clubs, and prodemocracy groups" (Hawthorne, 2004: 8). Chapter 1 highlights that certain preconditions are necessary to a successful democratisation process. Therefore, the breadth of civil society institutions described in Hawthorne's summary implies that, based on the assumption that a "political society" and state institutions must exist prior to civil society (Linz and Stepan, 1996a; Bodenstein, 2013), extensive state-building would not be required in Tunisia.

Analysis of history is not enough to understand political culture. While relevant historical experience is important to beginning a democratisation process, historical experience must not be over-emphasised as an explanatory variable to summarise a political culture, as per the historical-synoptic assessments of political culture. However, as Anderson identifies political culture as "the values that might support or undermine a particular set of political institutions, the particular distribution of patterns of political orientations-attitudes towards the political system" (1995: 7), the evidence of CSOs existing and operating, despite authoritarian conditions restraining their activities, could account for the basis of a civic culture.

The only way CSOs could operate in pre-revolution Tunisia was by working within the system as 'loyal' co-opted opposition. While the regional branches retained greater independence, the upper echelons of the powerful and mostly independent UGTT fell under government control (Perkins, 2014). Liberal-Associative forms of civil society were permitted to operate if their aims and goals were consistent with the regime's agenda. The public space was controlled by the regime and any opposition to the government or Oppositional-Resistance forms of civil society were suppressed or dismissed as enemies of the state. The false-liberalism and the end of Bourguiba's rule presented an opportunity for an opening in civil society. However, Ben Ali, using the threat of radical or political Islam, ensured pluralism did not develop. He used the same threat throughout his rule which meant that contesting the government through civic action remained effectively criminalised. National cohesion was gained by fostering tacit consensus.

Salamé points to how national unity has been a cloak for authoritarianism (1994: 4–6) while Sadiki describes it as a straightjacket that "has historically compromised pluralism and plurality" (2008: 113). Furthermore, the ethno-nationalism created during independence "lacked a democratic imagery" (Sadiki, 2008: 118). With the exception of the national organisation, prior to the revolution, Tunisian civil society was not entirely autonomous and therefore could not effectively challenge or constrain the state from a fully independent stance. Instead, their activity was constrained by the state because it was not sufficiently separate from the state. Therefore, civil society could perform a limited oppositional function, but not a truly democratic function. As far as can be ascertained, the patrimonial nature of the regime and influence of authoritarianism was reflected in civil society's political culture. There was mistrust and scepticism of the government and RCD due to civil society's experience with government manipulation tactics.

Civil society held an unclear position towards Islam as organisations like LTDH would have shown no prejudice towards Islamists and defended human rights of Tunisians regardless of political views. However, state-imposed secularism and the suppression of Islamism meant that all organisations had to appear secular as Islamist organisations would not have been permitted to exist under Ben Ali's rule, with the exception of pre-schools run by Imams to teach Arabic through study of the Quran.

What makes Tunisian civil society unique, however, is the manner in which its continuous evolution, which began prior to colonialism, survived through French occupation, and then became a vital part of nationalist struggle.

In post-independence Tunisia, civil society might have been weakened and depleted – through arrests, exile of key figures, and was heavily constrained by harsh authoritarian state repression – but it was never completely destroyed. Although it existed to serve the regime and appeared as a façade of liberalisation, it was organised and nationally networked, as opposition groups, at home or in exile, were connected. This meant that it was somewhat prepared for the revolution. The following chapter explains in depth civil society's unique role in the revolution and transition. Indeed, activists who had gained experience from operating in a restricted and co-opted civil society were vital at the start of the revolution. For example, the UGTT existed nationwide, but while the higher ranks were co-opted and close to the party-state, they were still connected to regional branches who operated with greater autonomy. Also, experienced activists who had been forced underground or abroad were prepared.

Notes

1 An Ottoman military commander rank who were recruited from the military and administrative elite and trained in the sultan's household (Moalla, 2014: 19).
2 The scholarly class of Muslims with specialist knowledge of Islamic law and theology.
3 From merchant families.
4 *Parti Liberal Constitutionnel Tunisien*, and in Arabic *Al-Ḥizb Al-Ḥurr Ad-Dustūrī*, was most commonly known as Destour which is Arabic for constitution.
5 Coastal cities of Tunisia's eastern shore; Hammamet, Sousse, Sfax, Mahdia, and Monastir.
6 A major mosque in Tunis and University of Islamic studies.
7 A central trade union founded in 1924.
8 An educational society that opened a window to the West for Arabic-speaking Tunisians (Perkins, 2014: 71) and was "designed to furnish the students at the Zitouna Mosque with a Europeans style complement to their Islamic education" (Anderson, 1986: 159).
9 "Independent reasoning" – an Islamic legal term.
10 Yahyaoui, Mukhtar (2001). Open letter to President Ben Ali. *Human Rights First.* Available at www.humanrightsfirst.org/wp-content/uploads/pdf/open_letter.pdf [Accessed 13 December 2015].

3 Civil society activism from revolution to transition

Ben Ali's superficial stability

Ben Ali's government appeared to be stable. It ticked all the boxes for successful maintenance of political stability through both carrot and stick approaches. It was an autocracy with a façade of democracy; legal opposition parties posed no viable threat opposition through the ballot box and dissenting voices were co-opted or stifled.

An industrial upgrading programme based on economic liberalisation through structural reform and export-oriented growth meant the Tunisian economy enjoyed sustained success (Murphy, 2006). This made it an International Monetary Fund poster child, the *bon élève économique* (good economic student), for its economic growth model. It was an efficiently run police state. The security sector that was overloaded with an estimated personnel of between 130,000 and 200,000 police officers on hand to survey and suppress the population. This is a "ratio of police officers to inhabitants that was three to four times higher than even the most heavily policed countries in Europe" (Lutterbeck, 2013: 1–2). The state monopolised the media sector and controlled the information flows.

Ben Ali's close relationships with France and the United States, based on trade, ensuring Islamists did not gain political power, and preventing extremist groups from establishing a foothold in the region, further added to his political stability as this meant that he had international partners who were complicit with his authoritarian practices.

Not only did Tunisia appear, on the surface, to be stable, but Tunisia had no history of violent or revolutionary transformation. "Reform, not revolution, was the core demand of Tunisian nationalists from the Young Tunisians through the Neo-Destour" (Alexander, 2010: 111).

However, Hibou argues Ben Ali's rule used the democratic façade and economic success to create a myth of "reform" in order "to disguise from the world the deepening corruption, nepotism and stagnation of a one-party state, dominated by what is, in effect, a president-for-life" (in Applebaum, 2007). This is why the bottom-up protests that began in December 2010 and led to a revolution took the world by surprise (Gana, 2013: 1). But the underlying problems of regional and youth unemployment meant that Ben Ali's control was not as stable as the regime had engineered it to seem.

The interior governorates of the country (Jendouba, Kef, Sidi Bouzid, Kasserine, Gafsa, Kebili, Tozeur, Medenine Tataouine) which had suffered from decades of neglect and underdevelopment, had higher unemployment rates than the capital and coastal areas (Boughzala and Tlili, 2014). Despite regime attempts to hide the correct unemployment figures, a World Bank report from March 2008 showed the number of higher education graduates out of work more than doubled over ten years from 121,800 in 1996–1997 to 336,000 in 2006–2007 (Aleya-Sghaier, 2012: 21). This increase in numbers is also matched by an increase in graduates' unemployment which rose from 8.6 per cent in 1999 to 21.6 per cent in 2008 (Haouas et al., 2012: 400). This was a five-fold increase in both the number of Tunisian graduates and the graduate unemployment rate from 1994–2009 (Broecke, 2012: 5).

As legal immigration to Europe became extremely difficult after the 2008 global economic crisis, the number of frustrated youths rose. Furthermore, when the "degree of luxury in which the privileged members of the regime lived (villas, private jets, palaces, luxury cars, private clubs, bank accounts in Tunisia and abroad)" (Aleya-Sghaier, 2012: 21) was exposed on the Internet, the rage against the system grew.

Foreign diplomats were aware of the socio-economic problems in addition to the ruling elite's fragile position. Robert Godec, US ambassador to Tunisia, highlighted major faults in the Tunisian system in his June 2008 report. His assessment later became infamous when it was released on WikiLeaks. He noted that "Many Tunisians are frustrated by the lack of political freedom and angered by First Family corruption, high unemployment and regional inequities" and that there was "little freedom of expression or association" in addition to "serious human rights problems" (*Guardian*, 2010). Regarding civil society, Godec highlighted that activists who participate in embassy activities are described as traitors in state-controlled newspapers and are intimated by plain-clothes police. The Tunisian government was also dissatisfied with the US embassy's contact with opposition leaders and civil society activists who were critical of the regime.

Bloody roots

The roots of the revolution can be traced to the 2008 mining basin uprising in the central eastern governorate of Gafsa. The uprising was a series of protests and riots due to levels of high regional unemployment, the worsening economic situation, and the corrupt recruitment processes of the Gafsa Phosphate Company (CPG). The Gafsa uprising was an expression of Oppositional-Resistance civil society activity. It demonstrated that civil society was active and, in the regional ranks, took an oppositional stance even when the co-opted central or head offices were too constrained by the authoritarian regime to take such a position.

In January 2008, CPG, the major employer in the mining region, opened a call for applications. Residents held that the recruitment process was nepotistic because over 60 positions were offered to citizens from a neighbouring governorate which was also the hometown of the Gafsa governor and his two cousins – the CPG president and the director of the local chemical factory (Bakchich, 2008).

In response to this injustice, four unemployed graduates began a hunger strike because their names were not included in the list of accepted applicants. This was followed by a peaceful procession by hundreds of high-school students, trade unionists, unemployed people and their families, and a one-hour sit-in opposite the CPG head office in Redeyef, one of the four major mining cities in Gafsa (*Révolution*, 2008). These protests continued sporadically until July 2008.

Regional General Union of Tunisian Workers (UGTT) members and leaders were active in organising the uprising, while Tunisian League for Human Rights (LTDH) Gafsa section leaders were active alongside demonstrators and "were sometimes able to serve as mediators in the negotiations with the local authorities" (Gobe, 2010a: 19). This level of civil society organisation (CSO) coordination and cooperation demonstrates the existence of tolerance and trust between different organisations' criteria of civility. It also demonstrates the agency of regional leaders.

Information surrounding the Gafsa uprising remains limited due to media blackouts and authoritarian constraints, therefore some details remain unclear. However, these events demonstrate that while oppositional civil society activism existed in the regions, it was largely covered up by the regime. Due to lack of access and information opacity, regional civil society activism remained understudied in the literature on Tunisian civil society.

A sycophantic report from the state-owned *La Presse* newspaper on 11 April 2008 stated that protesters were pro-regime, that they were marching in support of Ben Ali, were thanking him for initiating measures to improve the environment in the mining basin region, and were in support of his re-election in 2009 (*La Presse*, 2008).

In contrast, political prisoner Boubaker Akrem told Al Jazeera that "Protests were censored, there was no media and no Facebook, and people were scared to tell their stories because the regime was too strong" (Moshiri, 2011). As reports surrounding the Gafsa riots were spread on Facebook, the regime responded by blocking the site for two weeks. The extent of the online repression was reflected in the Freedom House Internet freedom index which ranked Tunisia lower than Iran and China (Freedom House, 2009).

The state also responded to the uprising with physical violence. Security and military forces responded heavily by firing live rounds at protesters, injuring 26 and fatally wounding two on 6 June (Nawaat, 2009). Tunisian CSO and news blog Nawaat reported that, between April and June 2008, 300 people were arrested across Gafsa including labourers, teachers, trade unionists, members of the Movement of Families of Striking Miners, and human rights activists. Many of the detainees were tortured, violated, and had family members threatened.

Another 150 people were arrested in Redeyef in June and July after demonstrations while at least 200 people were prosecuted in connection with the protests. Some were given eight-year prison sentences after unfair trials where defence lawyers were not permitted to present their cases or medical evidence of torture (Nawaat, 2009).

The UGTT pressured the government to release those arrested during the protests and the release of union activist Adnane Hajji demonstrates their success in influencing state decision making. This demonstrates a degree of civil society independence and showed how, even in heavily restricted conditions, the UGTT was able perform the "protection from despotism" function that writers like Paine attribute to civil society (1969).

The revolution

The revolution occurred because the economic based social contract between Ben Ali and Tunisians had been broken. The population's silence could no longer be guaranteed when high levels of state corruption, unemployment, disparities in wealth, and authoritarian practices negatively affected all sections of society outside the ruling family. Protests and demonstrations that spread across the country and calls for freedom, bread, and dignity brought down a seemingly invulnerable regime within a month. Feeding on local anger over high unemployment rates and a lack of political and socio-economic freedom, the Tunisian revolution would eventually claim 338 lives in the violent demonstrations where police and protesters clashed (Ajmi, 2012).

In the immediate months and years after the revolution, various published works have summarised these events. This has left the narrative of the revolution without a consensus. However, the act of self-immolation by street vendor Mohamed Bouazizi on 17 December 2010, outside the governorate office in the central town of Sidi Bouzid to protest against police interference and a lack of economic opportunities, certainly sparked the revolution. This was an act of defiance against the Tunisian state's undignified treatment of its people.

The early stages of the revolution were the result of individuals coming together in near spontaneous action. Unemployed and manual labourers in the interior regions and lawyers, doctors, and middle classes from the coastal cities all contributed to the uprising (Al Jazeera, 2011c). However, the overthrow of Ben Ali was driven to its conclusion by organised civil society.

The protests in response to Bouazizi's suicide demonstration did not spread like wildfire, as the more romantically constructed narratives suggest. Yet civic activism has been credited as a major factor in Ben Ali's downfall, particularly as military and foreign powers were apparently not involved. CSOs, which had become accustomed to state repression, collectively mobilised to form a protest movement against the heavy-handed response of the regime. The focus on opposition to the regime and the demand for rights united diverse groups around the common objectives of *khubz, hurriya, karama watanya* (bread, freedom, national dignity). "Tunisia's 'spirit of solidarity' signalled the start of the revolution and the starting point for freedom of association and institutional reform for civil society activity" (Deane, 2013: 5). Furthermore, Deane attributes the effectiveness of Tunisian CSOs as revolutionary actors to their homogeneity.

> Despite regime regulations and repression, Tunisia's civil society groups benefited from the relatively cohesive, tolerant make-up of Tunisian society, a society free from ethnically driven conflict. Historically, economic cleavages proved the most pervasive cause of social conflict in Tunisia leading to the revolution.
>
> (2013: 8)

General strikes and Ben Ali's departure

The UGTT played a fundamental role in the revolution through organising and coordinating demonstrations which represented 'grassroots' involvement. From the outset, after Bouazizi's self-immolation, local trade unions were echoing his sentiments of social and economic injustice.

On 24 December, when police opened fire on protesters in Menzel Bouzaienne, the UGTT disseminated news that two protesters had been fatally wounded. Major protests were held in Sfax, Kairouan, and Ben Guerdane on 25 December, then in the capital Tunis on 27 December next to the UGTT headquarters in the downtown area of the city.

On 28 December, the regime acknowledged the situation when Ben Ali addressed the nation in a television broadcast, warning that protests were unacceptable and would negatively impact the economy. Ben Ali criticised the "use of violence in the streets by a minority of extremists" and said the law would be applied "in all firmness" to punish the "thugs" responsible for the riots (Rifai, 2011).

Ben Ali later tried to pacify protests with financial and political concessions, in addition to dismissing the governors of the Sidi Bouzid, Jendouba, and Zaghouan governorates. He also dismissed the ministers of communication, trade and handicrafts, and religious affairs for reasons related to the uprising, the Arabiya news channel reported. Meanwhile, local union activists informed international news channels of their situation on the ground. UGTT management levels authorised the regional sections of Sfax, Kairouan, and Tozeur to organise strikes (Piot, 2011), and subsequently UGTT leadership called for a general strike on 6 January.

The protests were initially against corruption and demanding better economic opportunities. However, when the regime responded heavy-handedly, the nature of the protests altered to demanding political freedom, regime change, and an end to Ben Ali's rule in favour of a representative government. This occurred between 8 and 12 January after the killings in Kasserine and Thala by masked gunmen who shot at protesters from rooftops, killing 22 people and injuring approximately 200 (Ryan, 2013a). The UGTT leadership changed its mediating stance and fully supported the protest movement, calling for another general strike on 11 January. When the third general strike was called on 14 January, thousands took to the streets of the capital. Protesters gathered outside the feared Ministry of Interior on the central Avenue Habib Bourguiba to demand that Ben Ali stand down, famously chanting *Dégage* (get out). This marked the fall of the Ben Ali regime, as he fled to Saudi Arabia the same evening.

National Bar Association

Just like the influential UGTT, the Tunisian national lawyer's association (*Ordre National des Avocats* – ONAT) played a crucial role in the revolution. Under the Ben Ali regime, the judicial system remained controlled by the executive whose "influence over the judiciary persisted due to the failure to adopt long-awaited reforms of the judiciary" (Human Rights Watch, 2013). The judiciary, as a structure, was co-opted. But this does not, however, account for the agency demonstrated by lawyers who resisted the regime individually and collectively through ONAT.

Lawyers who were not loyal to the regime and opposed the system were arrested and the ease with which their protests were suppressed meant their politicisation and mobilisation failed to destabilise the system. Gobe (2010b) points to the lawyers' rebellious voting behaviour in elections for *Bâtonnier* (head of Bar) in 1998 and 2001 to argue that Tunisian lawyers were "not a homogeneous group" (2010b: 333) and there was growing discontent with the regime from within the profession. This dissatisfaction with the regime escalated to a lawyers' strike in April 2000, organised by the Bar Council. The strike aimed to protest against the physical assault of lawyers, who were defending opponent-journalist Taoufik Ben Brik, by uniformed and plain-clothed police (Ben M'barek 2003: 409). Further protests in the 2000s, such as the April 2005 sit-in to protest against the arrest of lawyer and regime critic Mohamed Abbou and the national day of protest in May 2006 by lawyers who rejected a new law which increased the executive's control over the profession, demonstrate the legal profession had been a vehicle to expression opposition.

ONAT, however, was able to work against the system. It became a limited space for dissent and "one of the few institutions of civil society that has managed to preserve its autonomy and independence" (Gobe, 2010b: 338). Gobe adds that it was "one of the only areas where politics can be expressed through professional demands ... [and] ... an arena of political protest by default, a sort of alternative political field" (2010b: 334).

This field became active during the revolution. Using their political leverage and professional duty as defender of rights, lawyers protested against the use of governmental repression against the uprising on 31 December 2010. This added significance to the protests as it meant that elites were joining the revolution. The protests could not be dismissed as a youth, working class, or unemployed phenomenon. Instead, the mobilisation of ONAT gave greater legitimacy and credibility to the protesters' demands. This strengthened the revolutionary process because it demonstrated that grievances with the regime cut across socio-economic cleavages and resonated with the middle class and the wider population. This sentiment was reinforced when the lawyers' protests were also subjected to police brutality (Ryan, 2010) and showed how the Ben Ali police state's coercive responses affected all Tunisians. Tunisian Blogger, Lina Ben Mhenni, argued that the 300 lawyers, who protested in front of the Court of Justice in solidarity with Sidi Bouzid, criticising the government, and asking the President to leave, represented a turning point in the revolution (Ben Mhenni, 2010).

This turning point demonstration was followed up on 6 January 2011 when 95 per cent of Tunisia's 8000 lawyers participated in an ONAT-organised strike. They protested against beatings they said they received from police at sit-ins in Tunis and other towns in the previous week and violence by security services against protesters (Al Jazeera, 2011c).

Diwan (2012) addresses the numerous factors surrounding the important role of middle classes in the Arab uprisings, arguing that the middle class, who were vital in helping Arab autocrats maintain their legitimacy, could no longer be co-opted. Economic liberalisation in the 1990s led to a market-oriented middle class and greater inequality led to the development of a wealthy Arab 1 per cent while insufficient job creation and high unemployment amongst educated youth created suitable conditions for uprising. Middle class youth, rather than hardened Islamists, leading the Arab uprisings (2012: 6) support his theory.

No independent press existed until after the revolution, only foreign press who worked with CSOs. Therefore, citizen journalism, blogging, and cyber-activism as well as investigative journalist CSOs, such as Nawaat, were pivotal in the revolution. The regime recognised their influence when bloggers Slim Amamou and Azyz Amamy, were arrested on 6 January (Al Jazeera, 2011c). While journalists were surveyed by the regime, social media could spread information from Sidi Bouzid, initially, and other protest locations, then upload the information to international media outlets such as Al Jazeera and France 24. In particular, Al Jazeera's coverage and broadcasting of citizen-generated media in the form of mobile phone video uploads from protesters in Tunisia helped spread awareness. Lynch adds that "Al Jazeera has played a vital, instrumental role in framing this popular narrative by its intense, innovative coverage of Tunisia and its explicit broadening of that experience to the region" (2011).

Cyberattacks from hacker activist group Anonymous crashed the websites of the Tunisian Stock Exchange, the Ministry of Industry, the President, and the Prime Minister (Kushner, 2014). Anonymous is not Tunisian but its activism inspired students who responded by protesting the following day in cities across the country. The importance of social media coordination, however, has been over-emphasised. Wolfsfeld et al. (2013) summarise the cyber-enthusiasts versus cyber-sceptics debate regarding the importance of social media in uprisings but argue that analysis of political context should take precedence and social media should be viewed as a dependent variable. Social media is only one channel of communication and just one aspect of the protest movements. Norris notes that "structural factors, such as corruption, hardship, and repression" were the overriding causes of the uprising (2012: 5). Furthermore, the same social networks that may contribute to empowering citizens, may also be used against them for control and repression (Benkirane, 2012).

Opposition political parties were mostly ineffective actors in the revolution. Their position was, however, complex due to the difficult situation the dictatorship had forced them into but opposition leaders were also entangled with CSOs. Classifying opposition politicians and parties as part of civil society is somewhat misleading. Ideally, civil society is separate from government and actors and organisations are not seeking to win elections. This definition would obviously exclude opposition politicians and parties.

However, the situation in Ben Ali's Tunisia was not as clearly defined. First, opposition politicians were certainly not in government. They were involved with the government as a loyal opposition and were complicit in the democratic charade that the regime presented to the world. Second, they knew, due to electoral and constitutional manipulation, their chance of winning an election, in addition to Ben Ali accepting the outcome, was almost impossible. This meant that Tunisian political parties were largely ineffective at counter-balancing or holding the government to account. Instead they were forced to tip-toe on the edge of opposing the government without over stepping the red lines and being too critical, which would inevitably lead to their arrest.

The alternative route to resisting the dictatorship and opposing despotism was through civil society. Therefore, civil society was politicised as opposition politicians were also members of major, legal CSOs such as the LTDH, the Tunisian Association of Democratic Women (ATFD), the Tunisian Association for Struggle against Torture (ALTT), the National Committee for Liberties in Tunisia (CNLT), and UGTT. For example, throughout his career, Mustafa Ben Jaafar remained an oppositional political figure through the Democratic Socialist Party and later the Democratic Forum of Labour and Liberty (FDTL) also known as *Ettakatol*, one of the few legal opposition parties under Ben Ali. However, he also held membership in the UGTT and LTDH.

Moncef Marzouki is another opposition politician who was forced to operate in and out of civil society. He was chairman of the LTDH but was pressured to leave. He responded by running for the presidency against Ben Ali in 1994, an offence that lead to his arrest. In 2000 he created the Congress Party for the Republic (CPR). The party was declared illegal by Ben Ali and so Marzouki operated in exile in France.

Maya Jribi co-founded the Progressive Democratic Party (PDP) and later became the first woman to head a Tunisian political party. She also founded the Association of Research on Women and Development. She suffered regime harassment and in 2007 went on hunger strike to protest against the regime's attempt "to marginalise political parties by moving the PDP's headquarters outside of the capital. This was a battle she won, she was not arrested and the regime backed down" (Al Yafai, 2018).

Other political figures were too critical for the regime's liking. Hamma Hammami, President of the Tunisian Workers' Communist Party (PCOT, *Parti*

56   Civil society: revolution to transition

Communiste des Ouvriers de Tunisie) and his wife Radhia Nasraoui (lawyer and human rights activist) became targets for state arrest, intimidation, and torture (Amnesty International, 1994). Under Ben Ali's rule Hammami was repeatedly jailed, tortured, and forced into hiding for his political views and activities such as running an illegal political party and publishing its party newspaper, *Al Badil*.

The difficult position these politicians were put in meant that, however hard they tried, they were certainly not part of "institutions and associations strong enough to prevent tyranny" (Gellner, 1996: 103). Yet, despite the realities of operating within the confines of a dictatorship, the connections between the political and public space had allowed civil society to remain in existence but, in some cases, on the periphery of political life under Ben Ali.

But when it came to the revolution, opposition parties that had remained operational through avoiding antagonising the regime, lacked the necessary infrastructure and grassroots support to play an influential role. In contrast, CSOs such as the UGTT, had the networks and organisational structures to unite people from different political and economic backgrounds, and in different regions, particularly the interior. As this narrative has shown, CSOs played a role in shaping the events leading up to 14 January through demonstrations, applying pressure on the government, and UGTT-organised and lawyers' strikes.

Degage: the post-Ben Ali era

In this period, opposition parties and CSOs were granted legal status which allowed them to perform a democratic role and contribute to the process of change. Civil society was effective at holding the interim government to account, amplifying popular demands, and ensuring the transition was not controlled by the old regime.

According to the collection of academic works that have been labelled 'transitology', the breakthrough in a democratic transition is "the collapse of the regime and the rapid emergence of a new, democratic system" (Carothers, 2002: 7). This description does not entirely apply to Tunisia in 2011 after Ben Ali departed for Saudi Arabia. Instead, there was a ten-month process of gradual change that led to the October 2011 elections for seats in the National Constituent Assembly (NCA) whose deputies would be elected to write the new constitution. This saw a change in ruling personnel but the regime's control was so comprehensive and omnipotent it did not 'collapse'. The head had been removed but the body was still working. Certainly more of the people's voices were included in this process but to call this a 'new, democratic system' would be a naively optimistic assessment.

Starting with the regime, Ben Ali and the close members of the ruling Trabelsi family had fled, but the Constitutional Democratic Rally (*Rassemblement Constitutionnel Démocratique*, RCD) state party was yet to be disbanded. Instead, members of the regime stayed in government and tried to control the aftermath of the revolution. First, the technocratic prime minister, Mohammed Ghannouchi, tried to assume the presidency. Popular protests forced him to defer to the correct interpretation of the constitution, that the Speaker of the Lower House, Fouad Mebazaa, was entitled to take the vacancy, because Ben Ali's departure was permanent, not temporary (Murphy, 2013: 232). The constitution had importantly prevented a power struggle and enabled a new interim government to be appointed. Second, Ghannouchi tried to use the regime's tactic of opposition co-option when he announced the new cabinet on 17 January. The inclusion of 11 leading opposition and civil society figures among its 23 ministers (Murphy, 2013: 233) was an attempt to control political unrest and ensure the RCD could retain power by incorporating the disaffected into the system and implementing just enough reforms to regain control of the country. Opposition leaders, familiar with the regime's playbook, saw through this move and objected to the inclusion of RCD members in the unity government while further protests sustained pressure on Ghannouchi.

These members of the old regime struggled to calm the storm caused by ongoing street demonstrations. On 22 January, approximately 2000 police officers, calling for better working conditions and a new union and seeking to disassociate from Ben Ali's repressive regime, joined the thousands of civilian protesters who were calling for the complete removal of all RCD members from the interim government (Al Jazeera, 2011b). The following day, members of the 'Liberation caravan', protesters who had travelled from different parts of the Sidi Bouzid governorate, broke the night curfew and joined the continuing protests against former RCD ministers who were remaining in government (Al Jazeera, 2011a). In response to these protests, on 24 January a group of politicians created the 'Council of the Defence of the Revolution'. Formed by 12 leading opposition parties and members of UGTT, ONAT, LTDH, and the Association of Judges, the council was tasked with overseeing the interim government and ensuring that reforms continued to be made (Reuters, 2011).

Tunisia's interim government was indeed effective in facilitating change from the old regime. They reformed state laws which encouraged greater civic participation and saw the creation of new political parties and civic organisations to support the development of democratic procedures. This also included the removal of certain individuals from government. Realising pressure from civil society and the wider population, which became progressively more organised, Ghannouchi increasingly surrendered control of the process. Further protests against the presence of RCD members in the cabinet resulted in the resignation of Ghannouchi and the remaining two ministers who served under Ben Ali, Minister of Industry Mohamed Afif Chelbi and the International Cooperation Minister Mohamed Nouri Jouini, on 27 February 2011 (Paciello 2011: 10). Beji Caid Essebsi, a politician who derived legitimacy from his long political career and held positions under both Bourguiba and Ben Ali, was appointed prime minister by Mebazaa the same day.

An important step in the transition was realised in early March when the announcement was made that the RCD would be formally dissolved, "thereby eliminating the key institutional bases of the ancien regime" (Murphy, 2013: 234).

Next, the Islamist Ennahda party was legalised on 11 March. This marked a significant change for pluralism and democratic participation.

Doubts remained, however, as to whether the 'old guard' of the RCD had been entirely removed from the new government. In particular, Prime Minister Essebsi was an RCD member and had served in Bourguiba's and Ben Ali's governments. To demonstrate that change from the old system was occurring, Essebsi dissolved the political police. It was an important break from the Ben Ali era and a step towards dismantling the tools and structures he had used to maintain power through surveillance, fear, and torture. In addition, as protesters and political forces had been demanding this move, Paciello argues it was an important move towards "building national consensus" (2011: 11).

In further reforms, on 18 February 2011 the interim government wrote Decree Law 6 to establish the "Higher Authority for the Realization of Revolutionary Objectives, Political Reform and the Democratic Transition" (Nouira, 2011). This body was created by merging the 'Higher Political Reform Commission' that Mohammed Ghannouchi had created on 17 January in order to control the transition, and the 'revolutionary' opposition forces led 'Council of the Defence of the Revolution'. The Higher Authority "became directly responsible for the political reform process to allow a democratic transition" (Nouira, 2011) and was vital for civil society as it "instituted new laws of association, providing a number of positive protections for NGOs" (Deane, 2013: 12).

As part of creating a 'new, democratic system', the Higher Authority wrote a new electoral law for the NCA elections. The elected members of the assembly would draft a new constitution. The law included 33 constituencies, a higher allocation of seats to south and south-western constituencies to redress the regional imbalance, and representation for Tunisian diaspora. To ensure female voices were included 50 per cent of nominations on lists were women. The youth perspective was awarded a token inclusion as one member of the party list had to be under 30 years old.

The electoral system was designed to increase pluralism and prevent exclusion. It featured the 'Hare Quota with Largest Remainders' proportional representation system to ensure no one party monopolised the election and smaller parties would also be represented. The decision to implement an electoral system that disperses power and fosters inclusiveness proved to be effective as it later prevented Ennahda, the strongest party in the 23 October elections, from dominating the assembly (Carey, 2013). In other measures to ensure fair elections and demonstrate a break from the old regime, "judges, regional governors, local officials, military personnel and former senior officials of the RCD were banned from running" (Murphy, 2013: 235).

To oversee the democratic elections, on 18 April, Decree Law 2011-27 established an Independent High Commission for Elections (ISIE – *l'instance supérieure indépendante pour les élections*) that was tasked with ensuring that elections were democratic, pluralist, fair, and transparent. ISIE scheduled the NCA elections for 23 October to allow adequate time for party preparation and voter registration. This enabled civil society to play a democracy promotion role by promoting the institutionalisation of inclusive democratic norms and practices. If democratic participation, such as voter turn-out, is high, it increases the legitimacy of the democratic processes. During this period, CSOs actively encouraged citizen mobilisation and voter registration, while also pushing Tunisians to defend their rights.

The establishment of these new and democratic institutional structures by the interim government was essential to oversee a democratic transition. Also, as "new democracies must be institutionalized, consolidated, and become legitimate" (Lipset, 1994: 7), institutionalising the democratic process, with the support of civil society, increased the new system's legitimacy.

In addition to legal democratic structures and procedures bestowing the new system with legitimacy, what can be said about the interim government's role in the legal establishment of civil political culture (CPC)? Murphy argues that

> the norms of civility – freedom, equality and tolerance of plurality, were woven into both the process and the legal construction, although retaining the role of the state in curbing uncivil behaviours, including those which might challenge equality on the basis of gender or religious belief and those who were implicated in the repressive incivilities of the ancien regime.
> (Murphy, 2013: 237)

A new legal framework for civil society

Civil society was strengthened on 24 September when Decree-Law 88 (2011) provided a new legal framework. It created a new context within which organisations could operate by providing clear requirements for CSOs and providing protection that was previously not afforded to them. It guaranteed the freedom to form and to join associations and to undertake civic activities. Decree-Law 88 (2011) strengthened the role of civil society and its development and enshrined its legal independence. CSOs became easier to establish, although they still had to be registered centrally. As a result, approximately 7000 to 10,000 new associations, unions, and professional organisations were registered within ten months of the revolution.

The law also helped influence the political culture of this 'new' civil society. This is a reminder that civil society is contextual and shaped by the government and laws. Article 3 of Decree-Law 88 (2011) directly encourages the criteria of CPC by stating that "Associations shall, in their bylaws, activities and funding, observe the principles of the rule of law, democracy, plurality, transparency, equality, and human rights." In conjunction with Article 3, Article 4 prevents incivility by prohibiting associations from adopting bylaws that call for "any incitement of violence, hatred, fanaticism, or discrimination of religious, racial, or regional grounds" (ICNL, 2011). Human Rights Watch commended the new law, stating that Decree-Law 88 (2011) "replaced earlier repressive legislation that criminalized participation in officially unrecognized associations. It had been hailed as an important step toward bringing Tunisian national law into line with Tunisia's obligation under international human rights law to uphold freedom of association" (2014).

The vital role of state institutions in the early stages of transition

Civil society can only operate if a functioning state exists. Thanks to Tunisia's state institutions remaining intact and not collapsing after Ben Ali left, the Tunisian transition did not require an institution-building process. The bureaucracy that the French colonial powers established remained after independence and placed a firmer grasp over the population throughout the dictatorship. Hibou noted the upholding of Ben Ali's authoritarian regime through his party's monopoly over state institutions, gradually becoming "a state bureaucracy regulating the whole of daily life and imposing its logic down to the smallest detail" (2011: 110). However, it was these centralised institutions that helped maintain stability through the revolutionary turmoil and prevented Tunisia from descending into chaos or civil war.

Driven by the desire to maintain their power and positions of privilege, RCD elites ensured a swift constitutional handover of power which enabled RCD to dominate, to varying degrees, the following two interim governments (Paciello, 2011: 10). This peaceful and leaderless handover of power reinforced the strength of state institutions and set the tone for a largely peaceful transition. As a result, the revolution did not immediately lead to the removal of the state's institutional foundations, which remained functional throughout and in the aftermath of the revolution. Indeed, "where in the world would you find a people who made a revolution on Friday and went back to work on Monday?" (Omri, 2013).

Tunisia's neighbour Libya demonstrated that despite removing the Gaddafi regime, democratic prerequisites are necessary for democratic transition. The lack of institutions and pre-existing structures, amongst other factors such as the new government's inability to control its borders or provide security for its citizens, has made its transition chaotic (Engel, 2014).

Transition could not have continued were it not for pre-existing political parties, institutional structures, and a democratic culture of compromise and consensus. The importance of pre-existing institutional power and the Tunisian tradition of constitutionalism and following legal procedures helped the transition, as laws were upheld, e.g. Ghannouchi complying with Articles 56 and 57 of the 1959 Constitution to allow Mebazaa to be President. The fact that "Tunisian politics had reverted to what it has historically known best – constitutionalism" (Murphy, 2013: 232) ensured that the following democratic transition was peaceful. The top two layers of the Tunisian state, Ben Ali's extended family and the RCD, were rapidly removed, but bureaucratic state institutions continued to function for a short period with an interim President and government.

The period between Ben Ali's departure in January and the October elections in 2011 was precarious for Tunisia. Although the transition period has been marked by a constant struggle to maintain a balance between breaking from old guard institutions and the "undoubted resistance of RCD elites to whole-scale change" (Murphy, 2013: 233), bureaucratic state institutions, active and organised civil society, the lack of military interference, and political culture of consensus, help Tunisia navigate the uncertain process leading to elections.

October 2011 National Constituent Assembly elections

ISIE oversaw the 23 October elections to form a 217-member NCA. The elected deputies would be tasked with drafting a new constitution that balanced power more evenly between the executive and the legislature than the highly presidential 1959 version. A total of 4,308,888 Tunisians voted (a 52 per cent turnout rate) in elections that were adjudged to have been free and fair by observers from the European Union (European Union External Action, 2011), the Carter Center (2011), and the National Democratic Institute (2011).

Ennahda won 40 per cent of the popular vote which yielded 89 seats. Due to the proportional representation election system, Ennahda was not able to dominate the 217 seat assembly but was required to create a coalition to meet the 109 seat target required to form and vote as a government. It formed a 'troika' government with the centre-leftist Congress for the Republic (CPR), which won 29 seats, and Ettakatol (FDTL), which won 20 seats. Although a coalition was a necessity for the formation of a government, it demonstrated and/or improved parties' capacity to compromise. As the parties had different visions for Tunisia, their cooperation set the tone for meaningful pluralism and tolerance of difference.

The nationwide, societal involvement in the elections suggested a "general consensus in favour of democratic politics" (Murphy, 2013: 239). A total of 113 political parties and independents representing a wide spectrum of political ideologies registered in post-revolutionary Tunisia, in comparison to only nine registered parties who participated in elections under Ben Ali's regime, demonstrated increased freedom. Electoral gender parity, which was enshrined in Decree Law 35 of May 2011, meant that 27 per cent of the seats were allocated to female candidates. This demonstrated an improvement in gender equality and ensured the constitution writing process would not be male dominated.

Civil society played a vital oversight role in the election process by observing practices at polling stations across the country. In addition to international observers, "A number of old and new civil society organisations had formed election observatories, including the Association Tunisienne pour l'integrite et la democraties des elections (L'ATIDE), Mourakiboun, Reseau Ofiya, the National Election Observatory and I-Watch Tunisia" (Murphy, 2013: 239).

These elections were a great accomplishment and another important step away from dictatorship. Stepan called this election a "successful democratic transition, albeit not yet a consolidation of democracy" (2012: 89). This assessment is based on the criteria of democratic transition that Linz and he prescribe. First, "sufficient agreement" on "procedures to produce an elected government". Second, a government that comes to power as "the direct result of a free and popular vote". Third, this government's de facto possession of "the authority to generate new policies", and, fourth, "the executive, legislative and judicial power generated by the new democracy does not have to share power with other bodies de jure" such as military or religious leaders (Linz and Stepan, 1996a: 1).

The Tunisian case certainly ticks Stepan's transition criteria boxes but would democratic governance and processes become the new norm in Tunisia? After only one election and less than a year after the revolution, there was no certainty democracy would remain the only game in town. There was still a strong chance that the country could return to authoritarian rule or end up in the "Grey Zone" (Carothers, 2002) of democracy with adjectives such as semi-, façade, pseudo-, weak democracy, partial democracy, illiberal democracy, and virtual democracy (Collier and Levitsky, 1997: 430–451).

After the October 2011 elections, further transition and change were required rather than consolidating the new democracy on the foundations of a bureaucratic, corporatist one-party state. The Tunisian government needed to reform the police, the judiciary, local government, and the state bureaucracy. Corruption and malpractice by the former regime also needed to be addressed in a transitional justice process. But the first major obstacle for Tunisia to overcome was to draft a new constitution that embedded democratic practices, liberties, freedom of expression, and freedom of information, separated and balanced executive and legislative power, balanced secular and Islamism aspirations, and enshrined human rights. To make the task even more challenging, the NCA deputies had been given a mandate of only a year to complete the process.

Interim government, the constitution drafting process and the 2011–2014 interregnum period

The constitution drafting process was a fragile time for Tunisia where the transition could have been de-railed and the newly elected entity could have used its democratic legitimacy to reinstate authoritarianism. However, a "spirit of solidarity" (Deane, 2013) and a desire for political consensus saw the country make strides away from dictatorship.

Civil society utilised the new freedoms it was afforded to positively influence the constitution drafting process. These freedoms already existed in the 1959 Constitution which guaranteed the freedom of political conscience; Article 5 emphasised the principle of pluralism and Article 8 guaranteed freedom of opinion and expression. However, the Ben Ali police state had suppressed these rights and forced the population to accept only the state-prescribed one-party inclusive secular republicanism. After the revolution, Tunisians could enjoy these rights which were further guaranteed in Decree-Laws 87 and 88 (2011) issued by the interim President.

Civil society groups were active in voicing their demands and disapproval against draft constitution articles they considered unsatisfactory. For example, OpenGovTN's campaign #7ell (Open Up), which was adopted by a number of NCA members during the constitutional drafting process, led to pressure resulting in the access to information laws (Decree 21) and Article 62 of the Constitution which states "Public information is the rule, secrecy is the exception" (Keskes, 2012). *L'Association Tunisienne de Transparence dans L'energie et Les Mines* (ATTEM) mobilised 14 CSOs focused on transparency in natural resource governance to work with the head of the NCA energy committee in the drafting of Articles 12, 13, and 136 which ensured "transparency and accountability in the governance of Tunisia's resources" (Karam, 2014) and that part of natural resource revenues were allocated to regional development. *Al Bawsala* played an important oversight role in enhancing transparency during NCA plenary sessions by "publishing NCA documents and posting on social media the attendance records of deputies and their individual votes" (Carter Centre, 2014).

The role of the also pre-existing and influential civil society that pushed the government for greater transparency ensured the constitution drafts met popular expectations. In 2013, the first draft of Constitution Article 28 included an ambiguous definition of the status of women as "complimentary to men". In response, women from trade unions and organisations of all political persuasions, such as ATFD, protested against what appeared to be an infringement on women's rights.

Outside the NCA, CSOs also continued to play an active role in the transition and fulfil an anti-despotism function in pressuring for employment and judicial reform. A report by Foundation for the Future (FFF) noted that many of the newly created, post-revolution organisations, were "heavily involved in the democratic transition" (2013: 11). The report cites unions – such as *L'Confédération Générale des Travailleurs Tunisiens* (CGTT), the UGTT, the Union of Tunisian Judges (SMT), the Union of Administrative Judges (UJM), and the Free Union of Industrialists and Traders (UICL) – and associations working for democracy, citizen action, transparency, and freedom such as the Tunisian League for Citizenship and Touensa. Unemployed youth associations, e.g. Association of Young Tunisian Democrats (JDT), maintained pressure on the government for employment and development while CSO networks like *Lam Echamal* worked on democracy promotion. Similarly, ONAT and the Association of Tunisian Judges (AMT), with assistance from the International Centre for Transitional Justice (ICTJ), helped effect transitional justice reform. In response, the Ministry of Human Rights and Transitional Justice signed an agreement on 16 May 2012 "with the United Nations and the Office of the High Commissioner for Human Rights to partially fund a much-needed judicial reform process that includes civil society in processes of transitional justice" (Freedom House, 2012: 11).

Civil society efforts during the constitution drafting process and pressure for overall reform created a public space that became an arena for debate, reconciliation, and learning to accept difference. *Al Bawsala* helped to provide this space by organising debates between politicians and members of the public.[1] A by-product of this opening was that action and direction for civil society during this phase became incohesive. Having worked together as a unified actor against Ben Ali, the free and open public space in which civil society could now operate lent itself to contradictions and discord. This left individual CSOs searching for their relative positions within this social habitus (Bourdieu, 1985). Some actors within civil society continued to act in a Gramscian, 'against the state' manner while others looked to work with the state. Despite this struggle to define themselves and their purpose, Tunisian civil society had a positive impact on the political transition and performed a collective pro-democracy function by holding the state to account. Nevertheless, civil society became a reflection of the national political situation: polarised.

Religious–secular polarisation of Tunisian society

The polarisation in the political and civil society spaces, largely due to Tunisians disagreeing over the extent to which religion should feature in politics and society, reveals a degree of political incivility.

The end of Ben Ali era oppression meant that civil society and political parties were no longer forced to adopt the government's state-secularist agenda. As a consequence, Tunisians exercised the newfound freedom afforded to them in expressions of freedom *to* (positive liberty) and pluralism. However, the expansion of freedom and pluralism led to a division as society learnt to accept the diversity of opinions in socio-political matters. This division largely manifested itself as a polarisation between secularists, who wanted religion to be away from state control entirely in the private space, and Islamists, who favoured the inclusion of Islam in the new constitution.

This secular–religious polarisation in society, which also manifested in civil society, confirms that the 'intolerance of opposition' legacy from the previous regime remained and that civil society was not entirely civil or democratic. A mistrust in the intentions of the political other led to a lack of tolerance and equality.

The polarisation did not, however, prevent civil society from performing an effective oppositional function that pressured and scrutinised the government and the NCA's progress therefore continuously driving the transition. Although civil society was assisting the democratic transitions and performing a 'protection from despotism' role, it was unable to entirely fulfil a democratising role because not all criteria of CPC were shared across civil society actors.

This social polarisation was a problem that Tunisia needed to confront and overcome in order to maintain the transition towards democracy. In addition to democratic transition, understanding and accepting the diversity of political and ideological perspectives was an essential part of Tunisia's "democracy learning" and local knowledge production process (Sadiki, 2015). Building trust and tolerance in harmony with freedom and pluralism, while also agreeing to equality for all, could be achieved through the open-ended, interactive, cross-cultural, and reflexive process Sadiki describes as the local level development of "intellectual and practical capacities, skills, [and] ethics" (2015: 706).

The main winner of the 2011 NCA election was the Islamist party Ennahda. It formed a 'troika' coalition government with two centre-leftist parties. This demonstration of parties with different ideologies working together in government might have allayed fears, for some, that the transition would be dominated by an Islamist agenda. Yet, for many it did not. Mistrust and suspicion existed throughout the Tunisian population regarding whether Ennahda's election victory was merely the first step in a long-term project with the intention of Islamising Tunisia or transforming it into a Caliphate.

Due to these doubts about Ennahda's true intentions, this period was fraught with delays and disputes over the constitution and charges by the secular opposition that Ennahda was packing the bureaucracy with its followers (Brown, 2014). As an Islamist party and holder of most seats in the troika, Ennahda was under greater pressure than other parties to prove its democratic credentials and ability to compromise with other political actors.

Secular civil society groups played an effective oversight role in the constitution drafting process as they worked towards ensuring Islamic law was not forced into the constitution. For example, the first draft article on blasphemy (Article 3) called for insults on the sacred to be punishable; "The state guarantees freedom of religious belief and practice and criminalises all attacks on that which is sacred." Concerned that this would lead to reduced freedom of speech, civil society drew public attention to the risks of including such an article in the constitution. In response, Ennahda removed 'criminalisation' and *takfir* (accusation of apostasy) was prohibited.

The previously mentioned civil society opposition to the inclusion of complementarity of women to men also led to the phrasing of Article 28 being changed to equality. Ennahda eventually compromised and confirmed it would not impose Sharia as the main source of legislation.

This appears that the Islamist side made greater compromises than the secular. However, the final wording of the constitution was not 100 per cent secular; "our people's commitment to the teachings of Islam" and "our Islamic-Arab identity" (Preamble), Tunisia's "religion is Islam" (Article 1), "The state protects the sacred" (Article 6) "To be eligible for President, your religion must be Islam" (Article 74).

Stepan argued that Tunisia adhered to the "Twin Tolerations" relationship between religion and politics during the 2011 elections. This is where religious citizens accept democratically elected officials of the state to govern and legislate while the state must permit religious citizens to express their views and values (Stepan, 2012). "In a democracy, religion need not be 'off the agenda,' and indeed, to force it off would violate the second toleration" (Stepan, 2012: 90). He argues that religion needs to be part of public discourse because the freedom *from* religion doctrines and "religion-controlling versions of secularism", such as Turkish Kemalism or French style *Laïcité*, are equally as illiberal as theocratic governance (Stepan, 2012: 90).

These 'Twin Tolerations' have been evident in the election process but the post-election, constitution-writing period was a time of misunderstanding, mistrust, and desperately needed reconciliation between the secular and Islamist differences in Tunisia's national identity. This societal divide also manifested in the civil society sphere where groups supported different ideologies and parties while tolerance was less prevalent. Secular civil society needed to exhibit tolerance towards not only the presence of Islamists in politics but also Islamists in power. Religion was not ready to be removed from the agenda, it was central.

This societal divide that also manifested in civil society, however, is another key part of the transition process. Understanding the difference between social and political activism is an aspect of a democracy learning process (Sadiki, 2015). In addition, CPC is not an inherent civil society characteristic but is also developed through the democracy learning process. As the theories of democracy and democratisation mentioned in Chapter 1 claim, civil society can be a contributor to democratic transition. But this can only occur if it also exhibits greater civility.

But how could social Islamic activism be different from political Islamic activism? Under Bourguiba and Ben Ali, social expression of Islam was prevented via state repression and societal exclusion of religion. In the political sphere, Islam-inspired political thought was branded a threat to the Tunisian economic model. However, Ennahda's election victory forced Tunisia to engage with the myths propagated by the old regime and also highlighted "the necessity for Tunisian society to reconcile its effective social and political pluralism not only with categories of Western modernisation, but also its Muslim-Arab identity" (Merone and Cavatorta, 2013: 254).

First of all, Ennahda was not representative of all Islamists' perspectives in Tunisia. Ennahda had accepted democracy in the 1980s and favoured embracing a civil state. Yet, despite Ennahda's statements and intentions, its credentials were constantly questioned. Tunisians leftists, such as the Democratic Patriots' Movement, remained suspicious of whether Ennahda, in conjunction with Islamist CSOs, were pursuing an 'Islamist project': with the eventual goal of turning Tunisia into an Islamic state.

The aftermath of the revolution enabled new-found freedom in Tunisian society and increased pluralism on the public scene. This allowed previously marginalised people and suppressed opinions into the political sphere, including Islamists who were aiming to apply Islamic principles of governance to post-revolution Tunisia. Salafism, an ultra-conservative and revivalist interpretation of Islam, was now part of the widened political spectrum and became an important political and social entity. Ennahda's pro-democracy stance, however, led to disagreement with pro-Sharia Salafists (Merone and Cavatorta 2013: 255). In addition, Tunisia's Salafists were not a unified body due to their competing understandings and methods towards implementing Sharia, such as using violence or not, and acting gradually or immediately (Wolf, 2013).

Reconciliation requires understanding and an important part of the reconciliation for Tunisians in the post-Ben Ali era was to accept that Salafism is the product of both external and domestic factors. There was an assumption that the differing versions of the Salafist ideology were imported after the revolution. In contrast to this, Merone and Cavatorta (2013) emphasise the indigenous origins of Tunisian Salafism but, also, that it represented a disenfranchisement with the dictatorship. Salafism was indeed another form of resistance. When Ennahda embraced democratic practices and ideals, members disaffected with this approach formed the Tunisian Islamic Front (TIF) in 1986 (Torelli et al., 2012: 148). These members were drawn from those who had been either jailed or engaged in jihad in Bosnia or Afghanistan/Pakistan. Tunisia's Salafi-Jihadists returned after the revolution and others were released from prison in amnesty. Ennahda, which "represent a new form of political Islam" (Torelli, 2012: 6), was a unique case of being an Islamist party that was playing a mediating role between Salafists and secularists.

Merone and Cavatorta argue that the political system needs to integrate Salafist demands, despite their incoherence, as the transition process will be strengthened by ensuring the disaffected are recognised (2013: 268). This, however, proved challenging. The Al-Islah party developed a political programme that addressed social, economic, and cultural issues while referencing respect for pluralism, alternating power, and non-violence. Yet their programme represented incivility as Islam took precedence over liberalism, the personal status code would be abolished, and the state would enforce only what religion has determined to be right (Torelli et al., 2012: 147).

Ennahda worked to dispel secularist fears of using Sharia as a source of legislation, while being the only actor capable of negotiating with Salafists (Torelli, 2012: 11–13). Rashid Ghannouchi, who was a compromising democratic Islamist and the focal point of Ennahda, was key to this mediation. "Ghannouchi, whose experience in exile during the Ben Ali regime, in particular, appears to have fostered a commitment to principles of liberal democracy and pluralism" (Carey, 2013: 2). Ennahda's attempt to moderate and include Salafists in the political process demonstrated an attempt at pluralism and accepting difference rather than exclusion. Ennahda tried to integrate Salafists into the political process as Ghannouchi had hoped they would become "moderate over time" (Merone and Cavatorta, 2013: 267). Ennahda legalised the Salafist Jabhat al-Islah party on 29 March 2012 as a representation of political pluralism, to mobilise ultraconservatives away from the violent approach of Jihadi-Salafism, and as an opportunity to embed non-violent Salafism into the political process.

Secular–Islamist tensions were expressed prior to the October 2011 NCA elections when Nessma television channel broadcast the animated film *Persepolis*, in which God is depicted as an old man. Perhaps this was a deliberate move by Nessma to test the limits of freedom and media censorship in the run up to the elections. Angered by this scene which they consider blasphemous, thousands of conservative Tunisians marched in defence of public Islam as they felt *laïques* (seculars) were damaging Tunisia's Islamic identity (Donker, 2013: 211). Some protests turned violent as 50 demonstrators were arrested and Nessma chairman Nabil Karoui's home was firebombed. Karoui was later fined 2400 dinars (£964) for "troubles to the public order" and "offence to good morals" (*Guardian*, 2012). This incident demonstrated that freedom of expression was not unlimited with regards to religious matters. US Ambassador Gordon Grey added that the conviction "raises serious concerns about tolerance and freedom of expression in the new Tunisia" (Fisher, 2012).

The elections may have been a representation of tolerance but civil society also needed to develop tolerance to effectively fulfil a democracy promotion role. This included toleration of the conservative Islamists elements. This became especially difficult when their agenda seemed directly undemocratic and contrarian to the democracy transition.

Part of Tunisia's social reassessment and subsequent need for reconciliation was the way Islamism had entered the political and public discourse. Public piety and levels of religious charity and education increased. The opening of political and social spheres meant Islamists were visible and active:

> more women began to wear the headscarf, more men started growing a beard and some started wearing *jalabas* (a long, loose-fitting unisex traditional North African outer robe) previously impossible in public. Mosques opened between prayers, religious classes started and attendance of mosque prayers rose markedly in the first period after the revolution.
> (Donker, 2013: 211)

Furthermore, use of Islam became more prevalent in public debates, including televised debates that gave Salafists a platform (Merone and Cavatorta, 2013: 252–253).

Similar to the UGET/UGTE clashes in the 1980s, the expression of Islam in universities focused attention on wearing the face-covering *niqab* in public institutions. Forbidden under Ben Ali, the *niqab* became an issue of freedom of religion and identity. These debates developed between those who believed in maintaining the secular character of higher education versus those who felt that radical secularists keeping elite positions, e.g. the university dean, represented maintaining the old regime (Donker, 2013: 217). Clashes at universities coincided with the re-emergence of the UGTE in the wake of the revolution. UGTE circles believed that "supporters of the Ennahda Movement remember very well that they managed to make their presence felt in the political arena during the 1980s and early 1990s, primarily through their activities within the university" (Zabas, 2012). The Manouba University demonstrations were a turning point but highlighted the fracture in Tunisian society. Salafists joined protests and threatened staff over the right for female students to wear the *niqab* and the right for prayer space, which spokesman for the Salafi students, Mohammed Bakhti, said was allowed in the United States, Britain, and Germany (Middle East Online, 2012). However, replacing the red and white Tunisian flag with the black, Salafist flag that bears the *shahada*[2] was controversial in Tunisia, especially in the midst of the polarised context which spread from Manouba to other universities as it mixed political issues with personal matters which "offended most Tunisians" (Mamelouk, 2012). Mamelouk summarised their difference as follows: "Secularists view the Salafis as long-bearded closed-minded intolerant religious zealots and in return the Salafists view secularists as atheistic Francophiles who are anti-Arab and anti-Islam" (2012). It was this unwillingness to accept difference that characterised the societal polarisation.

Despite Ennahda's efforts to appear moderate and committed to democratisation, civil society was divided along secular and Islamist lines. The ensuing dynamics between the two polarised camps suggested a relationship of intolerance and mistrust, which was exacerbated through violence. Mongi Rahoui, head of the Democratic Patriots' Movement, said he and other outspoken politicians experienced threats in what he viewed as a deliberate campaign by Ennahda to silence dissent (Ryan, 2013b). These threats were carried out by the Leagues for the Protection of the Tunisian Revolution (LPR); an example of violent incivility that was present in civil society. Formed in 2011 while Essebsi was interim Prime Minister and granted legal status in June 2012, the LPR "claim[ed] to fight corruption and old-regime remnants" (Belghith and Patel, 2013). However, these neighbourhood groups, who were often Ennahda members and former political prisoners under Ben Ali, used aggression and violence to support an Islamist cause. They were accused of trying to intimidate opposition parties and incurred hostility from more secular types. In December 2012 the LPR violently broke up a trade-union rally (*The Economist*, 2013) while a pro-Ennahda rally in February 2013 contained many league members (Al Jazeera, 2013).

The attack on the American Embassy led by Salafi extremists in September 2012 was the first incident in a series of events that altered Ennahda's relationship with Jihad-Salafists. The destruction clearly demarcated what were considered acceptable levels of protest or political expression. The attacks were a response to a US-made video that deprecates Islam but became a decisive moment in the relationship between Ennahda and Salafists, with Ghannouchi openly declaring that (Jihadi) Salafists were a threat to the nation (Donker, 2013: 220).

Freedom and pluralism existed which maintained an active civil society that could express itself and affect NCA proceedings but the lack of trust, tolerance, and equality in civil society meant that civility was only partially developing. The political assassinations in 2013 were a turning point in both Tunisia's transition and the development of political civility.

From deadlock to dialogue

Civil society protests became progressively less frequent from 2011 onwards but people continued to take to the streets when crises occurred. None more so than when Tunisia was rocked by the assassinations of leftist opposition politicians Chokri Belaïd and Mohamed in 2013. In response, protests were held against Ennahda on 25 July (Reuters, 2013). The Islamist party was blamed for the country's security failings and the perception it had been too lenient on hard-line Islamists. Protests developed into calls for Ennahda to step down from government. This led to a political deadlock where NCA members froze their membership and NCA activities were officially suspended. The constitution drafting process came to a standstill. Ennahda had already distanced itself from extremists and continued to do so, yet its members' perceived leniency on Jihadi-Salafism, meant other political actors and the general public lost faith in their ability to govern and maintain security. The assassinations, however, had an important effect of unifying the nation. Similar to the 2011 elections, it highlighted the vast majority's preference for a peaceful transition, regardless of ideological difference, and identified who was against democracy.

The four largest and oldest national institutions played a vital mediation role in overcoming the political deadlock. The LTDH, ONAT, the Tunisian Union of Industry, Trade and Crafts (UTICA), and UGTT, collectively also known as the 'the Quartet', established a 'national dialogue' (*hiwar watani*) to confront and address the issues the political transition was facing. The mediation process led by the Quartet represents civil society actors directly exhibiting CPC and also demonstrates the importance of civil society's role in playing a significant democratising role assisting the transition. The Quartet being awarded the Nobel Peace Prize in 2015 is a testament to the significance of their achievement.

The dialogue reduced political polarisation and paved the way for the Ennahda-led troika government to step down. In this process, major political party representatives were brought together to address the challenges posed by the deadlock and to negotiate agreements on how the transition could progress. This ad hoc civil society coalition was the only actor capable of securing the buy-in of all conflicting political parties, while simultaneously possessing the popular trust necessary to lead this process at such a critical juncture in the country's democratic transition.

There was scepticism from both government and opposition actors. But the initial recognition of interests was a key step to trust building between participants that lead to successful negotiations.

> Some members of the Quartet were also known to be close to the opposition and, as representatives of different sections of Tunisian society, all Quartet members had a stake in the outcome of the dialogue. For these reasons, Ennahda's leaders were sceptical that the process could lead to a fair outcome. Initial tentative discussions between the parties and the Quartet, therefore, focused largely on the Quartet's own interests in mediating. Only once the Quartet had explicitly acknowledged its own interests could it build trust and the discussions move forward.
>
> (Frazer, 2014)

Houcine Abassi, UGTT secretary-general, "initiated a marathon of negotiations with representatives of political parties, civil society organizations and foreign ambassadors" (Ben Hamadi, 2015). The hours of negotiations, which he personally oversaw, included a secret meeting between opposition party Nidaa Tounes leader Beji Caid Essebsi and Rachid Ghannouchi in a Paris hotel.

The successful dialogue led to Prime Minister and Ennahda member Ali Larayedh agreeing to step down under the terms of the UGTT proposed roadmap. This included the troika government being replaced with a technocratic government to complete the constitution and the formation of an independent electoral body to organise new legislative and presidential elections.

Ennahda relinquished power in government but only because the players in the system found a compromise that revived the process forwards towards finishing the constitution and the next round of elections. Pikard (2015) praises Ennahda for the concessions and compromises they made, including the removal of references to Sharia law, in order to ensure that a constitution could be drafted which included external and public input and satisfied the vast majority of the NCA. He also credits all Tunisian political leaders for their part in the constitution-making process. Ennahda's political action had a reconciliatory effect on a divided Tunisian society as it allayed fears from secularists that Ennahda's political intentions were to cling to power.

Regarding the role of the UGTT, Samir Cheffi, deputy secretary-general, stated that "National dialogue and national consensus are the best solutions to solve disagreement." Adding that Tunisian politicians had little choice but to engage in order to maintain transition, "away from making judgments about one party or another, we believe that our mission is to bring all parties closer, based on the initiative that we are proposing at the UGTT". Comparing Tunisia to Algeria and Egypt and noting Tunisia's lack of economic resources, Cheffi emphasised that "the most important thing for us right now is to save the country from descending into violence" (Ryan, 2013c). Sadiki argues that the UGTT's leading and moderating role in the National Dialogue process "has helped tone down ideologically driven divides and mutually exclusive political agendas, voices and forces" (Sadiki, 2014).

Ennahda stepping down was a major turning point in the transition and an indication of civility in the political sphere. The inclusion of disparate actors, including a major role from the Quartet from civil society, demonstrates pluralism and equality. It also implies that trust has been built; trust in the Quartet's mediation of the process and the roadmap, and trust in other political actors who would establish the new technocratic government. In addition, by demonstrating that the Islamist party had put Tunisia before its party interests, it helped develop trust between Ennahda and secular liberalists who feared the former was aiming to transform the country into an Islamic state.

A technocratic government and the new constitution

On 27 January 2014, the NCA deputies approved the new constitution. The draft was a suitable compromise for Islamist, secularist, right-wing, and left-wing politicians alike, in addition to civil society, insofar as it did not generate major objections. A total of 200 assembly members voted in favour, 12 against, and four abstained, therefore greatly exceeding the two-thirds majority required for passage (Dreisbach, 2014). Compromises had been made throughout the two years of drafting, including the removal of references to Islamic law, and a consensus was achieved.

Although a constitution is only meant to establish broad concepts, which require laws and decrees to codify and institutionalise them, the roles and rights of Tunisian CSOs are delineated in detail under Decree-Law 88 (2011), there is a fleeting reference to civil society in the 2014 Tunisian Constitution. Article 139 mentions that "Local authorities shall adopt the mechanisms of participatory democracy and the principles of open governance to ensure broader participation by citizens and civil society." Rather than guaranteeing rights to civil society, it enshrines its participation in the political process.

The creation of a liberal constitution represents a key part of democratic transition; the establishment of a democratic institutional structure (Carothers, 2002: 7). This, occurring three years after the collapse of the old, authoritarian regime, demonstrates that the pace of transition in Tunisia was not 'rapid'. It represents the time it took for sufficient socialisation and reflection in the democracy learning process to occur rather than forcing a 'ready-made' democracy designed by elites or exclusively from Occidental 'knowers' of democracy to agency-less Orientals (Sadiki, 2015: 709–718).

Ennahda stepping down enabled Mehdi Jomaa, a former Engineer for Total in France and Minister of Industry in Tunisia, to form a government that largely consisted of independents and technocrats. This new non-partisan government, worked to achieve the national dialogue's roadmap objectives of leading the country while parliamentary and presidential elections were organised. The Jomaa government represented the outcome of civil society action in creating, mediating, and encouraging debate between political parties that facilitated the resolution of a political crisis and enabled the democratic transition to continue. The non-partisan, caretaker government was more popular than the troika had been and did not divide Tunisian public opinion to the same extent. An opinion poll by the Sigma polling agency after Jomaa assumed office, showed that nearly 70 per cent of the public shared the view that the country "is heading in the right direction", compared to the previous October, when only 15 per cent shared this view (Romdhani, 2014).

The Jomaa government oversaw a step towards greater transparency through civil society oversight of government as Tunisia joined the Open Government Partnership (OGP) initiative. OGP was a cooperative partnership platform where government and civil society actors sought to "promote accountable, responsive and inclusive governance".[3] In order to qualify to join the OGP, the Tunisian government had to undertake reforms relating to transparency, openness, and citizen participation. The first two-year national action plan, finalised in September 2014, included the government's commitment to include CSOs in decision making and the OGP steering committee had to include both government and CSO representatives. The implementation of the first National Action Plan (NAP), which had 20 commitments related to public sector transparency reform, was monitored and later evaluated by CSOs.[4] The Tunisian government is currently working on the third OGP NAP for 2018–2020.

Further evidence that incivility and violence were not tolerated in civil society was demonstrated when the Leagues for the Protection of the Tunisian Revolution (LPR) was banned on 26 May 2014. The group was accused of using violence to advance its political goals (Ben Said, 2014).

CSOs also oversaw the implementation of the government agenda by maintaining a watchdog role on the progress of the reforms and commitments. For example, Tunisian youth CSO *I-Watch* established the 'Jomaa Meter'[5] to monitor government performance related to promises made.

October 2014 parliamentary and presidential elections to February 2015 inclusive coalition government

After overcoming a political stalemate and drafting a new constitution, a second successful post-revolution election was another important indicator that Tunisia was continuing to transition from authoritarian to democratic governance.

The 2014 parliamentary and, for the first time in the post-Ben Ali era, presidential elections, saw a double victory for Nidaa Tounes. Beji Caid Essebsi, the elder statesman who had served in both Bourguiba's and Ben Ali's regimes and had created Nidaa Tunis in April 2012, beat Moncef Marzouki in the second round with 56 per cent of the vote (Reuters, 2014). Nidaa Tounes won a parliamentary majority with 85 of the 217 seats (39.17 per cent) while Ennahda came second with 69 seats (31.79 per cent), significantly less than the 89 seats (42 per cent) it had held in the NCA following the 2011 elections (Martin, 2014).

In the build-up to the elections, civil society had encouraged voter registration and participation in the election process. Using their experience from 2011, civil society watchdogs and monitoring bodies ensured the election process was, once again, free and fair by designating more than 14,000 observers to supervise the elections in addition to personnel from the European Union and Arab League (Chekir, 2014: 4). Despite the large number of mobilised civil society actors monitoring polling stations, it did not prevent violations, which CSOs also noted. The National Democratic Institute (2014) credited the ISIE for overseeing "well-organized elections that earned the confidence of voters and political contestants", but recommended recruiting more campaign monitors. A report by the Tunisian Association for the Integrity and Democracy of Elections (ATIDE) also criticised ISIE for its poor management of the elections (ATIDE, 2014).

Despite its victory in the parliamentary elections, Nidaa was forced to form a 'unity' government with its main rivals, Ennahda. Prime Minister Habib Essid, an independent candidate, planned to form a minority government consisting of Nidaa Tounes and the Union Patriotique Libre (UPL) who won 16 seats. However, it was rejected because it fell eight seats short of the required 109 members needed to ratify the government. Assembly members rejected the two party coalition as they considered this arrangement to be unrepresentative (Amara, 2015).

An inclusive coalition government was formed on 6 February 2015 and was approved by 166 of 217 members of parliament (Al Jazeera, 2015). The two main parties united with two other smaller parties, Afek Tounes and UPL. Despite winning 103,000 votes and therefore eight seats, Afek Tounes's campaign focused on the party's identity and unique characteristics, rather than battling the two major parties. Likewise, UPL's 140,000 votes (16 seats) were largely gained by its promises to voters in rural and border regions (Chekir, 2014: 7–8). Although part of the opposition, the Popular Front's 124,000 votes (15) ensured leftist views were represented in the national assembly.

Critics called this unity government a return to the one-party state rule of the Ben Ali era. After splits and defections in the first years after the revolution (Sadiki, 2012), the Tunisian political party landscape began to develop a cooperative character and identity partly due to the institutionalisation of tolerance of difference, plurality, and a developing democratic culture beyond the former regime's myth of reform.

Comparing the 2011 to the 2014 elections shows that the polarisation was one of the community rather than political views and that Nidaa's victory does not represent the return of the *ancien régime*. The Mouvement Destourien, headed by Hamed Karoui, a former prime minister during the reign of Ben Ali, and Kamel Morjane, a former foreign minister, won four seats and performed poorly in the presidential election. "The victory also represents a change from the dilemma of Islam, the key word in the 2011 elections, to a new dilemma: that of the state" (Ltifi, 2014: 4) and from political Islam to national identity. Having already been removed after the national dialogue, the electorate registered its dissatisfaction with Ennahda's failures at moderating Jihadi-Salafists, preventing the violent acts from the LPR, and improving the faltering economy. Ltifi believes the results are a sign of Tunisia leaning "towards greater political rationalism and realism" (Ltifi, 2014: 7).

Despite the relative achievement of starting to overcome ideological polarisation, both Ltifi and Chekir (2014) recognise the significance of a lower youth turnout representing young people's dissatisfaction with the transition process, poor results in improving employment prospects, and lack of faith in political actors. Youth engagement in the political process is key for continued democratic consolidation and is another mission for civil society to address.

Conclusion

The Tunisian revolution was not a military or palace coup. It was a form of grassroots, civil action in response to worsening economic conditions, blatant state corruption by the ruling family, and police-state oppression which subsequently increased as a response to popular protests.

Civic action played a significant role in Ben Ali's downfall and pressure from a re-emerging and new civil society has continued to ensure reforms are undertaken. Deane describes a 'new social capital' of "social networks and associated norms of reciprocity created by activists and organisations, in the capital and the interior, united in their opposition to the Ben Ali regime" (2013: 15).

Sustained popular pressure on the government to implement reform led to pressure on political leaders. This popular pressure represented an oppositional-resistance manifestation of civil society action that demonstrated a confrontational relationship between the state and civil society. Top RCD figures, such as Mohammed Ghannouchi, may have played a role in encouraging Ben Ali to leave but continued protests also led to the RCD being dismantled in response.

In 2013, NCA members chose to suspend their activities but Ennahda stepped down in the face of continued civil action and mediation from the Quartet, demonstrating both confrontational and cooperational relationships between the state and civil society.

The role of civil society was significant during the revolution and fundamental throughout the transition period that followed. During the revolution, civil society acted together against Ben Ali and then the remaining RCD politicians who sought to remain in power. After the revolution, newfound freedom established by the increasingly less authoritarian state in Decree-Law 88 (2011) created a larger public space. This enabled civil society to dramatically expand and begin to perform a pro-democratic function by encouraging greater pluralism. Liberal-Associative CSOs operating in this space demonstrated democracy learning processes (Sadiki, 2015) within organisations through increased freedom and pluralism. However, variation in ideological perspectives caused polarisation across society and shaped the manner in which CSOs interacted with each other. Mistrust and intolerance existed in relationships between CSOs with vehemently secularist or Islamist agendas.

Tunisia's post-revolution freedom has been established in the context of an authoritarian government legacy. Political culture does not change suddenly with a revolution or elections and, as a consequence of the authoritarian legacy, the macro-level practices and discourses in Tunisian civil society have demonstrated political incivility during the democratic transition. For example, intolerance and mistrust of alternative socio-political perspectives, often regarding religion or support of political parties, has been evident. Nevertheless, civil society played a role in guiding Tunisia though the revolution and transition towards democratic consolidation.

Tunisia's democratic prerequisites have been vital to the transition's success. Extensive state-building procedures and programmes were not required, as major elements of a political society already existed, e.g. judiciary, state bureaucracy. After Ben Ali's departure, the Tunisian government proceeded to function effectively and the country did not descend into civil war. Although a new constitution was drafted and ratified in 2014, it was largely inspired by the 1959 constitution, a document that guaranteed individual and political freedoms but which had not been respected by the former authoritarian regime.

This chapter has demonstrated civil society has been present, active, and influential since the 2008 Gafsa uprising and throughout the 2010–2015 period. Civil society actors and organisations applied pressure on the government to democratise since January 2011, not only in the aftermath of the 2011 or 2014 elections, and the civil society-led national dialogue convinced the troika to relinquish power in order to overcome the 2013 deadlock and ensure that the transition continued. Watchdog organisations (*Al Bawsala*, *I-Watch*, *Mourikbouun*) and democracy building, *sensibilisation* groups that helped Tunisians transition from subjects to citizens and understand the meaning of citizenship, (CSID, JID, *Touensa*) had been working towards creating democracy in Tunisia since their inception.

Notes

1 MPs Citizens Debates. *Al Bawsala*. Available at www.albawsala.com/en/debats_elus_citoyens [Accessed 13 March 2015].
2 The Islamic declaration of faith: *there is no God but God and Muhammad is His prophet*.
3 Open Government Partnership homepage. Available at www.opengovpartnership.org/about/ [Accessed 18 March 2015].
4 Tunisia National OGP Action Plan, September 2014. Available at www.opengovpartnership.org/wp-content/uploads/2019/06/Tunisia-OGP-NAP_0.pdf [Accessed 18 March 2015].
5 Jomaa Meter. Available at http://jomaameter.org/?locale=en#.VcoERvNViko [Accessed 7 August 2015].

4 Surveying Tunisian CSO members' attitudes

Survey overview

If civil society organisations (CSOs) and associational life more generally can act like a school of democracy, as de Tocqueville described, is the learning process that CSO members are engaged in helping them learn about and embed the culture of democracy?

This survey is a fundamental tool for understanding the attitudes, values, and beliefs of Tunisian CSO members, which addresses the discourses half of understanding a political culture. It produced systematic data, which is a crucial aspect of understanding their political culture from a measurable positivist perspective of social inquiry. But, like any other survey in isolation, it is a 'snapshot' of Tunisian CSO political culture. Therefore, Chapters 5 and 6 engage with results from the interview and observation aspects of my research. In particular, the observation seeks to understand the other half of political culture; practices.

In terms of Tunisia's democratic transition, 2014 was a relevantly quiet period. The new constitution had been ratified by the National Constituent Assembly (NCA) and a non-partisan government was in power. The socio-political polarisation of society had given way to a greater spirit of cooperation. To reduce the risk of transitionary events, such as changes in government or the build-up to the next elections, influencing the research period, the 57-question, self-completion, anonymous online survey was available for seven months from 20 January to 20 August 2014.

The design process prioritised (1) constructing suitably worded questions to understand the criteria of civil political culture (CPC) – Tolerance, Equality, Freedom, Pluralism, Trust, and Transparency – (2) results that produce easily comparable, and (3) making the survey as easy as possible to complete. Therefore, the majority of questions were statements with close-ended, multiple-choice response options. I used a five-point Likert scale in the order of 'strongly agree, agree, do not know, disagree, strongly disagree' because it is less confusing than asking respondents to provide a 1–5 score or ranking. To prevent distorted responses, the 'do not know' mid-point option meant respondents were not forced to provide answers. A clear and attractive layout is especially important for a self-completion survey (Buckingham and Saunders, 2004: 84) so, rather than using a grid system, one question at a time is more aesthetically pleasing and easier for the respondent to understand. All the questions from each section (About You, Tolerance, Equality, Freedom, Pluralism, Trust, Democratic Practices, Financial Transparency, Your Civil Society Organisation, and What is desirable?) were placed on one page to help maintain respondent's focus.

In addition to demographic questions, some questions required a structure of unordered response choices. In particular, 'Describe your manager's leadership style', based on Lewin's leadership style research, had five options;

- Autocratic: makes decisions which reflect his/her opinions and personality.
- Bureaucratic: ensures procedures are followed.
- Delegative: gives responsibility to staff to make decisions themselves.
- Participative: acts as a member of the team.
- Laissez-faire: less controlling and acts more like a mentor.

Autocratic was used to see how many organisations are run like petit dictatorships where equality, freedom, pluralism, and trust would be lacking. Participative indicates higher levels of equality, freedom, and pluralism, and was the 'ideal' CPC answer. Bureaucratic was also included to see how much disparity there is between practices and discourse amongst CSO managers and to their adherence to rules.

For analysis of other aspects of the CSOs' internal operations culture, this survey also looked at the concept of institutional isomorphism. This phenomenon is where organisations become increasingly homogeneous and similar to one another in terms of their values and practices, due to their need for efficiency. However, this potentially constrains their ability to change in later years (DiMaggio and Powell, 1983: 148).

Language used

I decided to conduct the survey in Arabic for social equality reasons. The use of only French would exclude certain sections of the Tunisian population, particularly residents of the south where French is less commonly spoken. Tunisians are more likely to read Arabic fluently than French because the education system is more orientated towards Arabic than French. Public school students start learning French as a foreign language in the third grade while maths and sciences are only taught in French at the high school level. Furthermore, fluency in French is related to social class, making it an elite language. Despite French not being an official language, it is widely understood in Tunisia due to the French colonial presence from 1881–1956. Therefore, because French is the language of colonialism, its use in a foreign researcher's survey could have been seen as an Orientalist practice. Newspapers, television news, and official government statements in Tunisia are in Modern Standard Arabic (MSA) and using Arabic creates a more equal power balance between researcher and respondent. Also, the 2014 Tunisian Constitution says "Tunisia is a free, independent, and sovereign state.

Islam is its religion, Arabic is its language, the republic its system" and the 1959 Constitution states the same: "La Tunisie est un État libre, indépendant et souverain; sa religion est l'Islam, sa langue l'arabe et son régime la république". The use of MSA for written questions was more appropriate than Tunisian Arabic because the latter is considered a dialect and is not a codified language, which would have been problematic to create widely understood questions. Furthermore, the survey might not have been taken seriously since *Tunisi* is commonly used in informal contexts. Therefore, the survey did not benefit those who are more comfortable speaking French. Had the survey only been available in French, this would have been convenient for upper/middle class residents but not all sections of the population would have been able to complete it. Therefore, survey respondents would have been from a particular demographic of CSOs and would have been less representative of the wider CSO population.

Survey results

The survey results, summarised in Table 4.1, show an even gender distribution but a skew towards capital and coastal cities meaning the interior regions were less represented. The number of respondents was lower than anticipated which means the results cannot claim to be entirely representative of Tunisian CSO members. A total of 1000 responses would be representative of the approximately 18,000[1] CSOs in post-revolutionary Tunisia. This means that findings are not to be generalisable but should serve to generate inductive data which may inform further lines of inquiry. However, the regional, age, and gender distributions in relation to the Tunisian populations, the range of organisations represented, in addition to the inclusive factor of the survey being conducted in Arabic, means that the results can be viewed as indicative of Tunisian CSO members' attitudes rather than statistically significant.

The collected data also underrepresents Tunisia's interior regions and overrepresents the 18–35 age group. To address these representation issues

Table 4.1 Survey results summary table

Number of responses	102
Gender representation	51% men
	49% women
Highest represented age group	74.5% between 18 and 35
Age distribution	50% over 26
	50% under 26
Number of different organisations represented	55
Highest represented region	Greater Tunis (36.3%)
Educational level	89.2% undergraduate degrees or higher
Religious beliefs	78.4% Muslim
	21.6% agnostic, atheist, other, or not sure.

80 Surveying Tunisian CSO members' attitudes

and to produce more accurate analysis which would lead to more meaningful results, I re-coded these demographic variables. Question 2 demonstrated that the data is skewed because 50 per cent of respondents are under 25 years old and 50 per cent over 25. This was re-coded into a 'Youth vs Non-Youth' comparison.

Table 4.2 combines 2013 population census data, from the Tunisian National Institute of Statistics,[2] and Tunisian government data on registration of CSOs.[3] Question 5 demonstrated low responses from north, north-west, centre, south-central, and south regions.

Therefore, these were pooled into one group, labelled 'Interior', to create a more meaningful comparison to 'Capital' and 'Coast'. This may appear reductionist but the 'Interior' regions have been historically neglected and left underdeveloped by the former dictatorships, therefore the people may have different attitudes from those who lived in the more economically and infrastructurally developed Coastal and Capital areas.

Table 4.3 demonstrates a more even distribution of respondents over the three regions.

Overall, the survey data shows that the values, beliefs, and attitudes of the Tunisia CSO members who participated in this survey align with the values of CPC. This is evident from analysing both the answers to the individual survey questions and the indexes I created which relate directly to the criterion of CPC.

Indexes were created by pooling the survey questions about each criteria of CPC. For example, by merging the three questions from Section 2, Questions 7, 8, and 9, which address values and beliefs regarding tolerance, a Tolerance Index was created; thus averaging a range of variables into an index (see Figure 4.1). Indexing helped to highlight trends or associations between demographic variables

Table 4.2 Population percentage by region

Region	Governorates	Population percentage	Percentage of CSOs in region	Survey response percentage
Grand Tunis	Ariana, Tunis, Ben Arous, Manouba	23.4%	24.2%	36.3%
North	Bizerte	5.2%	2.7%	6.9%
North-west	El Kef, Béja, Zaghouan, Jendouba	10.6%	11.1%	2.0%
West coast	Nabeul, Sousse, Monastir, Mahdia, Sfax	30.7%	24.2%	29.4%
Centre	Kairouan, Kasserine, Siliana	11.5%	14.6%	4.9%
South-central	Gafsa, Sidi Bouzid	7.1%	6%	6.9%
South	Tozeur, Gabès, Kebili, Medenine, Tataouine	11.5%	17.2%	13.7%

Table 4.3 Survey results by pooled region

		Region			
		Capital	*Coast*	*Interior*	*Total*
What is your gender?	Male	23	11	18	52
	Female	14	19	17	50
Total		37	30	35	102

(Age, Gender, and Region) and criteria of CPC. Indexes for Tolerance, Equality, Pluralism, Trust, and Financial Transparency were created. It was not possible to create an effective or meaningful index for Freedom because the survey questions addressed different aspects of freedom; respondent's values of freedom and also the freedom they perceived the Tunisian state afforded them. Values and beliefs in freedom were instead analysed via descriptive statistics of Frequency Tables. Using the average scores from all respondents demonstrated which of the five (except Freedom) aspects of CPC are most prevalent in the respondent's attitudes. The score is from 1–5, 1 lowest and 5 highest, based on the five-point Likert scale choices.

A singular organisational culture is not evident in the results. This suggests that institutional isomorphism (DiMaggio and Powell, 1983) does not exist amongst Tunisian CSOs. This finding demonstrates the vibrancy and diversity of CSOs in Tunisia, as there is variation in how members perceive the way their organisation operates. Creating an index for institutional culture questions from Section 9, titled 'Your Civil Society Organisation' was also not possible because the questions' options were not all ordinal/numerical on a five-point Likert scale. Some were frequency questions, such as "43. For how long have you been active with civil society organisations?" and "45. How often do the organisation members meet?", and some were nominal variables, such as "47. Describe the process of decision-making in your organisation" and "49. Describe the philosophy and

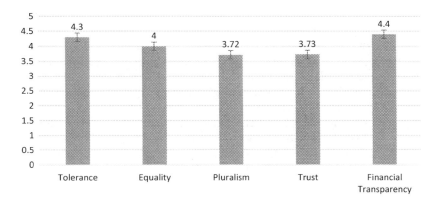

Figure 4.1 Survey results index scores.

culture of work within your organisation". These questions had options and "Other: please state" for respondents to select but produced answers which could not be grouped into an index.

Analysis of results

The demographic variables of Age, Gender, and Region helped to disaggregate the results and identify any differences or trends. The survey produced results such as women showed more evidence of tolerance than men, and over 26 year olds showed greater levels of trust than under 26 year olds. For further analysis of the results, it is easiest to separately examine each section of the survey. This analysis of the survey data includes results from statistical analysis t-tests and one-way analysis of variance (ANOVA) test. These statistical models and data manipulation tools helped show patterns and connections between key demographic variables of age, sex, and region and criteria of CPC.

Section 1 – Demographics (1–6) – shows that while Gender, Age, and Region were useful variables for comparison, Education level demonstrated that the CSO population is highly educated. Most respondents are practising or non-practising Muslims (78.4 per cent) while 21.6 per cent were Agnostic, Atheist, Other, or Not Sure. This indicates that personal faith and religious beliefs are not related to civil society values and that CPC is not at odds with Islam. Just as Islam is not a barrier to democratisation.

Section 2 – Tolerance (7–9) – demonstrates high levels of tolerance towards working together with other CSOs, cooperating for mutual goals, and other CSOs pursuing their goals on the condition that they are peaceful. This is represented in the Tolerance Index average score of 4.3. However, when the results are disaggregated by Gender, the t-test results demonstrate that women demonstrated more tolerance than men, see Table 4.4. The P-value of 0.011 is less than 0.05, therefore there is some evidence that there is an association between Gender and Tolerance. The comparison of means displays a 0.28 difference between men (4.17) and women (4.45). This indicates that male respondents demonstrate fewer values of tolerance than female respondents. I had expected to see some difference between men and women's responses but why did male respondents exhibit less tolerance? Tunisia's Personal Status Code of 1956 is progressive in terms of rights for women, but Tunisia has remained a patriarchal society. This t-test result might suggest men are less cooperative or might not be used to having their authority challenged. The implication being that women might show a greater affinity to democratic values.

Section 3 – Equality (10–16) – demonstrates almost complete agreement with equality to female participation, access to media, right to pursue cultural preference of choice, and non-Muslim Tunisians' participation in Tunisian civil society. There is less agreement regarding CSOs with secular or religious agendas and the inclusion of former Constitutional Democratic Rally (*Rassemblement Constitutionnel Démocratique*, RCD) members. The complete agreement in all but two areas is demonstrated in the Equality Index average score of 4.

Table 4.4 T-test results: Gender vs Tolerance Index (Q7–9)=Women>Men

Group statistics

	What is your gender?	Number	Mean Index score	Standard deviation	Standard error mean
Tolerance Index	Male	52	4.1667	0.62796	0.08708
	Female	50	4.4467	0.44979	0.06361

Independent samples test

	Levene's Test for Equality of Variances		T-test for equality of means					95% confidence interval of the difference	
	F	Sig.	t	df	Sig. (2-tailed)	Mean difference	Standard error difference	Lower	Upper
Tolerance Index equal variances assumed	0.081	0.776	−2.580	100	0.011	−0.28000	0.10853	−0.49532	−0.06468
Equal variances not assumed			−2.596	92.526	0.011	−0.28000	0.10784	−0.49416	−0.06584

Note
P-value of 0.011 is less than 0.05, therefore there is some evidence that there is an association between Gender and Tolerance. The comparison of means displays a 0.28 difference between men (4.17) and women (4.45). This means that male respondents demonstrate fewer values of tolerance than female respondents.

Questions 10 and 11 show no overall agreement regarding whether groups with specifically secular or religious agendas should be active in civil society. There is more acceptance of groups with secular agendas, 62.8 per cent (47.1 per cent and 15.7 per cent), than groups with religious agendas, 46.1 per cent (36.3 per cent and 9.8 per cent). This suggests Tunisian CSO members are unsure and in disagreement as to whether CSOs should be allowed to have political agendas but demonstrates less suspicion of secularist CSOs. This may indicate there is mistrust regarding the intentions of Islamist CSOs. In particular, that CSOs with religious underpinning are part of a broader Islamist project that seeks to 'Islamise' Tunisian society. Alternatively, this may indicate the assumption that Islamist CSOs were supporting the Ennahda party and were therefore politicised.

Question 12 shows no overall agreement regarding the inclusion of former RCD members in civil society. A total of 40.2 per cent (34.3 per cent and 5.9 per cent) agree with their inclusion while 43.1 per cent (22.5 per cent and 20.6 per cent) think they should not be included and 14.7 per cent don't know. This suggests that Tunisian CSO members are unsure and in disagreement as to whether former RCD members deserve to be active in the public space. To deconstruct this question, a cross-tabulation of the results question demonstrates there is slightly greater unfavourability towards former RCD members participating in civil society from respondents in the Interior; 48.6 per cent (28.6 per cent + 20.0 per cent) disagree, compared with the 37.8 per cent from the Capital and 43.4 per cent from the Coast. Also, fewer respondents from the Interior agree with their inclusion, 34.3 per cent compared to 45.9 per cent and 40 per cent. This may suggest there is greater resentment and less acceptance towards those associated with the former regime who should, therefore, be afforded fewer opportunities in civil society.

Section 4 – Freedom (17–27) – results appear somewhat contradictory. The majority is against government interference and 87.2 per cent believe the government should allow CSOs to operate freely. However, a vast majority also believes that the government should protect society from offensive opinions and 81.3 per cent think some groups are too dangerous to the common good to be allowed to operate. There is no agreement regarding whether the state should be determining what is offensive and whether respondents believe the freedom of association laws in Tunisia provide sufficient protection for CSOs. Questions 19, 20, 21, and 27 show almost complete agreement towards freedom of expression, that racially offensive views should be silenced, that religiously offensive views should be silenced, and in favour of the concept of universal human rights. This suggests the limits of freedom and that race and religion are taboo subjects. Question 17 shows 59.8 per cent of respondents (39.2 per cent and 20.6 per cent) support CSOs being allowed to pursue any goals they desire, as long as their means and methods are non-violent. A total of 27.4 per cent (23.5 per cent and 3.9 per cent) disagree, which suggests that there is not complete acceptance. Alternatively, the question could also have been too ambiguous.

Section 5 – Pluralism (28–32) – demonstrates that values of Pluralism are evident because respondents understand that disagreement is inevitable but they also believe that higher quality decisions are made by groups than individuals. Furthermore, 99 per cent have tolerance and respect for alternative opinions. Question 30, see Table 4.5, shows no trend towards CSO members changing their minds. This question sought to understand if respondents had the willingness to accept different views but this does not account for the quality of the argument.

The Pluralism Index average score of 3.72 is the lowest for the five indexes. This is caused by the inconclusive result to Q30. If this question is disregarded, there is strong evidence of other pluralistic values. The t-test results demonstrate that women expressed greater values of pluralism. The P-value of 0.022 is less than 0.05, therefore, there is evidence that there is an association between the Gender dichotomy and the Pluralism Index. The comparison of means displays a 0.24 difference between men (3.60) and women (3.84). This suggests that men demonstrate fewer values of Pluralism than women. This result, in addition to women expressing greater levels of Tolerance (Section 2), could be explained by a patriarchal mentality residing in Tunisia[4] that CSOs like the Tunisian Association of Democratic Women (ATFD) sought to highlight. Despite being one of the most liberal Arab societies, roles being defined by gender and male authority are common features of society (Ghribi, 2014). This confirms my expectation of a difference in results between men and women.

Section 6 – Trust (33–35) – suggests high levels of internal trust for other members of the same organisation, but shows no trend towards trusting other CSOs or their members. The Trust Index average score was 3.73, making it the second-lowest score. This is due to the lack of trust in CSO members outside the respondents' own CSO. Despite my prediction that trust would be low, the result that trust within a CSO (internal) is greater than trust in members of other CSOs is congruent with Putnam's "social capital" argument on the benefits of liberal-associational civil society. In *Making Democracy Work* (1993), he asserts that trust is fostered among people through their social interaction and cooperation in associations. This highlights a disparity between CSO members' discourse, regarding their willingness to cooperate and work with other CSOs, and their practice of not trusting other CSOs enough to work with them. The intention is evident, yet the practicalities may be more challenging. Perhaps because many associations had only formed within the past three years, and were relatively new, they had not spent much time cooperating and developing sufficient social capital to form alliances, coalitions, or even just working relationships.

Table 4.5 Survey question 30: results table

	30. I often change my mind when I hear other people's arguments.		
1	Strongly disagree	2.0%	2
2	Disagree	32.4%	33
3	I don't know	23.5%	24
4	Agree	39.2%	40
5	Strongly agree	2.9%	3

86 *Surveying Tunisian CSO members' attitudes*

The t-test result shows that Non-Youth (over 26 years old) respondents demonstrate greater levels of Trust than Youth respondents. P-value 0.014 is under 0.05 which means there is significance between 'Youth/Non-Youth and Trust Index'. The comparison of means displays a 0.3 difference between Youth (3.58) and Non-Youth (3.89). This may indicate that youth have less experience and are less acquainted with working in cooperation. This age difference is similar to the Pew Global survey 'Tunisian confidence in democracy wanes' (2014) which concludes that older Tunisians are more favourable towards democracy than the young. The question of why younger people in CSOs express lower levels of trust requires further research.

Roy describes how the youth in the Middle East and North Africa (MENA) region were changing and "feel less strongly bound to patriarchal customs and institutions that have been unable to cope with the challenges facing contemporary Middle Eastern societies" (2012: 8). Indeed, Tunisian youth are credited with instigating the revolution (Ben Hassine, 2011) and factors of globalisation and Internet exposure suggest the Arab Youth do not share the values of their parents' generation. Whether this makes the youth more or less inclined to exhibit CPC remains to be seen. However, for under 26 year olds, the definition of youth employed in this survey, their formative years were under Ben Ali rule. Therefore, their beliefs and values may have been shaped by dictatorship rather than global influences. While they might be quicker to reject dictatorship cultures, it is also plausible that youth have adopted individualism rather than the cooperative elements required to foster CPC.

Using the ANOVA test, the 'Region vs Trust Index (Q33–35)' test was the only one to show any notable difference.

Comparing the means of the Capital (3.63) and Interior (3.87) regions displays a 0.24 difference. The Interior has a higher index score which shows that, on average, respondents from the Interior regions demonstrate greater levels of trust or are more trusting than Coastal and especially Capital respondents.

A key part of political culture is discourses but also practices. What were the internal practices of the CSOs? Furthermore, how democratic were these practices? The content of Section 7 – Democratic Practices (36–38) – and Section 9 – My CSO (47 and 48) – are appropriate to be 'pooled' together. CSO leaders are not

Table 4.6 ANOVA test result: 'Region vs Trust Index'

Region compared to Trust Index				
	No. of respondents	Mean Index score	95% Confidence Interval for mean	
			Lower bound	Upper bound
Capital	37	3.6306	3.3743	3.8870
Coast	30	3.7000	3.4503	3.9497
Interior	35	3.8667	3.7115	4.0218
Total	102	3.7320	3.6050	3.8590

considered infallible rulers as, for example, 92.2 per cent believe in being allowed to express disagreement with their CSO's management. Questions 47 and 48 are related to democratic practices in decision making and selecting positions and/or leadership. Question 47 shows that 75.5 per cent say that the decision-making process is 'consultative at all levels'. Question 48 shows that 88.3 per cent use democratic methods to determine positions in the organisation; 60.8 per cent use 'elections' and 27.5 per cent use 'consensus after debate'. A total of 73.5 per cent believe their organisation has a well-defined organisational structure but this contrasts with 56.9 per cent who think job descriptions are flexible and authority within their organisation is questioned. As job descriptions of some organisations show fluidity, this suggests that there is flexibility in the appointment of roles and responsibilities. This could mean that either horizontal management structures are in place or could also imply internal disorganisation. Section 9 – My CSO (43–46) – assesses trends in 'organisational culture' and observes if there are similarities, or even cases of institutional isomorphism, within Tunisian CSOs. This section's results demonstrate no obvious trend regarding institutional culture which means the survey data does not provide firm evidence that institutional isomorphism exists.

Many of the questions in this section cannot be pooled; in particular, questions 43 to 51 require individual or paired analysis to make conclusions. It is not obvious what conclusions can be drawn from Question 43 apart from that CSO members have a range of experience and most have only been involved in CSOs in the post-revolution period; only 25.4 per cent (17.6 per cent more than five years and 7.8 per cent more than ten years) have been active pre-revolution. At the time of the survey, the revolution had taken place four years earlier. A total of 93.1 per cent of CSO members were volunteers with a smaller 6.9 per cent being professional, paid members. This 6.9 per cent might also include people are who unemployed but are paid by the Ministry of Work to work for a CSO. As 4.9 per cent of organisations meet daily, this suggests that a small, professional core of CSOs exists. There is no agreement as to a trend regarding the working environment of Tunisian CSOs. A total of 4.9 per cent and 6.9 per cent responded with 'very formal' and 'very informal' respectively, meaning the remaining 88.4 per cent was split between 'formal' (53.9 per cent) and 'informal' (34.5 per cent). Question 49 shows no clear trend in the culture and philosophy of CSOs, although *Person culture* scores highest with 44.1 per cent. Question 50 shows that 92.2 per cent of organisations have an internal law or constitution. This suggests that the remaining 7.8 per cent are either disorganised, are breaking Decree-Law 88 (2011), or are in the process of writing their internal law or constitution.

Section 8 – Financial Transparency (39–42) – shows 85.3 per cent of respondents know who funds their CSO and agreement towards practices of Financial Transparency in CSOs. A total of 80.4 per cent think funding that CSOs receive should be made public while some respondents in Q42 show unsureness (9.8 per cent) or reluctance (9.8 per cent). This is reflected in the Financial Transparency Index average score of 4.4, the highest Index score in the survey.

Section 10 asks 'What is desirable?' (52–56) and shows very strong approval of CSO independence, respect for other CSO objectives, and internal democratic practices. Question 54 shows 66.7 per cent disagreement that CSOs should be obedient to the government. A total of 20.6 per cent don't know and 12.8 per cent agree, which demonstrates a majority but no central trend exists. There was also no trend agreement regarding limitation to CSO activities.

Methodological limitations

There were two main criticisms of the survey which negatively impacted the number of responses; survey length and the religion question. Although my survey design and piloting process were rigorous, I could not have foreseen these criticisms.

This survey aimed to assess six criteria of CPC, plus organisational culture, with verification questions to ensure validity and reliability. In hindsight, this was too much to ask for a self-completion online survey and it should have been no more than 30 questions. The other surveys conducted in Tunisia that I reviewed while designing my survey were certainly not brief. Gallup, World Values Survey, Pew Global Attitudes Project, Zogby International, Arab Barometer, and BBC Media Action surveys include over 100 questions. These, however, were conducted face to face. For a self-completion, online questionnaire, 57 questions were enough to dissuade people from completing the survey. Four different people who had completed the survey told me that it was a struggle to complete.

Although common in UK social science surveys, Question 6 "How would you describe your religious belief?" was not well received. I received emails where CSO members did not want to complete or distribute the survey because it made them 'uncomfortable', they thought it was not relevant, and they simply did not want to talk about religion. A member of ATFD told me that religion is not part of their association and that "We are a secular society and our religious choices concern only us" (email, 13 March 2014). Also, a General Union of Tunisian Workers (UGTT) spokesman explained his issue with the question:

> With regards to the questionnaire, I think it poses a serious problem in the question relating to the faith. This is not an issue within the Tunisian society, or some parties would like to impose this issue that is foreign to Tunisia. The questions should be oriented towards the social aspects for NGOs [non-governmental organisations] dealing with social issues and otherwise for other NGOs. That's why I cannot disseminate the questionnaire.
>
> (email, 9 June 2014)

On reflection, I should have recognised the contextual sensitivity of this question. After years of state repression and control of religion, Tunisia's democratic transition was forcing society to confront its relationship with religion. In particular, foreign researchers and journalists were jumping to conclusions or making sensational assumptions about religion's role in politics and society. And my survey was part of that problem. Perhaps this question would have worked in an interview setting, but it was not a suitable question for an online survey. Unfortunately, the survey software I used, BOS, does not allow modifications to be made once a survey has been launched. Therefore, it was not possible to address or amend this issue once complaints were received.

The unwillingness to answer this question suggests to me that sensitivity regarding religion and 'religious belief' potentially indicates an underlying intolerance in a society; either by the respondent or how he/she will think others will perceive them. Of 102 responses received, only 2 direct complaints were made. It is possible that others chose not to complete the survey because of their sensitivity to this question but did not register a complaint. Although it proved problematic for the survey results, the aversion from some respondents to the religion question suggests that respondents who did not want to answer the religion question are sensitive about religion. It might also imply a default secular position that some CSOs hold. The UGTT email does not indicate a rejection of religion as a divisive political category, but rather that the organisation does not want to proliferate the existence of an Islamist/Secularist divide in Tunisia. On the other hand, it could represent their aversion to a white, European researcher trying to study them from within a narrow box defined by their supposed religion or trying to correlate their attitudes, values, and CSO practices with Islam.

If I repeated this survey, I would have to revise the structure to ensure a higher response rate. First, the religion question would certainly be removed to enable greater participation. This should mean fewer CSOs would have objected to distributing the survey. Although the refusal, by some, to engage with this question indicates the sensitivity surrounding this subject in Tunisian CSOs, its inclusion was detrimental to the completion rate. Second, for an online, self-completion, the length of the questionnaire would need to be reduced to no more than 30 questions. This would make the completion process less strenuous for respondents.

Conclusion

As this survey collected 102 responses, it is difficult to generate precise inferences given the sample size. It means that any conclusions cannot make overarching claims. Instead, the value of this research is the indicative data of the Tunisian CSO population's beliefs, values, and attitudes it provides. Indeed, they established some very clear results, quite notable trends, and trends that require further research to fully unpack their significance

The data collected in this survey addresses the three relationships of civil society – with the state, with other CSOs, and with organisations' own members. The results suggest that the criteria of CPC are evident in Tunisian civil society, which is enabling it to start fulfilling a democratic function. While CPC is generally evident in attitudes of CSO members, female CSO members are more likely to hold attitudes of Trust and Pluralism. Furthermore, Trust is more prevalent amongst respondents from Interior regions and Non-Youth respondents.

The frequency tables and bar charts suggest the following results.

- Section 2 largely suggests tolerance, respect, and cooperation in and between CSOs.
- Section 3 shows agreement towards female participation, accesses to media, right to pursue cultural preference of choice, and non-Muslim Tunisians' participation in Tunisian civil society but disagreement regarding politicised and religious CSOs and the inclusion of former RCD members.
- Section 4 suggests that Tunisian CSO members believe freedom should exist but it should be a freedom that has limitations such as causing religious offence, rather than American-style unrestricted freedom of speech at all costs. It is also expressed that the government has a duty to determine what is offensive or improper. Furthermore, CSO members express their unwillingness for the government to interfere but are also unsure that sufficient legal protection is given to CSOs. These contradictions might demonstrate the different understandings of freedom amongst CSO members with some preferring greater limitations.
- Section 5 shows agreement towards the value of including various points of view and collective decision-making processes but less towards this process swaying people's decisions.
- Section 6 suggests high levels of internal trust within a CSO but less towards other organisations.
- Section 8 largely shows agreement towards CSOs adopting financial transparency practices.
- Sections 7 and 9 show agreement towards the use of democratic practices within CSO procedures and decision-making processes.
- Section 10 shows very strong agreement that CSOs should be independent of the state, should respect the objectives of other organisations, and should operate with internal democratic practices. Also, there is strong agreement that CSOs should not be obedient to their government.

Overall, these results demonstrate normative acceptance of CPC. Tunisian CSOs are predominately run by voluntary members on a part-time basis. Regarding organisational culture, they are mostly consultative in decision making and determine positions through internal elections or consensus after a debate. Organisational culture and leadership styles vary between organisations.

By using SPSS software and running cross-tabulations and correlations tests, it was possible to analyse the survey responses more deeply by dividing the responses by demographic category variable. Furthermore, the indexing process allowed each section of the survey, corresponding to each criterion of CPC, to be grouped. This allowed for general trends to be observed. The indexes show there is evidence of CPC but that Tolerance, Equality, and Financial Transparency were more prevalent than, Pluralism and Trust. Financial Transparency

(Q40–42) was evident from looking at the frequency tables and bar graphs but SPSS analysis showed it was the most prevalent value. With the dividing and indexing processes used together, SPSS software data analysis was able to demonstrate where CPC was present or absent and who was more likely to demonstrate it.

Regarding any ambiguity in the results, SPSS could not add further analysis than frequency tables and bar graphs regarding Institutional Culture. The cross-tabulations were successful at disaggregating unclear individual responses, such as Q12 demonstrating that slightly greater unfavourability towards former RCD members participating in civil society from respondents in the Interior. However, the results from other cross-tabulations posed further questions or required additional hypotheses to understand the results.

T-tests and ANOVAs were useful for creating general trends, but the low-response, statistically insufficient and insignificant data means that these trends cannot be used to draw significant conclusions. The results are sufficient to suggest indications of attitudes from civil society members. The Interior's mistrust of the RCD party members in civil society and women showing greater CPC are similar to predictions made in the hypothesis. However, there were surprising results such as Youth scoring lower than Non-Youth. I expected Youth to demonstrate more democratic culture but, in all cases, except Trust, there was no association.

The t-tests showed that (a) Non-Youth respondents demonstrate greater Trust values than Youth and (b) women respondents demonstrate greater Tolerance and Pluralism values than men. The ANOVA tests showed that Interior respondents demonstrate greater levels of trust than Coastal and especially Capital respondents. The means difference from the t-tests regarding Gender across three indexes enables a plausible generalisation to be drawn that the responses in this survey from women in Tunisia CSOs demonstrate greater evidence of CPC than men in the areas of Tolerance and Pluralism. The t-test or ANOVA test results from Equality and Financial Transparency showed no level of association.

It is important to note some potential caveats with these results. Significance test analysis cannot be overly relied on because there are three implications regarding the data. First, the sample size means these conclusions should not be overstated. Second, as discussed regarding the sampling methods and despite the range of CSOs represented, it is also plausible that the collected population sample is not sufficiently varied enough to be entirely representative of CSO members in Tunisia. Third, although there is justification for re-coding the region demographic based on the Bourguiba and Ben Ali governments' systematic neglect of Tunisia's interior regions, the re-coded 'Interior Region' variable still groups together five separate regions and 15 governorates. To assume people from all these regions are like-minded would be making an over-arching claim. Despite these considerations, these survey results indicate evidence of CPC in Tunisian CSOs.

This attitude survey is a wide-reaching research method that identifies patterns and a broad spectrum of CPC values in civil society members. The operational use of Welch's (2013) theory of political culture, implemented in this book, recognises that discourse is only one manifestation of political culture analysis. These survey results demonstrate discourse rather than practice, although the practices in which CSOs engage were questioned. As this entirely positivist method of inquiry lacks nuanced and personalised engagement, the interview process in Chapter 5 enables greater insight into details of CPC gained through human interaction-based research. Answers to the inconclusive issues that the survey data produced can also be uncovered when compared with interview data results.

In comparison to the pre-revolution era, this survey indicates development and embedment of some aspects of CPC that would not have been possible in authoritarian Tunisia. Although the survey was not able to offer an assessment of whether CSOs are Oppositional-Resistance or Liberal-Associative, the questions help to provide assessments of the three relationships in which CSOs engage; with the state, with other CSOs in the public space, and the internal dynamics with their own membership. Indeed, the development of these CSO relationships indicates where CSOs self-consciously position themselves against the state and other CSOs, if relationships with others have developed, whether they discriminate or not: all of which would not have been possible in a restricted public space. This chapter has demonstrated that an attitude survey can be an important research method for providing a broad understanding of or identifying trends within the political culture of civil society. However, for a holistic understanding of political culture, additional micro-interpretivist approaches are required.

Notes

1 IFEDA (2014). Le centre d'information, de formation, d'études et de documentation sur les associations. Available at www.ifeda.org.tn/stats/francais.pdf [Accessed 11 June 2015].
2 Institut National de la Statistique Tunisie, Tunisia. Available at www.ins.nat.tn/indexen.php [Accessed 11 December 2013].
3 IFEDA. Le centre d'information, de formation, d'études et de documentation sur les associations. Available at www.ifeda.org.tn/fr/index.php?id_page=13&lang=fr [Accessed 11 December 2013].
4 ATFD (*Association Tunisienne des Femmes Démocrates*) (2014, 2 October). Enough condescension on the Tunisian women and people. Available at www.facebook.com/femmesdemocrates/photos/a.247294818675110.59337.153986931339233/732287603509160/?type=3&theater [Accessed 10 January 2016].

5 Interviews with CSO leaders

Survey overview

The survey demonstrated evidence of civil political culture (CPC) in respondents' discourses but the broadness of the research method also produced inconclusive results and raised further questions. The interviews provided human interaction with civil society organisation (CSO) leaders and provided an opportunity for them to explain their norms and values, through their discourse, and to describe their behaviours in greater details than from within the limitations of studying subjects from a removed position through surveys. For the collection of more nuanced and personalised data, the personal interaction also provided the opportunity for follow-up questions with CSO leaders. The face-to-face interview method, a micro-interpretivist approach, provides reciprocal interaction with subjects. This is essential for studying political culture in Tunisia because it reduces the risk of producing synoptic or culturalist analyses which can occur from only studying remotely or deducing from historical sources.

I interviewed CSOs that were important and influential during the revolution and transition process. The Quartet of UGTT, the Tunisian Confederation of Industry, Trade and Handicrafts (UTICA), the Tunisian League for Human Rights (LTDH), and the *Ordre National Des Avocats De Tunisie* (Tunisian Lawyers Association, ONAT) played a vital mediation role in overcoming the political deadlock of 2013. The UGTT had also been crucial in organising mobilisation during the revolution. *Al Bawsala* (The Compass), *Mourakiboun* (Observers), and *I-Watch* are political watchdogs that influenced the transition by holding politicians to account and observing constituent assembly and electoral procedures. *Destourna* (Our Constitution) played a leading role in arranging the Bardo sit-in demonstration[1] after the assassination of leftist politician Mohammed Brahmi in July 2013 which led eventually to the National Dialogue and the Ennahda-led troika stepping down from government.

It was also interesting to compare the methods, approaches, and perspectives of organisations that were active before the revolution, such as *Association Tunisienne des Femmes Démocrates* (Tunisian Association of Democratic Women, ATFD) and *Forum Tunisien pour Les Droits Economiques et Sociaux* (FTDES), to the hundreds of new organisations that were established in the post-revolution era.

To include Tunisian civil society's diversity, I interviewed organisations that were working on wide range of different causes, such as Charity (*Inara, Alwen Tounes*), Youth (Jeunes Independent Démocrates, *Sawty, Voix d'enfant rural, WeYouth*), Environmental (Network of Sidi Bouzid, Oxygen, We Love Sousse), Development and Training (Tunisian Association for Management and Social Stability, TAMSS), and Culture (*Verolution, Toupat Sidi Bouzid*, Sfax Outdoor Sports, *Sfax Mzyehna*). Many organisations who worked on raising awareness (*Sensibilisation* in French) regarding citizenship and the culture of democracy (*Qairawanioun, Association Tunisienne Pour La Promotion Du Droit à La Différence*, I-Lead). I also interviewed 'single-issue' groups like *Mnemty* (racism), *Esslam* (fairtrade for artisans), Reform (police and security sector reform), *Association Tunisienne Droits Constitutional* (ATDC) (legal reform), *Edupartage* (educational reform), and *Notre Santé D'abord* (free health care).

I spoke with two movements, which were not strictly CSOs but represented civic activism. Al Sajin 52[2] was fighting against the oppressive Tunisian laws against cannabis possession that were established during the dictatorship as a means of control, and OpenGovTN[3] was a network linked to the Open Governance Programme (OGP) that promotes transparency at national and regional government levels.

Although 36 of the 66 interviews were with organisations based in Tunis, the capital city, I ensured that the other regions were also represented in the interview process. Therefore, I spoke with organisations from Bizerte, Zaghouan, Sousse, Sfax, Sidi Bouzid, Regueb, Gafsa, Gabes, Medenine, and Djerba. Regional organisations often had more local and specific goals, such as *Sousse Demain*, Djerba Ulysses, Association Cepsa (in Gafsa), and Gabes Action, than CSOs that are based in the capital. *Association Amis Bassin Minier pour l'environnement* is based in Gafsa but is an environmental pressure group that addresses issues outside the region that are also affected by social problems related to mining.

I narrow the focus of this research, I chose not to interview CSOs with religious objectives. Quranic School and Islamic charity groups play a role in both the public and private spaces while *Dawa* movements are seeking to implement the political goal of Islamising the state. Donker (2013) identifies two types of Islamist activism in post-revolutionary Tunisia based on their goals: activism aimed at societal change and that aimed at political influence. Although not power-seeking, the objectives of these groups are blurring the lines between political and public space activism, therefore not entirely conforming to the definition of civil society established in this thesis. While religious organisations can add to a civil society's vibrancy, their position in Tunisia remains contentious due to accusations that they are supporting an Islamist project. Interviewing either of these types of organisations proved problematic because they did not publicly advertise their Islamist agendas making it difficult to identify them. The ruling Islamist Ennahda party was largely blamed for the rise of terrorism due to its perceived leniency towards Salafist Islamist groups. Ennahda was criticised for allowing groups such as the Leagues for the Protection of the Revolution

(LPR) to operate and spread political uncivil, even extremist, discourse and behaviour. The assassinations of secular-leftist politicians Chokri Belaid and Mohamed Brahmi reinforced the belief amongst many Tunisians that Islamist groups who were suspected of having ties with the ruling party were responsible for perpetuating violence and discrimination based on religious grounds. Within this context, CSOs were reluctant to publicise any Islamist agendas and actively distanced themselves from the 'Islamist' label. It is worth mentioning that Article 4 of Decree-Law 88 (2011) published on 24 September 2011 states that "Associations are prohibited from the following: One: Adopting in their bylaws, data, programs or activities any incitement for violence, hatred, fanaticism or discrimination on religious, racial or regional grounds." Of particular importance is 'discrimination' because CSOs that require members to be religious are not legally permitted to exist.

Interview methodology

CSO leaders, presidents, or members of the *bureau exécutif*, were chosen as interview subjects because they have an overview of the running of their organisation and can comment on relations with other CSOs and the government. I conducted one-to-one, face-to-face interviews for the following reasons. First, in one-to-one interviews, individuals' responses are not influenced by another person's presence, especially others in the organisation. This does not guarantee or increase honesty but it removes the possibility of influence from the other member of their organisation, respondents' opinions being swayed, and a 'groupthink' conclusion from being reached. Therefore, the expressed norms and values would be the interviewee's discourse rather than an influenced discourse. Second, it is also easier to probe and ask follow-up or concept checking questions to unclear and ambiguous answers to individuals rather than groups. Third, interviewees might not have agreed to conduct group interviews because, if they were not expressing the realities of their organisation, the other member would be aware their answer was insincere.

Where possible, I conducted one-to-one interviews but some were conducted as pairs as it would have been socially awkward and impractical to ask the other present members of the CSO to leave. In these cases, I conducted interviews with two people at the same time, from the same organisation, and it produced greater insight into Tunisians' perceptions of civil society's role. When I spoke to Khalid Ouazzani and Nizar Abdessaied from Associo-Med, for example, they had different ideas about what a civil society should be doing and how a CSO should engage with the government. Khalid regarded civil society as a means for engaging with the political sphere, whereas in Nizar's opinion, civil society's role was purely civic. This debate is not unique to Tunisia and is a reflection of how conceptualisations of civil society are understood. Nizar was sceptical of civil society working with the government or in political fields and thought civil society should be like a hobby, where friends meet to do what they feel, or undertake actions for the good of society that benefit the country; closer to the non-confrontational and associational life aspect of the Liberal-Associative model. Khalid thought differently and argued that civil society must have an impact on the government or the government would never address the problems of society. Also, he thought that civil society should be a power, which applies pressure to the government if required because otherwise there is nothing else to check the government's powers. De Tocqueville (2003) argued that civil society was required to counterweight government power and ensure citizens' freedom. Neither was right or wrong but the debate between these two medical students represented diversity in the understanding of civil society in Tunisia.

I started the interviews with easier questions, such as 'tell me about your organisation', so that I could build a rapport with my interviewee. Then the questions were structured relating to aspects of CPC, while sensitive issues, such as finance and documents from the organisation, were placed last. I conducted structured interviews, whereby the same questions were asked in the same order to produce systematic and easily comparable data. This was so that my research would produce greater reliability than unstructured conversations and using a consistent question order also reduces variation error (Bryman, 2001: 116). The use of structured interviews was specific to the research question as Hudson (1995) argues that political culture work is not fully developed in the Middle East, due to a lack of surveys and systematic interview data. Conducting structured interviews also addresses the 'conversational style' interviews that were considered a weakness of Almond and Verba's approach (Barrington, 2009: 108).

The interviews often lasted 45 minutes but varied from 30 to 60 depending on how much time the CSO members could afford. The headquarters of the CSO or a café were the most common interview locations while some were conducted in the members' homes. Interviews were conducted in English, if comfortable for the interviewee, otherwise in French or Tunisian Arabic with the assistance of an interpreter.

To verify my findings, I interviewed journalists, consultants, and members of non-Tunisian and international CSOs, and the member of the National Constituent Assembly (NCA) in charge of relations with civil society who all had experience of engaging with Tunisian CSOs. These interviews provided alternative opinions and more critical perspectives of civil society and civil society activities. The findings helped to balance to the research as there is a risk that CSO members had not been entirely honest about their practice, provided favourably optimistic views of civil society, or even especially favourable assessments of their own organisations. This verification is also necessary because I was not able to observe the behaviour (practice) of all the CSOs I interviewed.

I decided to conduct corroborative interviews after interviewing Intisar Kherigi from Jasmine Foundation;[4] a Tunisian Think Tank that brings CSOs, academics, and politicians together. Kherigi saw herself and her organisation as part of civil society yet separate and different from other Tunisian CSOs. She highlighted some problems with how Tunisian CSOs operate but also the conditions in which they operate. They are, in her opinion, poorly informed because the government does not release sufficient information and they do not conduct research. They rarely have solutions but often simply highlight problems. They spend too much time talking and not enough acting, and fail to run their CSOs efficiently. Finally, she believes that CSO members have an exaggerated belief in their impact and influence on public and political space.

Results and findings

Compared to the more easily separable quantitative data produced from the attitude survey, the interview process produced results that demonstrated the six criteria of CPC were more interconnected and expressed through different themes. Furthermore, the results showed neither clear evidence nor the absence of the six criteria of CPC but rather how the interviewees understood and demonstrated them while expressing their limitations.

The data was analysed inductively, by reading the interview data to look for emerging themes and patterns, and deductively, by searching for the criterion of civility, developed from the literature review, in the interviewee responses.

Tolerance through trust and transparency

The first finding was how Tolerance is linked to trust, transparency, cooperation and collaboration, independence, and the Islamist/secularist polarisation of society that occurs in civil society. It became evident in the interview process that Tolerance was a complicated criterion of CPC because it could not be understood in isolation and was interconnected with, and linked to, other issues. For the interviewees, Tolerance is conditional on the criterion of trust but also values, cooperation, collaboration, and to the secular/Islamist divide based on the long-term vision for the state. Furthermore, Tolerance is not simply either evident or absent, but rather on a scale and the degree to which CSOs express tolerance varies. The levels of Tolerance are therefore defined by different factors and Tolerance is a scale between CSO member's acceptance of other people's existence in the public space to a refusal to work with Islamist groups based on an assumption of the latter's long-term vision for an Islamised society. Therefore, the primary indicator of tolerance, of this research, is the Islamist/secularist divide in political ideology.

Democracy requires tolerance of voices and opinions that other members of society and the public space may dislike. This means that democracy is initially an internal process. Some of the interviewees, however, are externalising democracy but stating democracy starts with the other and whether they believe in democracy or not. The accusation expressed in interviews that "We believe in democracy, but they don't" is not a fully tolerant position because it fails to include others' right to espouse an alternative vision. People who take this position might think they are being tolerant but their unwillingness to accommodate, in their own vision of tolerance, views for the future of the Tunisian state that are fundamentally different from their own represents a degree of intolerance.

98 *Interviews with CSO leaders*

Emna Menif admits that Kolna Tounes can work with other CSOs, and even on different goals, but only if they have the same values. Emna is "not supportive of the normalisation of Islamists" and she qualifies this by saying those who are part of the 'Islamist project' are participating in politics and democracy with the ultimate objective of turning Tunisia into an Islamic state. She thinks their participation is just a strategy because they believe in something completely different. She says she has a Humanist and Citizenship background, they use the Quran. Emna is very pro-democracy but her fear of anti-democratic forces represents an intolerance towards difference.

In the political sphere and before these interviews were conducted, the Ennahda party was the major part of the troika government had constantly compromised on constitutional issues and stepped down from power to allow a technocratic government to rule. However, Islamist groups are not fully trusted. Adel Nagati of the Journalists Association of Kairouan states that "There are people who don't believe in democracy but are using it to attack democratic people, like *Hizb-Ettahrir* did." However, *Hizb-Ettahrir* (Party of Liberation) is a political party that was legalised by the Tunisian government on 17 July 2012.

Whether Islamist groups or CSOS are democratic or not is not relevant as there is an ideological position on the part of some secular CSO members that is fundamentally intolerant because it constantly assumes the Islamist 'other' is not democratic before the Islamist other acts. This represents a degree of intolerance. This research demonstrates that, for some, the boundaries of intolerance start when a group has, or is perceived to have, an Islamist vision or objectives. Those with Islamist values that underpin their civic engagement in the public sphere are then excluded from the vision and understanding of tolerance. Importantly, none of the CSOs I interviewed proclaimed to have an Islamist vision nor were any interviewees willing to label other CSOs as Islamist.

As mentioned with Emna Menif's position, the interviewees' understanding of Tolerance extends beyond the legal and legitimate existence of other CSOs in the public sphere. It also includes those who they actively cooperate with, and their willingness to work with, people who do not share their values, whether they are Islamists or not. CSOs recognise the existence of Islamist groups but some do not approve of them and have no intention of working with them. For example, Jaouhar Ben Mbarek explained that his organisation, Destourna had collaborated with UGTT, Tunisian Association for the Integrity and Democracy of Elections (ATIDE), Femmes Démocrates, LTDH, and stated, "We can collaborate with organisations that have different objectives but not with different values, for instance, we won't work with an organisation that defends the Niqab." He added, "We can debate or participate in a discussion with an association that has an Islamist background but not work on an action with them, it is forbidden [in Destourna guidelines]."

Marwa Mansouri from *Association Cultivons la Paix* seems to express a more open approach by stating, "For me, democracy is to accept the other who is different from you and work together for positive change." She added,

Interviews with CSO leaders 99

I think that if we are trying to establish democracy then we need to work with people from different backgrounds because that is how we move forward. Being different does not mean that we can't collaborate; there is certainly a minimum of common ground that we can find and work with.

However, she seems to contradict herself and echo Emna and Jaouhar's sentiment by also stating that "we work with other CSOs on one condition, they have to share our values". The bringing together of difference and the requirement of sharing values are mutually exclusive requirements. It suggests levels of Equality and Tolerance that are conditional on her terms.

In addition to Destourna and Kolna Tounes, a smaller number of CSOs expressed a view that they cannot work with CSOs who have an Islamist vision.

- "We don't work with organisations that have ideological backgrounds, like the Islamists." (Amira Achouri, Association of Kairouanees for a Culture of Citizenship)
- "The Quranic associations can't be considered part of civil society because they are working on their own agenda." (Kamel Abid, ATPC)

The majority of interviewed CSOs, however, express Tolerance through their willingness to work with other CSOs and in coalitions, despite differences, without mentioning the exclusion of any groups due to their long-term vision of the state. The following quotes are examples of this cooperative and inclusionary attitude.

- "We have to work altogether because we cannot work by ourselves, the impact would not be so good." (Selim Abbou, *Tounesa*)
- "The nature of our CSO obliges us to collaborate with the other CSOs in our network and they don't necessarily have the same objectives as we do. We also work with CSOs in partnership for certain projects in a certain amount of time." (Riadh Werghi, *Union des Jeunes Démocrates Tunisiens*)
- "We have to put our differences aside and work, which is, of course, difficult." (Amel Chaherli, *Alwen Tounes*)
- "We can collaborate with organisations that have different objectives than ours on certain occasions, for instance when we worked on elections, we collaborated with the medical association and student's associations and so on." (Imen Bejoui, *l'Association Tunisienne des Jeunes Avocats*, ATJA)
- "Yes, and it's happened a few times like when many work for the same thing. E.g. In the 1st draft – Complimentary to Women; FTDES worked with Women's groups etc. More than 40 organisations worked together. It depends on the issue, social and economic ones are popular." (Messaoud Romdhani, FTDES)

These CSO leaders recognise the importance and value of working together to increase effectiveness. Romdhani makes a salient point that civil society becomes effective when a large number or network of organisations can rally behind campaigning on a single issue, combined with media attention, then the government is forced to listen. For the majority of CSOs, the fragmented 'solo' campaigns are less effective, have less impact, and are easier to ignore.

CSOs recognise that working together is important for greater impact, but with which other organisation do they collaborate? Some CSOs expressed they only work with people and CSOs that they trust. This means issues of Trust and Tolerance are linked, not isolated. However, the nuance is that Tolerance is passive compared to Trust being proactive as the trust of another entity is not required to tolerate them operating. For example, interviewees express cases and examples of distrust but not intolerance towards a range of actors and groups such as a lack of trust in political parties.

- "Today civil society is in a much stronger position than political parties and in the most recent survey Tunisians trust 1st the army and 2nd the CSOs." (Samir Kilani, *Ofiya*)
- "I don't see them [political parties] as honest, they are not transparent enough, they are not trustworthy. Maybe some of them have changed a little but they still have the old way of building up a political party, they are hierarchical so it's very hard to climb the ladder, and are undemocratic and the decision-making is between 2 or 3 or 10 people and there are thousands in the party." (Zied Boussen, *Jeunes Independent Démocrates*)

Zied's points of being more attracted to civil society work than joining a political party and also of equating honesty and Transparency with Trust are reiterated by other interviewees. Interviewees also noted that people find that working in civil society is more comfortable than political parties. Parties are not that transparent which sets a bad example for civil society, and there is a lack of trust in political parties, for example:

- "Political parties have always been preserved as 'not so good to be part of'. We have always had a lack of trust toward people with a political agenda." (Jaouhar ben Mbarek, *Destourna*)
- "The people are sick of how bad the political parties are, so they go to civil society." (Mohammed Masri, Network of Sidi Bouzid Associations)

There is evidence that CSOs are not entirely trusted, by the government and the public. The following quotes are examples of cases where Trust is yet to be established.

- "Under Ben Ali, civil society was hated, but now it's tolerated but not taken into consideration. E.g. Terrorism and violence, 2 years ago when artists were attacked, that was a warning that was ignored by the government. Because the old reflex and mentality of 'you're with us or against us' still prevailed in the government. The mentality of the government did not change enough." (Messaoud Romdhani, FTDES)

- "The government nationally and locally still sees the civil society as the enemy. There is no trust between the two sides. In Sidi Bouzid there is some collaboration with the local authorities." (Aida Daly, TOUPAT)
- "Two months ago we invited the parents of members to a meeting and showed them the activities of the association, what we are doing, to break the ice between parents and our association, to let them talk to us and show we are like a second family for our members, and we have to have their trust in the association." (Anis Boufrika, We Love Sousse)

The interview data has numerous examples that demonstrate how Trust has developed between CSOs and other bodies, and additionally that trust is exhibited via cases of CSO collaboration and cooperation. *Mouraikboun, I-Watch*, and *Al Bawsala*, three influential, watchdog CSOs, mention how Trust has developed between the government and their organisation due to continued engagement.

- "We have daily contact with the Election commission, the election management authority, and parliament because we are monitoring them. It wasn't respectful in the beginning but after some months and years, when they understood that we are not 'against them', but just fighting for the rights of the people, open data, and transparency of the political process. And we proved that we are non-partisan, not fighting for any political parties, so I think they now respectful, and we don't have any problems." (Rafik Halouani, *Mourakiboun*)
- "I-Watch has a good reputation with the government. They know that we are neutral and independent and have no political affiliations. If you go to our Facebook page, for example, you will see criticism from us against the government and parties, but we don't belong to any. When there is something wrong, we say it strongly, when something is true, we say it. When something happens that affects the neutrality of Tunisian civil society, the government becomes suspicious and more scared it." (Mouheb Garoui, *I-Watch*)

What factors lead to increased trust for CSOs and state actors? Ghada Louhichi from *Al Bawsala* thinks the determination, perseverance, motivation, neutrality, and professionalism of the staff has made *Al Bawsala* a successful and trusted CSO. But she also adds that it is because *Al Bawsala* staff are paid full-time and can fully commit to their work that members of the national assembly were able to trust them.

I remember when we were first observing in the NCA, one of the deputies was angry with us, Tahar Hmila, he's one of the oldest, he doesn't like us much. He said to me and my colleagues "Go find a job", and she [one of Ghada's colleagues] said "this is my job". But we love our jobs. Every day we have something new, something different, or unexpected.

Then she notes how the relationship changed once the trust had been established.

Some of the deputies, when they introduce us to anyone, yesterday, for example, we were talking with some students from the United State who were in the NCA and one member said, "Ghada comes to the NCA even more than some deputies." This shows some confidence and trust we have built with the deputies. It wasn't easy, at the beginning they were suspicious, like "Who are you?" "Why are you here? What agenda are you implementing?", all these conspiracy theories, you know. For the commissions, we're there from the beginning to the end, even late at night. They saw us working and they know we are not just reporting on the bad things.

Furthermore, Trust and Financial Transparency are also connected and influence the potential for CSOs to collaborate and cooperate. This is based on Transparency providing a good impression because it implies Trust. The following quotes demonstrate how CSOs are unwilling or hesitant to work with other CSOs with opaque funding sources.

- "[Revealing sources of funding] is important for transparency and building trust between citizens and civil society." (Mouheb Garoui, *I-Watch*)
- "Now with the boom of CSOs the situation is different, there so many CSOs and they can't all be trusted in terms of funding so we continue to work with our historic partners." "[W]e collaborate with organizations that we trust like LTDH and Femmes Democrates." (Imen Bejoui, ATJA)
- "We can't really work with the newly created CSOs because we don't know where they get their funding from so we are very sceptical about it and also lots of political parties are behind some CSOs and that goes against our first value which is Independence. It is not up to us to say whether these small CSOs are trustworthy or not but we have a set of standards that we abide by and work with." (Boubaker Bethabet, ONAT)
- "There is a lack of trust between citizens and CSOs mostly because of the funding sources. People know it is all foreign funding and so they have doubts about it. And Political parties have also discovered that civil society can bring them money so they started CSOs of their own, this increased the amount of distrust between people and civil society." (Adel Nagati, Journalists Association of Kairouan)
- "We don't find it difficult to find funding because we have a brand and are a known organisation by funders and we interact with other funders, we have worked with funders and completed projects, they trust us and know how our work is." (Ghazoua Lteif, *Sawty*) Trust has been established between *Sawty* and funding bodies who they have been working with for two years.

The legal framework, established by Decree-Law 88 (2011), allows Islamist organisations to exist but Messoud Romdhani (FTDES) highlighted that Salafist groups who call for violence are breaking the law. Therefore, Romdhani understands the law as being the crucial criterion of Tolerance because Tolerance is defined by what is legal. Beyond the legal framework, there is no agreement of tolerance in civil society. While the law, indeed the Tunisian political system, remains in transition, discovering the limits of tolerance is a challenge for the new democracy.

Moez Ali of *Union des Tunisiens Indépendants pour la Liberté* (UTIL) claimed his rejection of Islamism is based on freedom of conscience. UTIL is a humanitarian CSO but worked on the 'Bus Citoyen' project with five other CSOs who all had different goals; *Sawty* (Youth), TOUENSA (Citizenship), ACT 'khammem ou karrer' (economic and cultural development of disadvantaged regions of Tunisia), *Femmes et Dignité* (Women's Rights), and ATIDE (Transparency and Corruption-fighting). Ali explained 'Bus Cityon' aimed to encourage voting because "Women's rights were threatened after the Revolution. Certain factions who do not believe in the role of women in society, Salafists and extremists, wanted women out of politics, cover their heads and to stay at home." This represents the ability of a CSO to cooperate and collaborate within its own circle of Tolerance. Ali explained his position and why the 'Bus Cityon' project took place.

> We are a country that has strong Islamic roots that goes back to the 14th Century, so we are not in a position to take lessons from others to bring other ways of thinking, other ideologies and insert them in our society. We have no lessons to take from others. My grandmother and mother grew up in a moderate state with a modern Islam, that respects women, values of the family, and people in general. And it gives freedom of thinking, it's mentioned in the Constitution as freedom of conscience. But people don't understand freedom of conscience, it's to be judged for what we do and not what we think. This is the Islam we know, and these are the values Islam we know. So the people who want to insert the Wahhabism, which was created in the early 19th century, so they are not in a position to give us lessons about Islam. We grew up knowing that the only one who can judge us is God, not people. This is how we grew up and how we want Tunisia to be.

This suggests that Ali's fundamental normative position is tolerant. His objection to Islamists is because, according to Ali, they do not want tolerance. Ali, therefore, cannot tolerate what he believes to be intolerance. Members of Tunisian civil society who reject what they perceive to be intolerant behaviour or attitudes demonstrates their 'externalisation of democracy'; how their understanding of tolerance begins with their assessment or judgement of others.

From the other perspective, Yassine Jebloui of *Notre Santé d'Abord*, a medical support CSO, was the only interviewee to explain any specific incidences of intolerance expressed by Islamists. This suggests that most interviewees exhibit bias against Islamists for only reasons of ideological difference. Yassine explained how his CSO was prevented from operating.

> We had one problem when we worked near Nabeul, people said you can't come here because there were religious people, you know extremists, who

> didn't want us to go. They didn't want us to help with giving out glasses and I think there are a lot of associations who work with Ennahda and work as religious associations who mainly work in this area [healthcare] and they do not want to have competition.

In addition to others attempting to benefit from the social capital gained by his organisation's work.

> There was another problem that we had, sometimes you make an action, and then after you have people who are from Ennahda who said that "we called them to help you". This happened in Manouba. ...
> In Nabeul, there are a lot of problems and a lot of extremists. They were governing there, and if they say you can't go, then you can't go. Sometimes you have associations who work there who say we only want the Islamic associations to work here, not the other ones.
>
> (Yassine Jebloui, *Notre Santé d'Abord*)

Despite interviewees criticising Islamists, the belief that Islamist organisations should be stopped or banned from participating in the public sphere was not expressed. This represents the attitude that freedom should still be afforded to these groups and an understanding of tolerance that is related to freedom of speech.

These results indicate that the boundaries of tolerance are dependent on trust, transparency, and exhibited through willingness or lack therefore, to cooperate and collaborate. Their approach to what should not be tolerated is certainly dependent whether other CSOs act within the law and, in some cases but not exclusively, whether the 'other' is classified as Islamist or not. The extent to which Tunisian CSOs exhibit democratic culture is shaped by the perception of Islamist groups. Some interviewees did not present in their discourse any expressed objections or reservations towards those with Islamist visions for Tunisia's future. However, for those who did, this means their perception of democracy is exclusive of the Islamists' vision. Islamism influences their understandings of and attitudes towards Trust, Tolerance, and Transparency. Furthermore, Islamism shapes whether a CSO is viewed as Independent or is considered plausible for cooperation and collaboration. Cooperation is a step further beyond tolerance as interviewees expressed that tolerance is a prerequisite for cooperation and collaboration. The reason some secularists express intolerance towards Islamist is that they are afraid of the non-democratic element of the Islamist vision.

Legally established freedom

Freedom and Tolerance are linked by the civil society member's understanding of the public space. Freedom to operate in this public space is a dramatic improvement in comparison to the Ben Ali era where even non-political CSOs were not granted legal status or were restricted. For example, Souhail Alouini from OpenGovTN was prevented from forming a medical CSO in 2006 and Sfax Outdoor Sports President Zaher Kammoun told me they were not permitted to engage in caving because the Ministries of Interior and Defence linked it to terrorist activities. Freedom is understood as a technical, more neatly defined legal issue regarding how much room CSOs are permitted and where the boundaries of freedom are marked as the use of violence and hate speech. CSO members recognise that freedom is required to ensure the quality of democracy. CSOs are protected by Decree-Law 88 (2011), therefore, interviewees explained that the government has not shut down their operations, they have not experienced interference from religious groups, and rather than being pressured by the government, they feel that they are the ones who are applying pressure. Amira Yahyahoui (*Al-Bawsala*) said "They wouldn't dare" while Faycal Labayed (*Sousse Demain*) rhetorically asked, "Do I look like I give in to pressure?" There were only two cases where interviewees mention state interference and interruption of their activities.

- "We wanted to work on the rural women health but we faced resistance from male farmers and even the Ministry of Health, so many hospitals didn't let us in. The Police as well were following us for a while." (Hachem Aydi, Cultural Association Mouwantaneen)
- "There is a lot of pressure on CSOs coming mainly from the ministry of interior, political parties, and some Salafist groups. Mainly Ennahda controls the south of Tunisia so they would vandalize our projects and events and they would even infiltrate the beneficiaries to sabotage us. As for the ministry of interior, there were always correspondences and phone calls to have us change or shut down a project and we were arrested a couple of times during events in Sidi Bouzid and Kasserine. They also shut down one of our projects for security reasons because the project was by Chaambi Mountain." (Riadh Wergi, *Union des Jeunes Démocrates Tunisiens*)

Cases such as the latter could provide a reason for intolerance towards Islamist groups that is based on a reaction and informed by experience rather than ingrained ideological intolerance. Riadh did not know if the people who have interfered with their work were connected to the Leagues for the Protection of the Revolution.

Interviewees understood that the freedom in the space that the state gives civil society is not limitless. The limits of the freedom afforded to CSOs are hate speech and calling for or implementing violence. The statistical results from the attitude survey in Chapter 4 also suggest that CSO members believe there should be limits to freedom of speech. Messoud Romdhani (FTDES) states that Salafist groups that are calling for violence and intolerance are breaking the law of associations. Indeed, Decree-Law 88 (2011) states, "Article (4): Associations are prohibited from the following: One: Adopting in their bylaws, data, programs or activities any incitement for violence, hatred, fanaticism or discrimination on religious, racial or regional grounds."[5] This demonstrates that the Tunisian state

106 *Interviews with CSO leaders*

has played a role in ensuring that civil society is legally civil. This is also in agreement with the argument Jamal (2007) makes, that civil society is not an independent variable but is influenced by the system of government.

Equality and pluralism identified in democratic practices, learning processes, and institutional culture

Equality and Pluralism are criteria of CPC that are expressed through the CSO's internal dynamics and therefore more easily identified. Equality is equal opportunity for anyone (gender, age, ethnicity, religion, or sexuality) to become members and, once a member, the chance to influence the CSO or gain executive bureau positions. Equality is indicated, internally, by equal opportunities and lack of exclusion in CSO membership. By contrast, inequality is demonstrated by friends and family members, certain age groups, a gender, or an ethnicity being given preferential treatment.

Pluralism is the inclusion of diverse opinions and the spread or decentralisation of power and decision making. Pluralism is indicated by consultative, collaborative, or democratic decision-making processes in which there are mechanisms for members to influence the decisions and the membership of the executive bureau. Power is multi-dimensional and distributed rather than concentrated in the hands of the CSO President or founder. If organisations have consultative decision-making processes or a mechanism for members to influence decisions, this suggests that they are Pluralist. Whereas, if decisions are top-down from the executive bureau or against the membership's wishes, this implies a lack of Pluralism. There are limitations to pluralism with regards to members who are from political parties. Decree-Law 88 (2011) states that party members are not allowed to gain executive bureau positions in CSOs. However, most cases of equality and pluralism were expressed through the CSO's institutional culture: the extent to which their practices and their decision-making processes were democratic. The composition of a CSO's *bureau exécutif* is also an indicator of equality and the following quotes highlight the extent of gender diversity in CSO bureaus.

- "We have an executive bureau that is composed of 7 members five of them are women and two are men. 30% of us are of youth. Every idea is welcomed whether it is coming from the executive bureau or the members, we don't make the distinction. We get together we talk about it and execute the plan." (Saloua Ghrissa, ATPDD)
- "The bureau is divided equally between both genders." (Yassin Nasr, President of Association Cepsa)
- "Democracy in Tunisia needs so much more time to be established. I think after the revolution women everywhere should be in decision-making position, you might say that I am only saying that because I am a woman but the truth is that I believe women should be given an equal opportunity to lead challenge because I believe in this transitional period we need finesse, flexibility and strength and women combine the 3." (Imen Bejoui, ATJA)

The power relations between the bureau and regular members also expressed the extent of Equality and Pluralism. Jaouhar's description of *Destourna*, as "a completely decentralised, network of small cells", was a unique case, but most CSOs described how their leadership takes the major decisions while being considerate to the membership. Amir explains how WeYouth's bureau is receptive to feedback.

> At the end of any project we made, we ask them [the members] for their opinions. Sometimes they are unhappy and say what they want. ... We have a good bureau but I support the idea that everyone is a normal member and we're all the same. It's not the era of the executive board giving all the orders. ... I was a member of another Tunisian NGO, so when I feel that my work was just the Bureau's gain and they want to force any idea or project, so I said I don't feel comfortable so I quit. So I don't want my members to quit.
> (Amir Ben Ameur, WeYouth)

Furthermore, interviewees' explanations of their CSO's decision-making processes and democratic practices, such as discussion, consensus, and voting, were also representations of Equality and Pluralism. The following quotes express how different CSOs implement inclusive practices.

- "If I want to take initiative, I present the ideas to the board members and we debate and have discussions about that initiative and if this project will be ok, what would be gained, what obstacles we may face. So we make a kind of plan about the project, basically, we support democracy in our NGO. ... I think leadership is not about taking decisions or being authoritarian, but you have to have influence, if you have an idea and support it with arguments and motivation, all of us work like this, if you have an idea just suggest it." (Amir Ben Ameur, WeYouth)
- "I'm a team player, not a ruler. The CSOs is happy because of the teamwork. We listen to each other, there no one person who decides. We vote for which theme we are going to work on, and then we select three themes that are the most relevant to Sidi Bouzid and proceed to vote on them." (Ghada Chokri, President of I-Lead)
- "Most of the ideas are from the bureau because we are part of this environment and we know the needs and what the region lacks and we try to stay apolitical and keep the association out of the political feud." (Abderrahamane Hadj Belgacem, Gabes Action)
- "As for ideas, they usually come from the members and also the ideas that our followers on FB might suggest." (Adel Nagati, Journalists Association of Kairouan)
- "We have a Facebook page and whoever has any suggestions or anything can send a message to the inbox. We also have meetings once or twice a month." (Amel Amraoui, Sajin 52)
- "There is no president who gives orders. We all are presidents and members." (Chedly Ben Messaoud, Association Djerba Ulysse)

- "We are a very Horizontal association." (Adel Hechimi, Friends of the Miners Basin)
- "Inside these walls, we practice democracy, we have a book for suggestions or we can also accept suggestions in our weekly meeting and then we vote to determine which ones to execute." (Naceur Yassine, Cepsa)

Sawty is a large CSO with regional chapters but Ghazoua explains the overall feeling of unity rather than having regional loyalty.

- "The members all feel like 'we are *Sawty*' first of all, they [each chapter] are not very independent of each other. They are trying to focus on each region because each region has its own specificities so they try to target the youth there and respond to their particular needs. But Chapters try to coordinate with each other when they work, and they all identify themselves as *Sawty*. The duty of the national board is to notice when a chapter is going far from the fields we work in and help try to remain focused on the collective aims. National projects and activities gather all the members." (Ghazoua Ltaief, President of *Sawty*)
- "We believe in unity, we have been trying to teach Tunisians to get over regionalism, tribalism, and nepotism." (Sami Tahri, UGTT Spokesman)

Institutional isomorphism (DiMaggio and Powell, 1983), whereby organisations hold similar attitudes, engage in similar practices, and operate with similar management styles, was not evident in the survey results of Chapter 4. The inquiry into the existence of isomorphism is relevant because it seeks to establish whether a central tendency or similar trends exist in Tunisian CSOs or whether they are varied and heterogeneous. Isomorphism is conventionally applied to institutional practices. However, this research applies it to examine the extent of political culture norms convergence between CSOs. The interview data largely confirms that organisations are not necessarily becoming increasingly similar or are adopting a certain, singular approach to civil activism. This is partly due to the varying objectives of CSOs which require different approaches. Delivering their message and initiating or implementing change is a common theme for CSOs. However, political watchdogs, awareness-raising groups, and charity or service providers operate differently, each according to their goals. Furthermore, how groups deliver their messages varies. Some use public displays in press releases and conferences or training workshops. Others target the general public through their projects. Some seek to influence NCA members through lobbying in person or sending written recommendations. Oppositional-Resistance approaches of protests, demonstration, or sit-ins were also employed.

Regarding management style, interviewees often cited *Al-Bawsala* as a great example of a CSO because it is effective and influential. However, its business model is not possible for all other CSOs to aspire to or even imitate. *Al-Bawsala* is a unique, professional reporting and watchdog association that became the most trustworthy information source on NCA activities. As the interview with

Amira Yahyaoui demonstrated, it may have a pro-democracy agenda, but its institutional culture has been centred around Amira's leadership and top-down mentoring rather than democratic practice and decision-making processes. Amira spoke candidly about her leadership of *Al-Bawsala* and noted that her philosophy behind the CSO was 'Accountability', which to her means "not letting Politicians get used to power". Therefore, all the ideas for the CSO's projects came from her. She attributed this to being the only member of the team who was an 'activist' under Ben Ali so she "grew up with real hatred for politicians and no respect for government".

In contrast, Ghazoua Lteif (*Sawty*) explains how she is inspired by various CSOs and tries to incorporate new ideas.

> "We are trying to build our own model, as a Youth organisation we are different, and there are not really a big number of youth organisations working with youth so we do not have a model in Tunisia because 90% of the NGOs you see today were created post-Revolution so we are all in the stage of learning. Even the old organisations, for me, are not very inspiring models. When I travel and see organisations abroad, I am inspired. There are great initiatives. Every time I go to a foreign training session or exchange programme, I try to learn new tools and skills, and then transfer them to members of Sawty when I get back. Even from the Arab World, not just European or American models. US models are very professional but I've seen some great initiatives in Jordan, Morocco, and Egypt."

In addition to different approaches civic activity CSOs seek to undertake, the variation in training CSOs receive adds to the diversity in civil society. The range of both Tunisian and international consultant-trainers and funding bodies that provide training for CSOs, such as the British Council, British Embassy, Department for International Development (DFID), United States Agency for International Development (USAID), U.S.–Middle East Partnership Initiative (MEPI), National Democratic Institute (NDI), International Republican Institute (IRI), Friedrich Ebert Stiftung (FES), Konrad Adenauer Stiftung (KAS), or GiZ (the German Society for International Cooperation), suggests a pluralism of approaches to civic activism.

Inquiry into issues of transparency demonstrated that most organisations require funding for their activities. CSOs demonstrated similar discourses regarding their acquisition of funding and that they must follow similar approaches to securing funding. Energy Sector INGO Associate, Lucy Kamoun, noted that some Tunisian CSOs understood the norms and the language they must adopt to be successful with their proposal applications.

> As CSO associate, I had to evaluate a large number of local CSO proposals for our small grants program. Our INGO's proposal template follows the same guidelines and structures many other international donors follow. I noticed that CSOs are aware of the 'donor jargon' and their proposals

usually reflect what they believe the donor wants to hear, from the way their proposal objectives and outcomes are phrased to the operational and financial management style they adopt for their proposed projects. It is not a surprise that the 'successful' Tunisian CSOs such as *Bawsala* and *I-Watch* are those well versed in grant proposal writing and who are more able to attract funding.

In addition to using the international standard terminology, some CSOs tailor their projects to align with the donor's requirements to gain funding. However, others reject funding if it contains conditions or does not suit their needs. Ghada Chokri explained how I-Lead refused support from a Danish organisation (VNG) because they could not agree on terms: I-Lead wanted training assistance but VNG could not provide it. Another CSO that did not bow to an international donor's requirements was *Inara* (Enlightenment), a charity organisation that aims to provide logistics rather than operating with a budget. The founder Sami Chaherli explained how low means can still have a high impact and that it is possible to make a positive change without huge budgets and international funding.

> I don't need money for the association; I can give you a list of 10 families, or 50 students, or schools. You can send them food, clothing, supplies, in the name of the association or by yourself. No money needs to go into the *Inara* account if people don't want.

Despite variations in these organisations' practices, similar trends in normative values were evident. Democratic practices, essential to CPC, were considered normatively desirable and appearing to be an independent was vital. Interviewees also conveyed the importance of members' inclusiveness and members having equality and freedom to express themselves. While institutional isomorphism was not clearly present, the diversity in types of CSOs and the methods they employed demonstrates the vibrancy of Tunisian civil society.

Women and racism: the limitations of equality

The limitations of equality were evident when addressing the status of women and the issue of racism. In contrast to the *mentalité* of male superiority that tangibly manifests within party leadership (Petkanas, 2013: 10), there are many female leaders in Tunisian CSOs and 22 of the 66 interviewees were women. Article 3 of Decree-Law 88 (2011) requests that CSOs observe equality and the interview data certainly suggests that women are not marginalised and gender equality is evident in civil society. CSOs were a driving force in protesting against the first draft of the constitution that included an article regarding Women's 'complimentary' status in relation to men.[6] Messaoud Romdhani (FTDES) explained how "More than 40 organisations worked together" on campaigning against this article. Women's rights are often vehemently defended in the liberal agenda against intolerance or Islamism. Anis Boufrika thinks the constitution is thanks to the hard work of NGOs and Tunisian women. He also is adamant that Tunisian women are a vital difference because "Women are harder to corrupt than men." The statistical results in Chapter 4 also suggest agreement with Boufrika.

Although the following issues cannot lead to generalisations but only point to underlying nuances, there were a few cases where gender-related issues were highlighted. First, the perceived threat that Ennahda poses to women's rights has made women an important post-revolutionary issue, but also something that can be exploited. Discussing why their organisation has refused advances from any political party, Wafa Garbout thinks parties try to work with CSOs for their own gains and to appear gender-sensitive. "They're using you just for their image, especially women, because they want to seem liberal and progressive" (Wafa Garbout, United Colleges Association, UCA). Second, both UGTT and LTDH talked about the need to change with the times, especially integrating more women and youth, which suggested these organisations are male-dominated. Third, although gender-parity exists in CSOs, women leaders still face the struggle of men challenging their authority. Imen Bejoui explained the difficulties she faces.

> As a woman, I have always felt that I was not in the decision-making process, I was respected but not included. Now being the president of ATJA I am the decision-maker and it is not an easy task but I am up for the challenge.
> (Imen Bejaoui, ATJA)

Fourth, despite being President, Amira Achouri explained, "I'm the only girl in the organisation, so it's difficult to manage things in a group of men" (Amira Achouri, Association of Kairouanees for a Culture of Citizenship). It was unclear exactly what she meant but it could imply a degree of sexism or that, as a woman, it is harder to convey authority, she is not trusted, or her ability to take the right decision would be questioned. Furthermore, nearly all of the female leaders are based in Tunis: Amira Yahyaoui, Selima Abbou, Emna Menif, Marwa Mansouri, Imen Bejaoui, Amal Amraoui, Intisar Kherigi, and Ghazoua Ltaief. As Amira Achouri is based in Kairouan, a more conservative city in the interior region, it possible that female leaders away from the capital are more likely to face these issues.

Hasham Aidi, President of Cultural Association Mouwantaneen, a CSO based in Reugeb, a small town the Sidi Bouzid Governorate, explained how participation in their organisation was appealing to women for social reasons.

> For us here, people, especially girls and women, join in because it is an opportunity for them to leave their houses, their daily routine and to meet up with people [friends of the opposite gender] who she can't meet elsewhere like in her house.

This is not to suggest that organisations express inequality but this case highlights that female inclusion can be limited by the conservative social conventions in some parts of Tunisia regarding a woman's role in society. Therefore, CSOs that have a neutral base of operations or headquarters (*locale* in French) have the social advantages of allowing women a more respectable location in the public space than the male-dominated café scene, thus potentially preventing further unequal participation. This suggests equality exists despite social norms. Besides, CSOs provide a democratic public space, which is a positive indicator of the role CSOs play in democratisation. Indeed, women's participation, particularly from conservative areas, in CSOs cannot be reduced to the availability of a locale. This issue is beyond the scope of the study, therefore it's not possible to make any wider claims about the status of women in Tunisian civil society.

No racism or race-related issues were expressed in interviews, except by Saadia Mosbah of *Mnemty*, an awareness-raising, pro-Human Rights, education, and development CSO. This is partly because Mosbah argues that racism is not recognised as a problem in Tunisia but that an underlying layer of racism exists in society and therefore civil society. She gave examples such as how slave names are still on birth certificates and how a teacher called a student using the term 'slave'. Mosbah explained how *Mnemty* asked the NCA to make committing racism a crime but it refused to discuss this topic. She thinks it contrary to the idea of human rights and equality if race issues are ignored. She acknowledges *Mnemty* is begrudgingly accepted.

> We are independent and that scares other organisations, so they feel obliged to invite us to their events, but at 11PM the day before it takes place. They are afraid that we will take the money of the funders, but we will prove them wrong, and we will show them that we can work without the money.

As Saadia was the only interviewee to address racism, it is not possible to make any wider claims about the status of racial equality in Tunisian civil society.

Independence and effectiveness: the limitations of pluralism

Interviewees noted that there were limitations on how pluralistic their CSO could be for two major reasons: first, in the prevention of politicisation and maintenance of independence; and, second, in favour of organisation efficiency where strong leadership, succession planning, and sustainability can take priority over democratic practices and therefore hinder the pluralism of the organisation.

Decree-Law 88 (2011) seeks to prevent the overlap between the political sphere and civil society activity by stating that "Article (9): Founders and directors of an association must not be among those who assume the central management posts in political parties." Furthermore, organisations pride themselves on their independence from control or affiliation to political parties for reasons relating to Trust. In spite of a legal limitation to complete inclusion and pluralism, Mouheb explained how *I-Watch* maintains a balance of independence without being exclusionary.

We have very strict rules, I-Watch doesn't accept members that belong to political parties, however, the main principle in I-Watch is 'No exclusion' so these members with political affiliations don't have access and cannot be involved in lobbying and advocacy projects. You can be a member and watch what we are doing but you cannot get involved in the projects, especially the elections ones. If you want to get involved in I-Watch, you must resign from your political party. We do not discourage young people from joining political parties but we believe that the two don't match or work together. Choose civil society or political parties. The board members are not in anyways allowed to join political parties, or even express on their Facebook page affiliation or alignment with political parties.

(Mouheb Garoui, *I-Watch*)

Whether an organisation that promotes or advocates for democracy has to be democratic itself is a contentious issue. However, interviewees largely agreed that it was the case and even viewed it as a requirement. Despite the normative desirability of internal democratic elections or voting procedures, either regarding the selection of leadership and bureau members or consultation with members regarding the organisation's decisions or actions, CSOs are seeking to strike a balance. On one hand, having skilled personnel is vital to making the organisation run effectively and bring sufficient stability to enable the organisation to develop. On the other hand, applying democratic ideals, such as pluralism and equality, and including democratic practices to determine which member is given decision-making authority may increase the CSO's credibility. Implementing too many democratic practices too soon can, in some cases, be detrimental to the CSO's effectiveness. Ensuring that the organisation is an established and functioning entity before power is transferred has been served to be a prudent approach for some. Presidents of professional (salaried) CSOs tend to have more expertise and have not stepped down because they are concerned that replacements would not have sufficient abilities to do their job. For example, while Amira Yahyaoui (*Al-Bawsala*) and Radwan Masmoudi (Centre for the Study of Islam and Democracy) were both looking to eventually step down and were in the process of training or looking for suitable replacements (Martin, 2015: 805), Yahyaoui left *Al-Bawsala* but Masmoudi remains the CSID President.

Of course I'm going to say it's very participatory [laughs]. Unfortunately, until today all the ideas for the projects were mine. When I talk about the people who will take over this NGO, they are excellent at doing the work but don't have enough initiative. In the beginning, I was involved in each detail, maybe this scared some of them because none of them were activists before. I am the only one who was active under Ben Ali, so they didn't have the same way of thinking and treating Politicians. ...

The big problem I had was *Al-Bawsala* was mine, and I used my name[7] to promote it, I mean if it wasn't me Sahbi Atig[8] would never have given up one hour a week. I worked on the ground a lot and then over time I had to stay more in the office because when you read what the press was writing about *Al-Bawsala*, its 'Amira's NGO' or sometimes just my name ... now the staff are becoming more independent and more involved, having more ideas.

(Amira Yahyaoui, *Al-Bawsala*)

Amira told me "Tunisians love to discuss, but never to work" and recalled an occasion when a CSO member told Amira she is like a TGV (French high-speed train), a testament to both *Al Bawsala*'s effectiveness and her strong leadership. She responded that they are like a yellow Tunisian bus; slow. If a CSO that has a strong leader with experience, expertise, and is effective at 'getting things done', democratic practices can sometimes be bypassed or overlooked in favour of efficiency and effectiveness in CSO activity, even if the CSO promotes democracy. In this case, equality and pluralism are compromised.

Some voluntary CSOs have decided to maintain stability and consistency with their managing personnel and leaders. Moez Ali has been the only President of UTIL, as the other founding members left or pursued a career in politics. His years of pre-2011 experience with USAID had enabled the members to re-elect him. His family members are also not involved in UTIL because he considered that "this isn't moral". He is not, however, overly controlling as he explains UTIL project managers are given complete control over their work. He explained that he is looking to step down to enable "younger people to take over". The presidents of organisations I interviewed generally had the intention of, eventually, resigning and transferring leadership, recognising it is the right thing to do. Many echoed the sentiment of Saadia Mosbah, President of *M'nemty*, "It's high time I stepped down at the next general assembly." This suggests that remaining in power indefinitely would no longer be considered an acceptable practice. Conversely, Chawki Gaddes (ATDC) told me, "I tried to step down in the last General assembly but the whole bureau refused" because they feared the organisation would not function as effectively without him (Martin, 2015: 805).

Having democratic practices within your CSO is a normatively ideal position, indeed many interviewees state we have to 'practice what we preach', for example, "You cannot advocate for transparency and participatory democracy if you are not applying this internally" (Mouheb Garoui, *I-Watch*). Anis Boufrika (We Love Sousse) concurs; "I am very convicted to democratic ways and democratic values, and if we defend these values, we have to apply them." However, the balancing act between democracy and effectiveness is a logical and practical explanation for where the limits of pluralism exist.

What CSO members have been learning about democracy reveals the processes of change they have been undertaking and indicates degrees of Equality and Pluralism. Attempting to implement democracy has made members realise they need to be pluralistic and treat members equally. The following quotes demonstrate what and how CSOs have been learning about democracy in addition to how it is practically implemented.

- "For us, democracy also means involvement, if you are the president of a CSO that does not mean that you are always right when you discuss your ideas with others and listen to their ideas, that is when you have better results." (Radwan Fatnassi, FTDES)
- "The most important thing we have learned is the practice of democracy, the acceptance of other views and the tolerance and the importance of consensus." (Zouhayer Hammoudi, Government Participative)
- "There are a lot of values that you might be totally convinced are correct and would be willing to fight to see implemented. However, because of democracy, other people may be convinced of the opposite, and if the vote favours them, you find yourself losing the battle. Learning to accept defeat is important." (Mohsen Mhadhbi, ARAA Pour la Civilisation et Citoyenneté)
- "We learned democracy in theory and we have the chance to practice it our CSO while having our elections, writing our status and discussing projects. We learned how not to be afraid to disagree and say it straightforward." (Aida Daly, TOUPAT)
- "We learned that we have to listen to each other and that there should not be one person who decides." (Ghada Chorki, I-Lead)
- "Decisions should not be taken vertically and there should be room for debates. Voting should be the way to solve our disagreement and we should resort to voting if consensus can't be reached. Also, working with other CSOs contributed to our learning about democracy, doing this kind of activities should be very collaborative and so no CSO should dominate the decision making." (Adel Hechimi, Friends of the Miners Basin)
- "For me, civil society is like a smaller prototype for society. If we can work on being democratic in our organisation it is a start, and then we can move to applying democracy in the family and schools. So we don't take unilateral decisions, we use voting instead." (Myriam Belhaj, OVC)
- "We can say 'no' and we are allowed to disagree. The President of the CSO can be challenged and should listen to what other members have to say and do what the majority decides. We often disagree, so we resort to voting." (Wissem Ksiksi, Oxygen)

Jaouhar Ben Mbarek (*Destourna*) found that the application of democracy is also different from how he had previously understood the concept.

> I thought that democracy was about laws and texts and I found out that is a culture of the people. The problem is we live in a country where the culture of people is not democratic so we need to rebuild this society.

Other interviewees concurred, describing how they understood that a specific culture is required to support the processes and institutions of democracy.

- "Elections are not the definition of democracy." (Marwa Mansouri, *Association Cultivons la Paix*)

- "Democracy is a process but it's also a mentality. This is something you hear in lots of NGOs, that it's about a revolution in mindsets, like a Cultural Revolution, and this is something we're struggling with, how do we achieve this?" (Intisar Kherigi, Jasmine Foundation)

Furthermore, interviewees who described democracy as something new or unfamiliar to Tunisia, indicate that change and learning are occurring, despite the process being slow.

- "We are not used to democracy, before the revolution we didn't have any, not in our political life and not even in our family life." (Houda Khalil, Zaghoun Centre for Development and Democracy)
- "We learned a lot. In the beginning, there was a 'diarrhoea of democracy' where people don't know the limits. Democracy is good, but there are limits of liberty; everyone has to know that your liberty stops where other's starts. We learned through our organisation that you cannot ask for everything, there are limits. But we're still learning. The process of learning democracy is not finished, it will take more time. We're quick, for sure, but I think it will take 5 to 10 years and the new generation will fully understand the meaning and the rules of democracy." (Souhail Alouini, OpenGovTN)

In conjunction with the democracy learning processes, interviewees expressed the training opportunities with which CSOs can engage. These were chances for members to increase their organisation's capacities in addition to their understanding of democracy. Interviewees indicated that knowledge and skills are passed on within CSOs, from trained to untrained, while CSOs are helping mentor others.

- "We were present at many conferences and capacity-building training sessions. We learned about democracy and elections. We even organised an event about how to do elections and the role associations play during elections, and how they must be equal and neutral but must observe." (Abderrahamane Hadj Belgacem, Gabes Action)
- "Civil society is about 'enabling people' by giving them practical skills, and I think civil society is the perfect antidote to the education system. The Tunisian education system teaches people how *not* to think, it's about groupthink and how to answer the question exactly the way they want you to answer it: memorise and regurgitate. Civil society is providing a much bigger space where people can do things in different ways and even fail. Our education system doesn't allow failure. If you're a failure it's stamped on your forehead because everyone knows who repeated a year. Our education system is really theoretical, it's abstract and lacks practice but civil society is an arena for tangible learning." (Intisar Kherigi, Jasmine Foundation)

This learning process that all these CSOs describe relates to de Tocqueville's (2003) idea that civil society is a school of democracy. In this process, CSO members are learning that disagreement is not a problem but it can be overcome, learning to accept defeat, learning the practical aspects of democracy, learning the culture of democracy, and learning to be organised in order to be able to perform a democratic function towards the state. Rafik had a particularly interesting point about what democracy can reveal.

> I have discovered the real face of human beings. We are working on sensitive issues, elections and election results, sometimes people try to corrupt you, to bribe you, to threaten you. How people talk behind your back. It's not easy, we discovered another face of people, and we learned how political parties and MPs are working. It confirmed suspicions and allegations I had about politicians.
> (Rafik Halouani, *Mourakiboun*)

Conclusions

This chapter reveals that the criteria of CPC are evident in the discourses of the interviewed Tunisian CSOs members. Simultaneously, a process of active, bottom-up democracy learning process, "through discovery in context specific experiences via socialisation [and] reflection" (Sadiki, 2015: 709), is also evident.

The interviews produced evidence of Equality and Pluralism as most CSOs express a degree of consultation between leaders and members and inclusive decision-making procedures. The quantitative survey sought to independently measure each criterion of CPC in CSOs; however, the interviews discussed in this chapter demonstrate that CSO members view some of these criteria as interconnected. The limitations of Tolerance in civil society are linked to Freedom, Trust, and Transparency. This impacts on the relationships between CSOs and is evidenced by the fact that CSOs' ability to collaborate and cooperate is shaped by the perception of whether the 'other' in civil society is Islamist or not. This is a key factor of local knowledge production for context specific democracy learning (Sadiki, 2015: 703).

Regarding the internal dynamics of CSOs, despite recognition of the importance of practising democracy, certain organisations sometimes chose to overlook Pluralism to a certain extent by focusing on efficiency and effectiveness of their work and the development of their organisation. This means practices and decision-making processes of a democratic nature are being bypassed. The learning process that CSOs are undergoing requires addressing how to balance "habits of co-operation, solidarity, and public-spiritedness" (Putnam, 1993: 89–90) and internal democratic practices within the organisation with simultaneously running an organisation efficiently. Indeed, the Liberal-Associative 'schools of democracy' model of civil society may help members understand democracy through participation in a CSO, but, unless the organisation is effective, it struggles to fulfil a democratic function towards the state and other CSOs.

The interview results show that some organisations are performing a democratic function though performing a watchdog function which holds the state to account through Oppositional-Resistance means. For example, *I-Watch*, Open-GovTN, and *Al Bawsala* are seeking to enhance Tunisia's democracy by making electoral and parliamentary processes more transparent. While Tunisian civil society played during the revolution and transition, these results evidence how civil society vibrancy has developed. Furthermore, the data reflects a genuine understanding of the Oppositional-Resistance role CSOs perform. Liberal-Associative organisations are also performing a democratic function and influencing their members and society through a democratic learning process. The vibrant discussions, that would have previously not been permitted to occur, represent progression that is changing the nature of discussion in the public space. Civil society is filling the public space with discussions that are, in part, deliberative and democratic.

The drawback of the interview method, that any researcher conducting interviews faces, is how it possible to tell if interviewees were being completely honest and providing objective, unbiased accounts? The inconclusiveness of the interviews for assessing the extent to which Tunisian CSOs exhibit CPC lies in the fact that they assess the discourse and do not observe the practice of CSO members. Therefore, it was not possible to verify if interviewees 'do what they say they do' or whether their discourse is at odds with their practice. How was I really to know what happened inside these CSOs? How was to know they were really being honest? Were they just presenting a version of themselves and their organisations that they think I wanted to hear? Recognising this potential disparity between discourse and practice, it is possible that interviewees could have presented a version of themselves and their organisations that they think I wanted to hear or a more positive image of Tunisia. This suggests how they think or want Tunisian civil society and CSOs to be.

Therefore, the methodology based on Welch's dualistic understanding of political culture, that this book operationalises, addresses this disparity. The interviews with non-CSO members helped provide a balanced perspective but this research also requires ethnographic observation to assess practice.

Notes

1 *Huffpost Maghreb* (2013). Tunisie: sit-In au Bardo, devant le siège de l'Assemblée Nationale Constituante. Available at www.huffpostmaghreb.com/2013/07/29/sit-in-bardo-tunisie_n_3669208.html [Accessed 8 February 2014].
2 www.facebook.com/AlSajin52/ [Accessed 16 March 2014].
3 www.facebook.com/OpenGovTN/?ref=page_internal [Accessed 3 April 2014].
4 www.jasminefoundation.org/en/ [Accessed 2 May 2014].
5 Decree Number 88 for the Year 2011 Pertaining to Regulation of Associations. Published on 24 September 2011, trans. International Center for Not-for-Profit Law. Available at www.icnl.org/research/library/files/Tunisia/88-2011-Eng.pdf [Accessed 14 December 2013].
6 Al Jazeera (2012, 19 August). Wording on women sparks protest in Tunisia. Available at www.aljazeera.com/indepth/features/2012/08/201281981854620325.html [Accessed 20 June 2013].

7 Amira is famous in Tunisia because her father, Mokhtar Yahyaoui, a judge and human rights activist, was a vocal opponent of the corruption undertaken by the Ben Ali regime.
8 Ennahda NCA member for Ariana and chair of the Ennahda parliamentary group in 2014.

6 Inside a CSO
An ethnographic study

Overview: why observation

Political culture is dualistic and manifests as discourses and practices. So far, my research has captured discourses. But the study of practices requires the anthropological technique of ethnographic participant-observation. The focus of my work is to observe the internal operation of a Tunisian civil society organisation (CSO), the behaviour of its members, and assess the development of its democratic culture and knowledge.

Ethnographic observation can be described as "immersion of the observer in the social setting in which he seeks to observe the behaviour of the members of that setting and to elicit the meaning they attribute to their environment and behaviour" (Bryman, 2001: 163). It is largely an anthropological method but is key to observing and understanding cultures and cultural phenomena. It helps to understand what people "do" rather than what they "say" (Welch, 2013). Culture is not always easy to verbalise but can also be expressed through behaviour. Bryman notes the advantages of observation; that it is "almost certainly more accurate and effective than getting people to report on their behaviour through questionnaires" (2001: 166).

My research methodology rejects synoptic and essentialist understandings of political culture, and also recognises that political culture is not static and does not require generations to change. This ethnographic research chapter implements Geertz's approach to understanding culture, as approved by Said in *Orientalism* (1978: 326), that emphasises close proximity to research subjects.

This chapter addresses the inadequacies of studies in political culture and those specific to the MENA region context. Anderson's (1995) critique of political culture studies in the MENA context and Hudson's (1995) recommendations for a more sophisticated approach, including disaggregated political culture by focusing on groups rather than the national level, has informed the development of the methodology in this thesis to incorporate ethnographic work.

Almond and Verba (1989) established the concept of civil political culture (CPC) in *The Civic Culture* and identified the criteria through which democratic culture can be measured. The reliance on their work on questionnaire data makes it appear weak in light of Anderson and Hudson's contributions. This chapter of the book expands Almond and Verba's work by using ethnographic observation to further uncover the criteria of CPC.

Case study: *Jeunes Indépendants Démocrates*

Due to the diversity of Tunisian CSOs, the study of one organisation could not produce findings that would be representative of all. I worked with *Jeunes Indépendants Démocrates* (JID) because it was a group that was consistent with this book's theoretical understanding of a CSO: non-governmental, represents the will of a section of Tunisian citizens, and is working towards achieving civic goals, be they minority views or not. The group didn't need to be a voluntary association; however, the majority of Tunisian CSOs are. However, the group must not be 'power-seeking' and looking to become part of an elected or appointed government. I sought to work with an organisation that was new, Tunisian, not a branch of an international organisation, and not affiliated with the Tunisian government. Working with a new association allowed me to observe the steep learning curve that a CSO established after the revolution would experience in the undertaking of its democratic function.

JID, Young Independent Democrats, is a youth-led CSO from Tunis. The organisation is independent, meaning members are not allowed to be members of political parties. There are three membership requirements; (1) Young: between 18 and 35 years old, (2) Independent: no political party membership, and (3) Democratic: belief in democracy. JID was formed after the revolution in 2011, by a group of young Tunisians living in Tunis, mostly students of different disciplines (Law, Medicine, Languages, and Sciences) with shared civic and democratic values. Some members had experience from pre-revolutionary involvement in civil society through activity in university campus clubs, but not through activity in established and more militant CSOs that were active during the dictatorship e.g. trade unions, *Union Générale des Étudiants de Tunisie* (UGET), *Union Générale Tunisienne des Etudiants* (UGTE), or *la Ligue Tunisienne des droits de l'homme* (Tunisian League for Human Rights, LTDH). Civil society activism in a free political environment is a new concept (three years old at the time of the study) to Tunisia. JID is one of the many new, post-revolutionary associations whose members were learning how to engage in civil activity as they progressed.

JID has branches in two governorates, Tunis and Monastir, although during my observation an attempt was made to create a branch in Gafsa. The observation was almost exclusively conducted with the Tunis branch (JID Tunis). Members of JID Tunis resided in the northern suburbs of the capital Tunis. These areas of Menzah 5, Menzah 6, Menzah 9, and Cite Ennasr are largely middle class with white painted gated and guarded villas and high-rise apartment block residences, modern shopping malls, private clinics, boutiques, and chic coffee shops, restaurants, and patisseries. The streets are well-lit at night and noticeably less littered and dusty than the less affluent neighbourhoods of Tunis. JID members, who largely come from those neighbourhoods, are from families that are certainly above the Tunisian average income. Indeed, JID largely represents a specific section of the population; middle-class youth from Tunis who are successful products of the national education system. The founding members are from the same neighbourhoods and universities. Although JID expanded to Monastir, the majority of JID Monastir members are from Tunis but are based there studying medicine, dentistry, or pharmacology.

JID combined typical and atypical Tunisian CSO characteristics. In addition to matching the aforementioned criteria of a CSO, JID was a suitable and typical example of a Tunisian CSO to study for the following reasons. First, it is one of the 10,000 organisations established post-revolution.[1] Second, JID is one of the many part-time, voluntary organisations, a majority within Tunisian civil society. Third, as many CSOs claim to be politically independent and considering that 'independence' is JID's middle name, it was interesting to discover the extent of its independence. Fourth, JID is a Tunisian organisation, not the office or chapter of an international CSO, therefore does not represent a re-creation of an international institution's culture. Fifth, JID is a pro-democracy advocacy organisation and, since there are many CSOs promoting citizenship and political awareness, its message is not a minority view.

JID is also an atypical CSO for the following reasons. Many CSOs talk about youth, however JID is one of only a few that are youth-led and entirely youth-focused. Furthermore, studying a youth-led CSO is an interesting aspect of this research because it examines the new generation that has only recently become politically active in the post-revolution context. JID was not part of the old regime or pre-revolutionary CSOs, which have different habits but represent a group engaging in a "mutual, equal and reciprocal" (Sadiki, 2015: 716) learning process with the practice of democracy.

JID was a suitable CSO to work with for this study because its focus is on democracy promotion. This means it is more likely to be focused on the issues relating to democratic culture; pro-democracy, political aspects, and practising what they preach. In comparison to other types of CSOs, service providing and charity organisations are more likely to be concerned with the practical, on the ground, work they are doing rather than their own democratic functioning and procedures. The regional CSOs tend to be focused specifically on their region, governorate, or city. JID actively attempts to expand across Tunisia and its projects aim to address national, rather than regional, issues such as participation in elections.

In addition to its apolitical position, JID retained its independence by sourcing funding from various donors, although it is often funded by GiZ and Friedrich-Ebert-Stiftung. One drawback of JID's independence was that its activities were not funded by one specific donor and its diverse funding does not include operational costs. Therefore, JID could not pay for a permanent HQ (*locale*). Instead, meetings had to take place at members' houses. The majority of meetings were held at Zied's parents' house, while he was President, but Mohammad also hosted. Both these large wall-surrounded villas with polished stone floors and bright, spacious *salons*, were well above the Tunisian average. Otherwise, meetings were held in middle-class, stylish cafés with glass tables, comfortable booths, and cushioned seats in the Ennasr, Bardo, or Menzah suburbs.

JID was a voluntary organisation. Therefore, the members either had jobs or were university students. The *bureau executif* consisted of a President, Vice-President, General Secretary, Treasurer, Spokesperson, Human Resources Secretary, Internal Communication Officer, and Website Editor. According to the JID Charter, their objectives are to:

- Educate Tunisians (firstly the youth) on the issues of our revolution to encourage them to make their contribution to the building of our emerging democracy.
- Educate and communicate to all young people who want political, civic and citizenship education that is a necessary act to master;
- Inform about the evolution of political, social and economic events which Tunisia is going through and share with all the youth of this country information whose reliability has been verified;
- Bring the voice of young people that we represent to the highest levels of the State to enforce our rights and our will.

Fieldwork ethics

Ethnographic observation yields important results but also requires ethical sensitivity. I made my presence and the task of my research obvious to the JID members from our first meeting when I explained who I was, the nature of my work, and its purpose. This honesty helped develop trust and facilitated the observation process by making members at ease with my presence and reducing any suspicion about my study's intentions.

I set out to act as 'observing participant' because I intended to participate in JID work as part of my observations. I was an active member because I attended their meetings and tried to be part of their cause, in addition to paying the mandatory 10 dinar membership fee. They understood that I was always willing to help them and I tried to help improve the organisation in any way I could. They were very grateful for the essay I wrote for them; a comparison between British and Tunisian civil society. I enjoyed working with them but wished I could have helped more. For the majority of the time, however, I was a 'participating observer' due to JID being a part-time organisation.

In the years following the revolution, a considerable number of journalists and academics have travelled to Tunisia to conduct research. Initially, people were enthusiastic to tell their stories but, after a few years, a degree of exhaustion was felt by Tunisians as foreigners attempted to neatly summarise their experience. Furthermore, as highlighted in Abaza's 2011 article "Academic tourists sight-seeing the Arab Spring", foreign academics have been guilty of utilising the local experts without giving them sufficient credit for the knowledge acquired from those locals, instead only portraying them as the subject. This approach can be especially troublesome if these foreign academics only travel to a place once and then proceed to create a narrative based on a portrayal of their findings from a particular point in time. Living in Tunisia for a year and my ongoing work with JID enabled the members to distinguish me from the aforementioned researcher. Rather than treating JID as a laboratory experiment, I believe I was seen as a committed academic who was seeking to acquire a more sophisticated understanding of the changing contextual dynamics and to present nuanced findings.

How to conduct a participant-observation?

This participant-observation study focuses on how individuals may undergo democratic learning, therefore acknowledging that this process can be observed. Referring to changes in political structures in post-cold war Poland and the Czech Republic, Goldfarb discusses the reinvention and the radical transformation of the political culture in addition to the impact of CSOs in this process (2011: 36, 63–67). The learning this CSO is going through is based on its own 'trial and error' processes and also from interaction with trainers and external consultants.

This ethnographic case study is to observe absence or presence of the elements of CPC, expressed through the same set of criteria of CPC as in Chapters 4 and 5; Tolerance, Equality, Freedom, Pluralism, Trust, Transparency, and Democratic Practices. It is a focused study in which only one Tunisian CSO is observed. It looks to observe the political culture of a CSO by asking the following:

- *Tolerance* – How are different opinions treated? Can ideology be observed?
- *Equality* – Who works for the CSO?
- *Freedom* – Are there any preventions or restrictions on its work?
- *Pluralism* – Is there any evidence of diversity?
- *Trust* – Is there internal trust between members? Does JID work with other CSOs?
- *Transparency* – How much of its work or accounts are publicised?
- *Democratic Practices* – How are decisions made? What processes are used?

I sought to identify uncivil practices by asking the following questions:

- Are voices excluded?
- Is any form of intolerance or prejudice expressed?
- Are undemocratic practices evident?
- Are certain members afforded preferential treatment?

I observed JID for over eight months. JID is a part-time CSO that only met at weekends on an ad hoc basis, usually every other weekend. This meant that prolonged or daily observation was not possible. During my observation period, in addition to meetings, I attended a conference hosted by *Sawty* where Zied spoke and represented JID, and at a music concert/event that JID Monastir had organised. Using ethnomethodology, studying actions and practices of everyday life

(Garfinkel, 1967; Atkinson, 1988), as a basis for the observation, the methods I employed were, for the most part, systematic. I used a template to guide the observation. It featured the subheadings of (a) Date, Location, and attendees, (b) In meeting discussion/agenda, (c) Interaction style, (d) Out of meeting discussion, and (e) Personal feelings. Wherever appropriate, or if I was asked explicitly, I would contribute to the meetings and offer my opinions or suggestions. The majority of the time I would not because I was conscious not to interfere in their work or be perceived as another Westerner in Tunisia telling them 'how to do democracy'. I would also ask questions during and after the meeting. I would not always ask the same informant to clarify the discussion or further develop an idea. Initially, I was most comfortable asking Zied, as he was the point of access but I also asked Oussama or Emir if they were giving me a lift home. After JID held internal elections for bureau positions in February 2014, Sara and Souhayel, the new President and Vice-President respectively, were patient and conscientious to ensure that I understood what was taking place in the meetings. These five had very good spoken English skills which made them the most useful informants.

The use of literature produced by JID also aided the observation process. During the period of my observation, JID became increasingly efficient at posting the minutes (*procès-verbal* – PVs) from their meetings on the Facebook group page. These became a useful tool for noting any disparities or discrepancies. The PVs do not address the style and manners of interaction. I also translated JID's charter to allow an analysis of its discourse and observe consistencies, or inconsistencies with its practice and assess whether the members followed and adhered to its charter.

My major contributions to JID were based on my academic knowledge and English language skills. I researched theoretical understandings of the concepts of political violence, structural violence, and violence against women for its project. I also met Dr Christian Olsson (University of Brussels) to propose a training workshop. I suggested and researched foreign funding sources and proofread letters to funders. Vice President Souhayel asked me to write a paper for JID that compares British and Tunisian CSOs. He also asked me to include recommendations for JID based on this comparison. Engaging in these tasks enabled me to be a participant-observer, rather than just an observer. This was important for trust-building, showing my commitment to JID, and getting closer to 'insider' status.

One-to-one interviews with JID members

I complimented and verified the observations with one-to-one, semi-structured interviews with eight JID members. These were not a method for observing the members' behaviours and practices, but I used them as an opportunity to comprehend the issues and the conversations that I did not understand and to verify or clarify information and incidents from meetings I observed. The observation data must be verified due to potential misreading or misunderstanding. Also, the interviews revealed new information and enabled a greater understanding of their more personal thoughts. These interviews also address the critique Crapanzano makes regarding Geertz' ethnography which, he argued, only includes "a constructed narrative of the constructed native's constructed point of view" (1986: 74). This ethnography, in contrast, includes an understanding of the JID members from their points of view and their voices.

Like the structured interviews with CSO Bureau members in Chapter 5, these also had a devised set of questions specific to uncovering aspects of CPC; to what extent the interviewees are tolerant, pluralistic, act and protect freedom and equality within JID. For example, I asked "Do you ever feel ignored?" to assess levels of pluralism and tolerance. But, due to the familiarity between me and the JID members, these interviews were more conversational. The interviews took place in cafés, either one-to-one or with an interpreter present. I trusted the information I was given in the interviews as JID members trusted me because they saw me at meetings, knew I worked for JID, and saw me as a member on the inside of the organisation. They also knew I saw some of the events and situations they discussed in the interviews. I had already established some rapport with the members so I felt that allowed them to speak freely. The interviews did not yield particularly surprising results and often confirmed what I had observed. Members did not overly present critical perspectives of JID but admitted some of the deficiencies and areas which require improvement.

I also interviewed Moujib, a consultant in communications and Middle East and North Africa (MENA) CSOs who had worked with non-governmental organisations (NGOs) and associations in Jordan, Lebanon, and Morocco in addition to Tunisia. He used to live in France and Washington, DC, but he came back to Tunisia after the revolution because he wanted to help; specifically, NGOs that represent the LGBT community. Moujib explained to me that he developed his own methodology and approaches to CSO work and created his own training manual for CSOs. JID member Cyrine contacted him asking for help, explaining it was a new CSO that required institutional capacity building. He had been working with JID for two years. Moujib held a unique place in the research because, as a qualified NGO consultant, he is a non-member but is also an insider as a Tunisian. His responses during the interview were highly critical and offered more insight, as he could also offer perspectives from both insider and outsider positions. He informed me of issues that had not come to my attention through observation or interviews, such as the negative attitudes of certain members. He suggested certain members should leave JID because they were only seeking personal gain or to bolster their CV.

Results and findings

Projects

Through ethnography of CPC, I was able to observe the projects and campaigns that JID undertook. There were three major projects that JID undertook before my observation.

1 '*Ikhtiar* (Choice)' was a questionnaire platform to help guide people in their decision of who to vote for in the October 2011 National Constituent Assembly (NCA) elections and featured a 30-question questionnaire[2] that determined the Tunisian party whose agenda is closest to the respondent's answers.
2 'Forum 1.0' (2012) was a five-day conference that collaborated with associations from different parts of Tunisia to exchange knowledge and build relationships. The conference aimed to help CSOs understand how to function and work together, especially regarding work in the less developed southern Tunisian governorates. Four workshop sessions within the activity focused on issues regarding society, politics, economics, and culture, and featured relevant experts in each session. By the end of the event, participants completed the drafting of a set of recommendations for the constitution. The expected impact of this project was to make the youth heard regarding the writing of the constitution. Therefore, members of the NCA from Ennahda, Ettakatol, CPR, and Nidaa parties were invited to the event to convey the recommendation to the NCA. However, JID members went to the NCA and saw that the documents and recommendations produced by Forum 1.0 were not presented to the legislature.
3 'High Schools' (2012) was an educational project to inform high school students of the importance of voting, how it is a right in a democracy, and the duty of citizens.

During my observation period, JID planned two projects. *Ikhtiar* 2 (launched in October 2014) was a revised and repeated project for the 2014 parliamentary and presidential elections. This focused on the registered voters, especially youth, by helping them find a political party that matched their interests. This required JID to meet with politicians from ten political parties to devise questions and answers that reflect their platforms. I observed the process of the website's redesign. 'The fight against Political Violence' (2013–2014) aimed to raise awareness about what constitutes political violence, training the citizens in the fight against political violence; educating the general public about the forms of political violence and the dangers it represents to Tunisia. However, this planned and proposed project did not materialise because JID could not find a funder willing to support it.

Internal elections and transition

During the period of my observation, JID went through a major leadership change through *bureau exécutif* elections in February 2014 that brought in the third elected bureau. I refer to the three different bureaus as JID.1, .2, and .3 respectively. Before the general assembly meeting in February 2014, there were 25 candidates for nine positions. However, none of the members wanted to be President. They all thought they were not ready, needed more experience, or were too shy. This is partly because Zied (JID.2 President) was an effective leader and other members were apprehensive about following in his footsteps. The JID charter permitted him to run for a second term but he declined. Zied also discouraged the other members of the JID.2 bureau from running because he wanted new active members to run for JID.3 elections. Instead, he wanted the JID.2 bureau to mentor the new bureau members through the training and handover process. JID.1 and JID.2 were roughly the same members in different positions. For example, Hela and Zied were President and Vice-President respectively in JID.1, and then they swapped positions for JID.2. For this reason, Zied told me he wanted to have a change of leadership and a completely new bureau with no enduring members. He did not have the authority to prevent current bureau members from running for election but they obliged.

JID wants Tunisia to embed the concept of gender equality in all aspects of society and politics. Therefore, it operates accordingly, applying these principles to be an example for others. One manifestation of said gender equality is male/female rotation of the presidency. After Zied, there must be a female President. Two members from *Al Bawsala*, a watchdog and political monitoring CSO, were present as observers to ensure election fairness by counting votes and observing the election box.

On the one hand, this transition allowed other members to 'lead'. Zied was able to distance himself from being the face of JID but remained an active member and helped with the transition. This was important because of association personalisation. Indeed, as Moujib noted, by that time JID Tunis had already become 'JID Zied'. On the other hand, by determining who should or should not run in the election is a limitation on pluralism and is to an extent undemocratic because it limits the choice of candidates. This was not a written rule but a decision that Zied thought would benefit JID and to which other members did not object.

Also, JID.2 bureau members Hela, Khalil, Mohammed, Ines, and Salma became far less active after the election of JID.3. A drop in activity is a problem for voluntary associations, as members are under no obligation to attend or be active. However, it inhibited the transition. The old *bureau exécutif* was supposed to have the duty of training the new bureau members. Ahmed, Treasurer in JID.3, told me of his disappointment and frustration with the change of leadership, as the old members did not support or pass on the skills and knowledge they had developed and were not attending meetings. He expressed the most dissatisfaction with regards to the lack of information handed over to him by the previous treasurer, implying that CSO members do not work as hard when they are not in the bureau of an association. This might be the case for JID but further observation or interviews would be required to verify this claim for other organisations. After stepping down as President, Zied remained active and present at meetings and Emir is an active member and works hard to promote JID through his position as an adviser to the Minister of Youth and Sport.

Confirming Ahmed's account, Moujib thought JID members seem to stop working when they no longer have a title or a *bureau exécutif* position, e.g. Ines, Mohammed, Hela, and Salma. They all had a sudden drop of interest and he could not understand why they did not give the tools to the new bureau. After the February elections, Moujib thought the only hard-working people were Souhayel, Yasmine, Khalil, Aicha, and Oussama. He credits Souheyel and Yasmine for being hard-working, preparing in advance, and taking the initiative. Towards the end of my observation, the aforementioned members were playing a more prominent role in the organisation. The election of a new bureau caused disruption but allowed new members to develop and grow into the 'power vacuum'.

Expansion and restructuring

JID was founded on 15 January 2011 by seven members in Tunis. Therefore, it operated as both a local and national bureau. They attempted to change the structure of the organisation during their 2014 general assembly to create a Gafsa regional bureau. This would have been a significant step in decentralising power from Tunis and empowering Monastir and the new Gafsa bureau. The attempted expansion to a JID Gafsa bureau was stifled and then halted indefinitely. This was due in part to insufficient trust developing that was required to form any agreement. JID Tunis thought JID Gafsa was only seeking money while JID Gafsa was concerned that JID Tunis wanted to dominate and exploit them. JID Gafsa members were insistent on being supplied with sufficient funds to have their own office. Gafsa is a more conservative region of Tunisia than the capital where it is less acceptable for women to meet in public cafés or non-family members' houses; hence their demand for an office. JID has multiple donors who fund specific short-term projects rather than the organisation's operational costs and overheads. Therefore, JID Tunis does not have sufficient funding for its own HQ and does not have the funding necessary for a Gafsa bureau. As this situation could not be resolved, JID Gafsa suspended its operations. The lack of funding and organisational difficulties affected JID's ability to expand. However, the attempt to expand signifies the level of JID's ambition. Furthermore, not conceding to JID Gafsa's financial demands demonstrates that JID Tunis did not compromise its principles of remaining independent, as it believed having a semi-permanent donor (e.g. funding for a three-year project) would compromise its independence. After the 2014 general assembly after the election of JID.3, JID Tunis became increasingly focused on its internal matters, such as task delegation and roles and responsibilities. Moujib confirmed that, as a result, JID Monastir and JID Tunis began to act increasingly independently. In comparison to *Sawty*, a similar youth organisation, the latter's regional chapters were more closely coordinated.

JID charter

Analysis of the JID charter is important for the observation of rule use and identifying consistencies, and inconsistencies, between the organisation's discourse and the members' practice. I translated JID's charter with the assistance of Myriam, my interpreter and research assistant. She found the process annoying because the flowery, vague text was frustrating to read and translate. JID seemed to be trying to make the organisation sound more important and grandiose but produced a document that is imprecise and ambiguous.

JID's objectives seem quite general but the projects demonstrate how members attempted to implement them. The 'High Schools', *Ikhtiar*, and political violence projects were ways of 'informing' and 'educating', while to "Bring the voice of young people to the highest levels of state" was attempted through Forum 1.0. Article 1 of the JID charter addresses the age limit for members (35) which ensures the 'youth' element of the CSO. Independence is maintained with the requirement for members to remain "completely independent of political parties". Aspects of CPC are guaranteed through articles such as Article 23: "All decisions must be taken by consensus or by vote", which ensures pluralism and equality. Similarly, Article 26: "For each project, a project leader will be elected by a majority vote of the regional office" entrenches democratic processes. As the *bureau exécutif* consists of five members, it demonstrates 'power-sharing' and pluralism is also embedded in the annual meeting of the general assembly where "an item must be included in the agenda if it is proposed by at least three (3) members" (Article 3). A degree of equality is implied in Article 4: "All members of the assembly may also propose projects for the Association." Transparency of their work is not addressed. On the contrary, Article 32 states "confidentiality is a requirement of all members vis-à-vis internal meetings of the association and projects that are carried out by it". This encourages a lack of transparency. The concepts of Tolerance and Freedom are not explicitly mentioned. Regarding rule use, the roles of bureau members are clearly defined and, during my observation, I saw members conform to these roles.

The focus of my interview with Yosra (JID Monastir) was ascertaining where JID's discourse matches its practice. She admitted that its charter is not clear and there are problems with it, but added that JID is learning how to be an organisation and the charter amendments that have been introduced are further evidence of this learning process. She added that they have improved how their meetings are conducted but were not always so effective at putting their ideas and planning into practice. In the meeting on 19 April 2014 where JID members discussed amendments to the charter of separation between national and regional bureaus, they mostly seemed disinterested in making amendments and wanted the meeting to finish as quickly as possible. Moujib had comments on the charter, adding "it doesn't matter how good the charter is, people only turn to it when there are problems, like all CSOs in Tunisia". He thought that a 'set of internal rules' would be more effective because he thought JID is defined by its lack of rules.

In comparison to other charters I translated (*Mnemty*, *Cepsa*, and Friends of the Mining Basin), JID's contains far fewer rules and does not include the responsibilities and rights of members. *Mnemty*'s charter, which seemed to be written following the Law of Associations (Decree 88), was stricter than JID's, including a set of rules with references to punishments or disciplinary hearings. *Cepsa*'s charter included elements of freedom, equality, and tolerance, Article 11: "All members are bound to respect the thoughts and the decisions coming from colleagues and to speak civilly." It also placed greater emphasis on pluralism, Article 8: "Suggestions are to be written in the book of suggestions in the headquarters, or during the regular meetings, or on the Facebook page." Furthermore, the *Cepsa* charter clearly explains the financial aspects of the association. The Friends of the Mining Basin charter made more references to finance. Article 18 states that the association is a non-profit and defines financial rules and regulations, the duties of the accountant, and reporting of public funding were included.

Sawty President Ghazoua Ltaeif said its internal code is discussed and sometimes amended at each general assembly but some parts remain fixed. With the assistance of TAMSS and with MEPI funding, a mentor was assigned to *Sawty* to help them develop a manual of 'procedures' that is given to each new member and contains general rules. This is also updated and modified when deemed necessary. Chapter 5 demonstrated that other CSOs considered *Al Bawsala* to be an important and influential CSO. However, Ghada Louhichi (project manager) discussed the consistency between *Al Bawsala*'s practice and discourse and, although she had not even read it carefully, its charter was informal but had some general rules. "Being young, fresh, and flexible is important for the current climate in Tunisia" she added. *Al Bawsala* also holds evaluation sessions every six months which provides the opportunity to make amendments as they learn more and evolve.

Upon examining these CSOs' charters to extrapolate consistencies between discourse and practice, the following conclusions can be made. CSOs are required to create a charter by Decree 88 and seem to recognise that some rules are required and that some principles or values should be included. These cases demonstrate that CSOs maintain some flexibility and are open to change or adapt to the times. They are not a helpful indicator for JID's practice, as members seldom referred to their charter. However, the use of the charter by JID members when "things go wrong" indicates its use as a legalistic device to settle disagreements and as a tool for checks and balances, rather than a code that informs their commonplace practice.

Decision-making processes

The decision-making processes in JID seem to be consensual. I witnessed a common trend of ideas and suggestions for projects being accepted or rejected depending on the strength of the argument the member presents. For example, Salma has a strong personality and is a charismatic debater. She told me how she managed to convince the JID members in a meeting to side with her point of view. However, she also acknowledges how debates lead to decisions.

> I'm very vocal so I haven't felt ignored. I always try to convince them. We once had a debate about participating as JID in the Bardo sit-in. We had a big debate about it and eventually we agreed that we shouldn't participate.

Another example: congress against violence. 8 people were against participating in it as UGTT partners, I wasn't. They were against it because UGTT is big and always tends to be dominant. JID participated in organising the event without even showing our logo. The UGTT liked the concept we proposed, but before we did all this, all of the members were against it because they were afraid that the event is going to be politics heavy. They said that we're independent but this event is going to include Islamist associations and parties etc. so they wanted it to do it differently. So we debated it and I was successful in convincing everyone to participate, I told them that we can expand our network and that the workshops about political violence can be beneficial for us, and even if this event doesn't work out, we can take what we learn and apply it in our projects against political violence. So personally, my voice was always taken into consideration. For example, USAID suggested that we distribute flyers to promote power separation during the constitution. I said that the project is sloppy; they would give us $20,000 to create and distribute the flyers without having a say in the content. I said that we don't do sub-contracting, it should be up to us to create the content of the flyers and the sponsor should only provide the funds. I don't like working with sponsors that tell us what to do. I said no even though they were going to give us a big amount of money.

Emir's proposition to advocate against the harsh Tunisian law on cannabis was rejected. Emir argued that people caught in possession spend a whole year in jail. They often re-offend and get sent back to prison, proving that this aspect of the justice system does not work. He added that it is related to citizenship and that law 52 (relating to cannabis) is a form of structural violence and oppressive regime tactic. JID members decided they did not want to get involved with this because it does not fit with their objectives and Emir had to accept this collective decision. Although Emir's idea was considered, the discussion did not require a vote because no one else sided with him.

I did not observe cases of members being excluded from debates but there was an occasion, during a planning meeting for *Ikhtiar* 2, when Cyrine felt that the point she was trying to make about the layout of the website was not given due consideration. When we adjourned the meeting, she and I walked to a nearby *hanout* (small grocery shop) to buy some drinks. She said she understood that the meeting had to move on, especially because foreign trainers from GiZ were present, but she still felt a little bit overlooked.

Interpretations of results

From my observation and from what most members have expressed, it is possible to summarise JID in one sentence; too much talking and not enough action. Although they realise their lack of ability and admit to lacking expertise, JID members recognise that they are undergoing a learning process. This is akin to the constructivist democratic learning 'cycle' Sadiki describes where participants

Inside a CSO: an ethnographic study 133

make sense of and meaning out of their world by learning through socialisation and reflection on their experiences (2015: 709).

Considering that the organisation's goals are focused on raising awareness, their projects require a more 'intellectual' approach than, for example, a service-providing charity organisation. JID members struggled with the difficulties of turning ideas and concepts, like democracy, into workable awareness-raising projects because they need to be better prepared and have a greater understanding of both democracy and Tunisia. Therefore, they were open to new ideas and understood that they needed further training. Moujib points out two types of members in JID, (1) the logical and realistic who know what is going on and how to work, and (2) those who think they know what they are doing but they lack the capabilities and instead challenge everything but offer no solutions. He also added that there are opportunists in JID who are only looking to participate in an organisation or training sessions so it would look good on their CV.

The major issue Moujib highlighted was JID members' (mis)understanding of what they were working towards; democracy. To be working in democracy promotion, groups need to have a better understanding of democracy itself. Some members did not understand that democracy is accepting something with which you disagree in addition to respecting all human rights. In a training session that Moujib ran, he used his own methods where he trains people from the perspective of a homosexual to help them to understand what it feels like to be persecuted and treated as an outsider. This training exercise demonstrated that some members had homophobic attitudes. I was unaware that some members knew little about tolerance towards homosexuals. Moujib highlighted the importance of LGBT issues in relation to a CSO promoting democracy.

> You can't not respect human rights or LGBT community and say we're working for democracy. How can you work on democracy and human rights if you have problems with homosexuals? Where's the acceptance and tolerance of difference? Imagine if a sexually confused student asked a JID member 'What about the right to be homosexual?' and the JID person says 'it's wrong' or 'they have no rights', this means JID are preaching intolerance.

Therefore, before he could engage in any strategic work with JID, Moujib told me he focused training sessions on educating them about democracy. In a later training session, these members had become less homophobic. This demonstrates part of the democracy learning process these members had experienced and how they were developing an understanding of tolerance and equality by learning to treat people equally and by understanding that democratic culture is not exclusionary to anyone. On a personal level, Moujib is proud of making members more tolerant and less homophobic. As this book argues, the development of tolerance and equality are criteria of CPC. Before interviewing with Moujib, I was entirely unaware of the homophobia that some members had expressed. This is because issues of homophobia were not brought into the conversations and the members who had particularly homophobic feelings had no reason to express these issues. This demonstrates that, as Crapanzano (1986) indicates, talking to people and engaging with them about what is occurring is an essential part of ensuring that an ethnographic inquiry is representative of the subjects' perspectives. Conducting interviews and verifying information with informants does not necessarily undervalue the observational status.

After the February 2014 election and the change from JID.2 to JID.3, the terms 'professional' and 'professionalisation' became used more frequently. This did not refer to making JID a professional and salaried organisation as JID remained a part-time, voluntary CSO. There had been discussions about hiring a manager for a project, which would have been the first step towards financial professionalism, but a suitable project had not been devised. For JID, professionalisation involved defining clearer job descriptions and more evenly delegated work and tasks. In JID.2, Zied, Farah, and Selma had been doing most of the work. Sara positively described Zied and Farah as "the Superman and Wonder Woman of JID" because of what they had achieved. However, as a consequence, Moujib thought that the transition from Zied's to Sara's presidency was poor. He argued that Zied did not seem to trust others to satisfactorily complete the work. Therefore, he did not share or delegate tasks or allow others to work and acquire skills and experience. Also, Salma did not trust others to complete tasks correctly, so she did too much herself. Moujib thought Zied and Salma were guilty of caring too much, "When you love an association too much it can destroy it because you think it's 'your' association."

The move towards professionalisation in JID.3 was not meant as an expression of criticism of the JID.2 leadership, but rather a recognition that practices had to change. This is primarily because, unlike JID.2, the members of the JID.3 bureau were not old friends. Therefore, the style of interaction at meetings needed to be different. Throughout my observation, I largely witnessed respectful, tolerant conversations at JID meetings. Two conversations taking place during a meeting is quite common. I did not interpret this as impatience or impoliteness but that members were enthusiastic to contribute and that the atmosphere was generally relaxed. There were heated moments during meetings, but I interpreted these to represent passion and interest rather than intolerance or incivility. Founding members, however, interacted in a different way to newer members. They were friends long before they were colleagues in the same organisation. Therefore, their behaviour was different and they made more familiar comments, e.g. sexual innuendos and minor insults. For example, during one meeting Zied covered Salma's mouth so the debating on that issue would end and the other points of the meeting could be addressed but this was done in jest. Salma knows she's argumentative but justified the interaction; "Given the fact that we're friends, sometimes the behaviour, when seen from the outside, looks strange. We had a debate about Egypt and it got intense. They're not professional relationships [laughs]."

Towards the end of a long meeting when people were getting tired and a point was being argued, Mohammed told Zied to "Sakker fammek" (shut your mouth). This is normally considered a rude phrase in Tunisia, but due to their long friendship, Mohammed knew he could speak to Zied in this manner without any repercussions. Oussama told me that "old friends can be rude to each other, that's normal", but he added that he would not accept being spoken to this way by the members of the JID.3 bureau. Therefore, as JID.3 interactions were still friendly but more formal with less bantering and joking insults, members considered this behaviour more professional.

Regarding meeting practice, professionalisation also referred to the efficiency of meetings. In JID.2, Zied had the 'final say' but that was also because members looked to him for decisive leadership. In contrast, JID.3 more frequently came to a group decision without referring to an arbiter. On 20 April 2014, after discussing the responsibilities of each member, members decided that a clearer description of each bureau position was required, as the charter does not provide clear definitions. This demonstrates a step towards sharing responsibility, distributing power, and professionalism. JID.3 also held more organised meetings that were chaired more effectively and had specific agendas. On a few occasions, Souhayel even allocated time limits to each point to make meetings more efficient, which also encouraged decision-reaching discussions. The following are notes from a March 2014 meeting:

> The meeting was under a time constraint, therefore, it was interesting to see how well JID worked under pressure. I think they worked efficiently in this meeting; all eight of the issues on the agenda were covered in just over an hour. Souhayel chaired the meeting; he was very effective at making sure the meeting kept to time and issues that were not on the agenda were not discussed. He even set a timer on his phone to make sure the meeting stayed on track. This seems to be a new 'norm' for JID meetings; letting everyone know the agenda at the start. It was interesting to see that Zied has returned to 'member' status and didn't try to control the meeting. He was asked for his views and opinions, like any other member, but Souhayel led the meeting. I think that holding the meeting at Cafe Bonzai in Bardo, rather than at Zied's parents' house, changed the power dynamics as it did not give anyone host status.
>
> (JID Meeting, 23 March 2014)

As JID.3 was operating differently from JID.2, professionalisation was also utilised rhetorically as motivation for being more active, making a difference, and having an impact, rather than just holding meetings and talking about issues. An aspect of the lack of action is based on the concern with maintaining a 'good' public image. Considering JID has a good external image, members are hesitant about engaging in an unsuccessful project for fear of damaging it. This highlights the point Intisar Kherigi makes (see p. 116) that the Tunisian education system discourages students from learning through trial and error for fear of being labelled as failures. Regarding their efficiency and effectiveness, or lack thereof, there is a struggle with the part-time nature of JID's work and members' other commitments. Despite this balancing act, there were mixed opinions amongst members as to whether JID should professionalise and have permanent, salaried members of staff or remain voluntary.

Zied's leadership and the transition from JID.2 to JID.3 redefined the organisation's democratic function. In JID.2, Zied was an effective leader. He was very approachable, pleasant, and welcoming, considerate and a team player but also ensured tasks were achieved. He was fluent in English, French, and Arabic and he had the personal skills necessary to develop good relations with funders. The drawback to this positive leadership was that it led to a cycle of members expecting Zied to undertake any task and Zied pre-emptively addressing tasks without asking others. This is not to say JID was acting like 'petit dictatorship' because freedom, pluralism, equality, and tolerance were evident in its interactions. It meant that members had become increasingly dependent on Zied.

Although the JID charter entitled Zied to run for a second term as President, it is notable that Zied did not want to hold on to power. He told me that people in other CSOs had begun to associate JID with Zied. For this reason, he thought JID certainly needed a new President. He said it was usually the case in Tunisia that CSOs are mentioned in the same breath as the President and he was keen to avoid this type of personalisation in JID. Indeed, Moujib confirmed this as he said "JID Tunis had become JID Zied". Zied wanted to avoid further personalisation as he was aware of the dangers it posed to JID's external image. For the internal operations of a CSO, if the leader is doing everything by him- or herself it creates a delegation problem. Other members are not given the opportunity to learn to do things and thus all the skills become concentrated in one person. This leads to the personalisation of the CSO and makes a future handover difficult. The dilemma for CSOs is whether they continue with someone who knows how to run a CSO and is an effective leader, or democratically change leadership to give others a chance to learn leadership skills.

The CSO leaders I interviewed recognise that transferring power is normatively the 'right thing to do' but this ethnography has identified that personalisation, due to an effective leader in a CSO, can lead to stagnation or the concentration of skills and expertise with a few members. Although in the case of JID this personalisation did not lead to a reduction of democratic practice in the long term, as Zied chose to step down, other CSOs did not have a change of leadership in over three years. The two-term limit in JID's charter prevented this from occurring in the long term. However, signs of this phenomenon could be observed during the JID.2 term. Other members did not want to run for President because they did not think they could do the job as effectively as Zied. This is also due to other members not developing the CSO knowledge and skills during Zied's leadership before an election, either because they did not feel the need to learn or because these tools were not shared. I could also see, from our conversations, that Zied was becoming tired of being President and running JID. He had been interning with Democracy Reporting International[3] but was looking to move his career forward. After the observation period finished, Zied became a full-time Advocacy Officer at *Al Bawsala*.

The problem at JID was the quality of their transition. The intentions of power-sharing and giving other members a chance to lead were beneficial for

JID's democratic credibility. When Zied stopped being President, it allowed the opportunity for others to participate. However, this was problematic because they were less effective. Zied made sure JID.2 bureau members did not run for JID.3. In some ways, this is limiting the election by determining who can and cannot participate, but it was to ensure non-bureau members were given the opportunity to lead. It was a good intention, in terms of democratic practice, but was a tactical mistake because the transition overlooked the importance of skills and the handover of CSO skills did not occur. Moujib explained that Zied, Selma, and Farah, who were proactive members that completed most of the tasks, made way for Sara, Souhayel, and Oussama. The first three were trained by Moujib, who had given them the tools, documents, and work strategies, but these have not passed on their knowledge to the new three. After they were no longer in the *bureau exécutif*, their presence at JID meetings dropped remarkably. Ahmed, the JID.3 treasurer, was particularly annoyed by the insufficient handover of tools and skills from the previous bureau. Zied's intent on the renewal of leadership and depersonalisation of JID led to a transition of power but did not ensure a transition of skills.

However, despite their struggles, JID has stayed true to the principles established in its charter. The political independence of members is paramount and is a rule that is observed, while political neutrality in their work remains highly prioritised. The environment of long-term friends and family-like interaction is changing to become more colleague-based and professional, but their friendliness remained despite the decreasing levels of 'bantering'. Members became increasingly included in decision-making processes. However, being an effective debater remained a helpful attribute in determining JID's policies. The middle-class bias is recognised but it is something they admit they would like to address but remains a challenge.

Conclusions

"What Tunisians are experiencing is the smell of democracy but the problem is that too many people are waiting for change rather than working for change" (Moujib). The members of JID do not fall into this category. The democracy learning process they have undergone in a CSO meant that, on an internal level, they developed aspects of CPC. Lacking knowledge of both democracy and the complexities of their own country has meant that JID was not able to accomplish as many projects as members had hoped, which reduced its external influence. However, the limitation of JID's impact on the public sphere does not diminish the impact that participation has had on the members. The positive impact for JID is the Tocquevillian, school of democracy learning process that they have undergone in this period. This study demonstrates the learning progression that has taken place regarding the internal relations of a CSO. JID has therefore performed a democratic function predominantly through a Liberal-Associative form of civil society. In this school of democracy, the majority of the lessons were learned by the members as they tangibly engaged in embedding the values of democracy. In addition to the norms JID members developed, it was evident that trainers and consultants have a role in this democratic learning process. Members benefited on a personal and organisational level from the capacities they acquired through their associative work through conscious and subconscious learning. Souhayel, for example, pointed to crisis management within a team, budget management, civil rights, voting rights, and how to write 'realistic' funding proposals as vital knowledge and skills he developed. Whether they use these skills to improve JID, another voluntary CSO, or to enhance their careers, the democratic values and organisational skills they have developed will have a positive impact on their role as members of a democratic system.

My observation period witnessed a developmental change from a group of old school friends to a more formal, colleague style organisation who also managed to stay true to their conviction of remaining politically neutral. They appear to be pluralistic with very few cases of members' views being sidelined in discussions, and I observed evidence of equality, gender in particular. Some members were more socially conservative than others, but this did not impact on their work. JID members were aware of the middle-class bias within their organisation but attributed it to the location of their organisation; a middle-class area of Tunis. During the observation I did not witness any expressed prejudice, only during an interview was the issue of homophobia from two members brought to my attention. Decisions were most often made through agreement after discussion, often leading to consensus, but voting was implemented for elections. JID.2 was strongly led by Zied and Farah, where Zied often had the last word and in 2012/2013 JID undertook more activities. They recognised that personalisation was occurring and sought to address it. The leadership learned that taking on too much responsibility can hinder a CSO and is certainly not sustainable for a voluntary CSO. Although the leadership transition process could have caused less upheaval for the CSO if JID.2 leadership had transferred their skills and knowledge to the new bureau more systematically, the leadership of JID.3 made the organisation more pluralist as responsibilities were shared and further personalisation was prevented.

The publishing of JID PVs online increased the group's transparency. JID did not experience any limitations to its freedom to operate in the public sphere. The preventions or restrictions to its work only occurred by the prohibition of CSOs from entering schools, which applied to all civil society. Internal trust between members was very high, which I experienced after being welcomed so quickly to the CSO, in addition to new members who joined during my observation period. Regarding their relationships and cooperation with other CSOs, JID showed its willingness to work with other CSOs who shared its values, such as *Sawty*. JID's attempt to expand to Gafsa demonstrated further willingness to work with others and also address its middle-class bias. However, like the political violence project, it was largely financial issues that prevented this extension from manifesting but sufficient levels of trust to cooperate were not established either. JID's engagement with the state was more limited as it only worked with the state through Forum 1.0 and when conducting interviews for the *Ikhtiar* project.

The timing of the research was also significant as the majority of my observation took place during a politically quieter period. In 2014, the constitution had been ratified, the Ennahda coalition had stepped down, and a non-partisan technocratic government was running the country. There was less for CSOs to be active about. The revolution was now three years old and JID was somewhat reactive to the political situation. In addition, the first half of 2014 saw a degree of civic action fatigue and a dip of enthusiasm. JID.3 was unsure of how to progress as an organisation in this period and was already somewhat reinventing itself through professionalisation. Towards July 2014, civil society became more active in the build-up to the October 2014 elections and JID started to implement *Ikhtiar* 2. Interestingly, Zied played a prominent role due to his experience in organising the first *Ikhtiar* and his connections with the donors.

This ethnography demonstrated that practising democracy helps to embed the values of democratic culture. JID was engaged in a learning process involving the intricacies of democracy, the tolerance that is required, and how to implement democracy. This ethnography has also made it apparent that civil society members must improve their organisational skills, at personal and associational levels, to influence the political and public spheres. JID's organisational difficulties affected its efficiency and effectiveness, as proven by the failure to implement the political violence project. CSO impact and effectiveness are also dependent on securing funding, and JID has been successful at acquiring funding for some projects. However, even if JID has not been as successful or influential as its members had hoped, individuals have undertaken a learning curve through which they acquired organisational skills, and a deeper understanding of democracy, and the contextual intricacies of where they want to make an impact: Tunisia.

Regarding rule use, the charter was almost never referenced and I did not hear anyone quote it. The norms of respectful interaction had been established. The moments of disrespectful interaction appear uncivil but were representative of the way old friends can interact rather than JID being an uncivil organisation. In spite of all their problems and the fact that JID members do not always follow his advice or the methods he prescribes, Moujib was surprised that JID still managed to function as a CSO. This implies that he admits there are alternatives to his approach.

Notes

1 Le centre d'information, de formation, d'études et de documentation sur les associations (IFEDA). Available at www.ifeda.org.tn/ [Accessed 20 July 2014].
2 Available at http://2011.ikhtiartounes.org/ [Accessed 12 August 2014].
3 Democracy Reporting International. Available at http://democracy-reporting.org/ [Accessed 13 June 2014].

Conclusion

This book has demonstrated that the role of civil society has been important as Tunisian civil society organisations (CSOs) have played a democratising role in the country's transition through activities aimed at the monitoring and oversight of governmental decisions and procedures and through engaging in a process of bottom-up, reflective democratic learning. Through their practices in the revolutionary and transitional periods, CSOs have exhibited attributes of civil political culture (CPC). Oppositional-Resistance type CSOs, that challenge the state's monopoly and pressure the government, and Liberal-Associative types, that seek to inform the citizenry and protect their freedoms from elected despotism and an overbearing state, are present in Tunisia. Both these types of CSOs can play a democratising role in a transition from authoritarianism to democracy. However, this democratising role can only be fulfilled if CSOs exhibit attributes of CPC. After the 2011 revolution, decree-law 88 provided civil society with an increased public space, which civil society used to perform a democratic function by facilitating a balanced relationship between the state and non-state actors.

This research project was informed by the functions of civil society, as defined by civil society theory, by democratisation theories, and by CPC theories. These theories enabled the development of six criteria of CPC (Tolerance, Equality, Pluralism, Freedom, Trust, and Transparency) to be employed as an analytical tool to measure CSO civility: the extent to which CSOs demonstrate CPC. These criteria were applied through quantitative, qualitative, and ethnographic research methods to assess civility in the three relationships in which CSOs engage; with the state, with other CSOs in the public space, and their internal dynamics with their members. The major finding from all three research methods is that CPC, required for a stable democracy, is developing in Tunisian civil society.

Theoretical summary

The understanding of civil society has evolved to culminate into a modern, pro-democratic force. Both Oppositional-Resistance and Liberal-Associative conceptualisations are equally significant to enabling civil society to fulfil a democratic function. Oppositional-Resistance CSOs perform a democratic function by pressuring the state, ensuring the maintenance of democratic procedures, and acting as a more vigorous check on state authority while posing a greater challenge to ideational state hegemony. Liberal-Association CSOs can pressure the government but also offer a supportive stance for a liberal government but also encourage citizens to engage in a democracy learning process through participation in associative life. Civil society is not, however, intrinsically a force for democratisation. It can only perform a democratic function if it exhibits CPC (civility). This applies to both Oppositional-Resistance and Liberal-Associative forms of civil society. By denoting the importance of political culture, this book has demonstrated that political culture cannot be disregarded in the analysis of a political transition. This book contributes to civil society theory by highlighting the theory's linkages with democratisation theories and CPC theories.

Democratisation theorists Diamond (1999) and Linz and Stepan (1996a) argue that civil society remaining independent is vital to it performing a democratising role. Authoritarian government structures prevent civil society from freely existing and operating independently. Public space is largely restricted or co-opted by the government and the development of political civility is not encouraged. Therefore, studies of civil society in the Middle East and North Africa (MENA) context have been shaped and limited by the persistence of authoritarian governments and have instead sought to explain how religious, kinship groupings can perform a civil society function or resorted to using culturalist, macro-interpretivist approaches to argue that the region's culture prevents the existence of civil society and democracy. Other works disregarded the importance of political culture by focusing on structuralist explanations for political conditions.

Methodological summary

The methodology developed for this book sought to overcome the shortcomings of other political culture studies, in particular those in the MENA region, and can contribute to the study of political culture, civil society, and democratisation. Implementing Welch's (2013) theory of political culture, which asserts that political culture is exhibited through practice and discourse, a methodology was specifically developed for a political culture research project that captures the two expressions of culture.

Therefore, this book has operationalised Welch's theory into a practical methodological approach to studying political culture which posits the need to collect multi-layered data to gain a greater understanding of political culture. The use of Welch's theoretical conceptualisation of political culture enables a more sophisticated analytical approach for assessing a political culture than works that do not sufficiently engage with the concept or only view political culture as either discourse or practice.

The understanding that political culture manifests as discourse and practice is the fundamental epistemological grounding of this book. Therefore, although ascertaining practice through asking subjects about their practice is sufficient to a certain extent, there is a discrepancy between what people say and what people do. This means that observation of practice is also required and a triangulation of methods, or at least two, is necessary for the process of inquiry that requires the researcher to both ask about and observe a political culture. The triangulated, mixed-methods approach is implemented from the theoretical requirement to understand practice and discourse, rather than motivated by the novelty of using three methods. The three methods have enabled an investigation of civil society that addresses the three relationships in which CSOs engage; with the state, with other CSOs in the public space, and with their members and the internal dynamics. This multifaceted approach has created a greater understanding of how CSOs see themselves and how they internalise democratic attributes. By enabling CSO members to reflect on their processes, it has facilitated investigation of civil society not only in terms of what it does but how it sees itself. This degree of reflexivity has enabled investigation into how CSO members envisage their attributes internally.

This approach offers an improvement on political culture works that use a single method, a macro-interpretivist approach, or seek to make overarching generalisations, by focusing on a micro-interpretivism approach that employs three separate methods for measuring political culture. The recommendations Hudson (1995) makes regarding the study of political culture in the MENA region context, including the disaggregation of culture, are implemented as the research focuses on the political culture of CSOs specifically. Further claims regarding a Tunisian national culture are not made from the collected data and results.

This book has demonstrated that the analysis of political culture requires a multifaceted approach. The use of survey, interview, and observation methods combined is an optimal approach to studying political culture because it comprehensively addresses practice and discourse. The six criteria of CPC were used to structure the method of inquiry. Questions and observation plans were designed regarding the extent to which Tolerance, Equality, Pluralism, Freedom, Trust, and Transparency were present or absent in Tunisian CSOs. Addressing a CSO's internal practice is vital to the assessment of civility. To understand a CSO, the internal operations need to be analysed. This research has demonstrated that not only do the relations between CSOs and between civil society and the state matter, so too do the internal attributes of CSOs.

The methodological approach of this book contributes to an alternative understanding of civil society. The methodological approach was possible due to the lack of authoritarian government structures in place in Tunisia. This enabled an online survey and ethnographic-observation to be conducted without suspicion or censorship from subjects or state interference.

Historical summary

Tunisian civil society was limited and restrained under colonialism and authoritarianism yet it played an influential role during the revolution and in the democratic transition. A civil society had existed, survived, and developed from Beylical rule via French colonialism to the twenty-first century. The Tunisian monarchy, which was semi-independent from Ottoman control, allowed civil society to perform an independent financial function that limited the potentially despotic government tendencies of the Bey. During the French protectorate, civil society, which included oppositional political parties, developed an Oppositional-Resistance function to the imperialist presence. This developed into the independence movement, which, crucially for the development of political civility, did not engage in guerrilla warfare and was almost exclusively non-violent.

The vibrancy of civil society that existed at independence was lost in the post-independence era. The dictatorships of Habib Bourguiba, and later Zine El-Abidine Ben Ali, controlled the population, restricted the public space, and ensured that CSOs were largely co-opted by the regime or determined a threat and therefore crushed. National trade unions played a vital role in the independence struggle, but their leftist tendencies posed a threat to the one-party rule. To prevent challenges to the state, their leadership structures were co-opted and constrained. Islamist organisations, previously permitted to exist as a counterbalance to leftist thought, were subsequently suppressed. Oppositional-Resistance forms of civil society were forced underground and some adopted oppositional political agendas as the political system did not permit pluralism. Liberal-Associative groups, which remained uncritical of the regime or whose goals aligned with those of the regime, were permitted to exist and provided some degree of consultation with the government. Ben Ali used the number of these loyal, largely uncritical CSOs as a false indicator of Tunisia's democratic credentials. Neither form of CSO could effectively perform a democratic function due to the constraints of authoritarian government and the lack of political pluralism.

Despite these constraints and lack of independence, major civil society groups who were organised and nationally networked as opposition groups, at home or in exile, were connected before the 2011 revolution. Although their leadership was largely co-opted by the regime, the General Union of Tunisian Workers (UGTT) could claim some independence and could mobilise its large membership base. The 2008 Gafsa uprising demonstrated that a disparity existed between the UGTT's co-opted upper-echelons and the oppositional stance of the regular members.

Tunisia's historical experience and strong institutions placed the country in a position that was more conducive to the successful completion of a democratic transition. The extensive building of state institutions would not be required. Furthermore, this book has demonstrated that the foundation for an organised civil society and Oppositional-Resistance CSO activism existed before the revolution. The revolution and the subsequent transition process demonstrated the importance of civil society in generating change. After the 2011 Revolution, the interim government provided civil society with a new legal framework (Decree 88) with fewer constraints and greater freedoms, which allowed it to develop a democracy promoting capacity.

The behaviour and decision-making processes both of political party leaders and members of the NCA in this transition period influenced the development of a CPC in Tunisia; for example, the formulation of coalition governments, the

144 Conclusion

desire to achieve consensus in the constitution-writing process, and Ennahda's agreement to relinquish power to a technocratic government.

The work of Tunisian civil society in this transition period was also vital for the development of civility. The use of violent conduct and methods in civil society, such as that exhibited by the Leagues for the Protection of the Revolution, who were consequently outlawed in 2014, was not accepted as evidenced by its prohibition under Decree 88.

Chapters 2 and 3 use a macro-interpretivist approach to address the history of Tunisia civil society and civil society's role in the revolution. Although this book considers this approach insufficient for understanding the contemporary dynamics of a political culture or representing findings of the book, this broad synoptic analysis represents an important overview for establishing a historical background and providing context to the research period.

Results

This research demonstrates that political civility is growing and developing in the discourses and practices of Tunisian CSOs, enabling them to fulfil a democratic function. The six criteria of CPC are evident, to varying degrees, in CSOs in the Tunisian transition. Despite the interconnectedness of these criteria, this research has demonstrated that they do not develop simultaneously. Furthermore, the six criteria should be considered in gradual or nuanced terms rather than understood in the absolutist binary of present or absent.

Key to this development is the Tunisian state's relationship with civil society. It is vital because civil society exists in relation to the state with the state regulating the space in which CSOs operate. Although aspects of Decree 88 are imprecise, particularly those in relation to financial transparency, this legal framework provided freedom, equality, and the foundation for CSOs to operate in post-authoritarian Tunisia. CSOs expressed the absence of state interference in their activities.

How CSOs engage with each other is important for understanding the extent of their political civility. The coalitions and collaborations between CSOs, or at least their willingness to work with each other, demonstrate increasing levels of trust. Conversely, factors such as a CSO's perceived political allegiances or ideological tendencies, the sources of its funding and the degree of its transparency, and the degree of its membership's involvement with the former regime, cause suspicion on the part of other CSOs. This can lead to intolerance or a lack of trust or equality amongst other civil society actors.

The internal operations and procedures of CSOs are also significant in this research. The results showed that CSO members recognise the normative importance of democratic practices and values while embedding democratic culture has been a more gradual process. For some, in particular, participation in a CSO has been akin to a Tocquevillian 'school of democracy', whereby both individuals and organisations engage in a process of democracy learning through their actions and interactions. Therefore, understanding the institutional culture

Conclusion   145

and internal dynamics of CSOs was important in assessing their political civility. This required addressing decision-making processes, how internal disputes are overcome, and the organisation's structure. The research showed that management styles largely included consultative processes that afforded pluralism and tolerance to members. Also, positive relations between *bureau exécutif* and the membership suggested equality amongst members. In some cases, depersonalising the leadership, establishing routine practice, or creating a clearer definition of roles and responsibilities from a CSO's charter or internal rules were required.

Chapter 4 demonstrates that civility is developing with separate analysis of each of the six criteria and the high-scoring criteria indexes created. These quantitative results demonstrate that greater levels of trust are exhibited towards respondents' organisations than externally to other groups. General trends of tolerance, equality, and pluralism were exhibited, but disagreement regarding politicised and religious CSOs and the inclusion of former Constitutional Democratic Rally (RCD) members was also evident. While agreement towards the implementation of democratic practices and independence from the state was expressed, respondents also preferred some limitations to freedom.

Chapter 5 utilised a set of interview questions specifically designed to assess the existence of the six criteria of CPC. Unlike Chapter 4's analysis of each criterion in isolation, these results demonstrate the interconnectivity of the six criteria of CPC, in particular, the linkages between Trust, Tolerance, and Transparency. Therefore, the improvement of one criterion is linked to improvement in the others. CSOs become aware of the importance of Transparency because it leads to greater Trust, which leads to greater Tolerance. Conversely, the limitations of Tolerance in civil society are linked to Freedom, Trust, and Transparency. In particular, CSOs' ability to collaborate and cooperate is shaped by the perception of whether another CSO has Islamist sympathies or not. CSO operations and projects have meant that in some cases Pluralism is overlooked, to a certain extent, as leaders focus on the development of their organisation and the efficiency and effectiveness of their work. This may occur at the expense of democratic practices, which can reduce the development of democratic culture. However, aspects of the Liberal-Associative 'schools of democracy' model of civil society are evident as interviewees explained how they have gained a greater understanding of democracy through participation in a CSO.

Chapter 6 presents the ethnographic participant-observation results, which were essential to the theoretical understanding of the practice of CPC. These single case results from working with one youth-led, pro-democracy CSO, *Jeunes Independent Démocrates* (JID), are less generalisable, but the previous two research methods were not able to verify if interviewees 'do what they say they do'. Therefore, the observation of internal behaviour was the most effective and most valid method for understanding internal interactions.

The observation data demonstrates the problems of personalisation of leadership or when too much responsibility remains with a few members. To a certain extent, a lack of trust in other members of the CSO was evident as members may not trust others to perform tasks. This meant that the transition of leadership was problematic as somewhat personalised leadership could reduce the democratic function of the CSO and lead to anti-democratic outcomes. This can be manifest in leaders who seek to retain their positions or refuse to delegate, which in turn makes the CSO dependent on its leader for expertise, skills, and institutional memory.

The members' partial but developing understandings of both democracy and the complexities of their own country meant that JID's impact in assisting the Tunisian transition had not met members' expectations. However, the observation period established that JID members were engaged in a democracy learning process. Practising democracy was assisting JID in embedding the values of civility. Learning to work, cooperate, and collaborate with other members, through inclusive rather than exclusive interactions, encouraged tolerance and acceptance of other views. Furthermore, the organisational skills they were developing, especially the sharing of roles and responsibilities, helped make the organisation more equal and pluralistic.

Potential further research

There were two issues that this research could not answer but require further investigation. First, the question of whether the authoritarian state has been entirely dismantled and overthrown or has only been forced to retreat. Although the authoritarian character of the Tunisian state has been changed, the extent to which a 'deep state', a political elite, or a particular socio-economic group remains in control of the country needs to be addressed. From a legal perspective, the authoritarian state has been overthrown. Ben Ali, the dictatorial figurehead of power, was removed and the Trabelsi clan was forced into exile, while the network-structure of control, the RCD party, was dissolved. Opposition political parties were legalised, new leaders elected, and the constitutional changes that include a greater separation of powers demonstrate that political structures have been changed. However, the networks of corruption and patronage that include politicians, business people, officials, and security officers, who are determined to keep their privileges, remain. For example, former RCD members have formed new parties. Even President Essesbi was a member of the Bourguiba government. Therefore, "the Tunisian revolution was largely peaceful, but it also meant that we inherited the whole administration intact and many of these civil servants are trying to hold on to the past and the privileges that they received" (Hussein, 2013). As this book has addressed the political culture of CSOs, rather than government or business circles, further research would be required to assess if an old elite is still entrenched in the country and to what extent this is obstructing the democratic transition.

Second, this book addressed the relationships between CSOs and the state, other CSOs, and its own members. It has not addressed the relations and interactions between CSOs and the Tunisian general public. A further study into the relations between CSOs and citizens could ascertain whether CSOs are embedding

CPC in the population. It would assess the impact of CSOs on encouraging democracy learning amongst Tunisian citizens or whether the practices and discourses of CSOs, whether they are politically civil or not, are influencing citizens and vice versa.

This book has also opened the potential for further ethnographic studies of CSOs to be conducted for deeper assessment of local democratic knowledge production. The participant-observation was a single case study of one organisation. Additional secondary or tertiary ethnographies with different organisations would have been helpful for a comparative aspect to be included. Various comparative studies could be conducted with potentially illuminating findings regarding CSO political culture. For example, a comparison between JID and organisations from less affluent areas or the interior or coastal regions in Tunisia could address the middle-class and regional biases JID represents. The regional variations highlighted by the findings of the Chapter 5 attitude survey demonstrate that perceptions of democratic values differ across regional lines. Other possible comparisons could be drawn from observing an organisation with greater experience in civil society activity, such as a CSO that was established pre-revolution, which might have established rules and procedures but also potentially show less flexibility or willingness to adapt. If an organisation with different objectives is observed, such as a charity-based organisation, its focus might be on the delivery of aid or services rather than internal democratic practices. A unique further case study would be *Shams* or *Chouf*, two organisations that are fighting against homophobia and working for the decriminalisation of homosexuality in Tunisia. It would be interesting to focus on CSOs that are a target of prejudice (Tounsi, 2015) and could demonstrate a lack of tolerance or represent the boundaries of CPC in Tunisia.

This book concludes that civility is developing in Tunisian civil society as CSO relationships with the state, other CSOs, and its own members evolve, which has enabled CSOs to fulfil a democratic function.

Epilogue

For their "decisive contribution to the building of a pluralistic democracy in Tunisia",[1] the Quartet was awarded the Nobel peace prize in October 2015. Interviewees noted that the Quartet (UGTT (General Union of Tunisian Workers), LTDH (Tunisian League for Human Rights), ONAT (Tunisian Lawyers Association), and UTICA (Tunisian Confederation of Industry, Trade and Handicrafts)) were of vital importance in pushing the Tunisian transition forward. This collaboration of four major civil society organisations (CSOs), responsible for steering Tunisia through the National Dialogue process out of a political deadlock, was rewarded and received international recognition for their invaluable contribution towards safeguarding the country's democratic gains. This award was welcomed by the Quartet as recognition of the efforts of the Tunisian civil society in playing an oversight and support role throughout the most critical junctures of the country's democratic transition. The Quartet, and in particular the UGTT, however, has a greater influence on political decision making than any other CSO and function more like a counterpart to the government. Therefore, their actions and achievements are not characteristic or representative of Tunisian civil society.

Despite progress, Tunisian civil society faces ongoing challenges in the political transition, particularly amid the current volatile security context, which provides the state with the pretext to reduce the public space in which CSOs operate. This reinforces the ongoing importance of Oppositional-Resistance CSOs performing a democratic function.

Protests on the fifth anniversary of the revolution, however, reminded political leaders that issues of economic disparity, unemployment, and corruption – the original causes of the revolution – have yet to be sufficiently addressed. The 2016 protests started in Kasserine, a neglected region with the highest national unemployment rate: 30 per cent.[2] The regime responded with the imposition of curfews but recognised the validity of the protests. This represents the degree of change that has occurred in leadership but the extent to which protesters feel that not enough has changed and corruption still exists, implying that the deep state is still being removed five years on.

Furthermore, the securitisation of the state is threatening the public space in which civil society operates. An issue of current importance is the state's security discourse in its response to terrorism, as civil society activists and human rights advocates have sounded the alarm about this discourse's potential for limiting civil society freedom. National security and counter-terrorism issues have become a priority for the Tunisian state. Since my research period ended, Tunisia has witnessed an increased number of attacks by Uqba Ibn Nafi Battalion militants that have taken place against Tunisian soldiers at checkpoints in the Chaambi Mountains in 2014; 2015 saw three major ISIS-claimed attacks: the Bardo museum attack, that resulted in at least 22 deaths, the Sousse beach resort attack that claimed the lives of 38 tourists, and the Mohamed V Avenue bombing which targeted presidential guards, killing 12. The March 2016 failed ISIS incursion into the south-eastern border town of Ben Guardane was the last of this series of attacks to date. The government's response to each of the attacks has proven the state's willingness to sideline individual and civil society freedoms on the account of combatting terrorism. The counter-terrorism bill advanced by the government in the wake of the Bardo attack was largely denounced by civil society for its infringement on individual rights and due process.[3] Furthermore, the state of emergency, which has been the government's kneejerk response after each terrorist attack, has been used to quell and disperse legitimate and peaceful civil society movements and protests (Keskes, 2015). President Beji Caid Essebsi used a speech following the Sousse attack to accuse civil society groups, namely those responsible for "Winou El Petrol?", a CSO social media campaign demanding transparency in natural resource revenue management, of destabilising the country and making it more vulnerable to terrorism.[4]

Civil society has suffered previous government crackdowns using the pretext of counter-terrorism. In the wake of a 22 July 2014 terrorist attack that killed 16 national guardsmen near the Algerian border, the Jomaa government forced 157 CSOs to suspend their activities "for security reasons" and some were sanctioned for financial irregularities.[5] Nawaat noted that the suspensions were based on Articles 10 and 11 of Law 52, dated 1975 (Bellamine, 2014), a vague law that grants power to Governors to "ensure the implementation of laws, regulations and government decisions" and "maintenance of public order".[6] However, this executive decision breeches CSO Decree 88 which gives the judiciary exclusive authority to determine whether a CSO should be dissolved, through a process that includes issuing a warning to the CSO in question, before suspending its activities for 30 days and dissolving it as a last resort.[7] CSO freedoms have been negatively affected by government measures to counter terrorism and extremism and legal reforms have taken a backseat to security issues. CSOs have a new role in ensuring anti-terrorism laws do not contravene the 2014 constitution, reduce the newly acquired public space, or jeopardise the recently gained liberties.

Finally, a notable achievement is the progress civil society has made with regards to the range of social problems it is addressing. Civil society is now tackling issues of homosexuality and racism, matters that were previously considered off-limits. Five years after the revolution, civil society groups have succeeded through continuous mobilisation, awareness-raising, and advocacy, putting a spotlight on issues and rights long neglected or regarded as taboo by the society and the legislature. Homosexuality is perceived by most Tunisians as violating the Quranic scripture and thus being against Islam, leading some to note "LGBT Tunisians are treated as second class citizens" (Samti, 2015). Furthermore, Article 230 of the Tunisian Penal Code criminalises "homosexual acts" with a punishment of up to three years in prison. In 2014, JID's external consultant told me that LGBT CSOs operate "underground" because Tunisia was not ready for their activism. Two years later, regardless of the social stigma and the severe state penalisation, *Shams*, a group of young Tunisians committed to de-stigmatising homosexuality and advocating for legal rights for the LGBT community persevered in demanding its legal right to exist as a CSO. After having been refused authorisation in December 2014, in May 2015,

> in what seemed to be a landmark victory for sexual and gender rights in the Middle East and North Africa, the Shams organization for LGBT rights became the first group of its kind to receive official authorization from Tunisia's interior ministry.
>
> (Kilbride, 2016)

This victory, however, revealed the intolerance of Tunisian society and an unwillingness to respect pluralism in beliefs and lifestyles. This was evidenced by the ensuing "rampant homophobic abuse in Tunisia's national news, social media outlets, and community mosques" (Kilbride, 2016). Members of the group who appeared on national TV reportedly received death threats.[8] The smear campaign that the CSO was subjected to culminated in the Tunisian authorities filing a complaint to the judiciary to suspend the group's activities. Article 45 of Decree 88, which "allows the executive to request the judiciary to suspend the activities of a registered NGO when it breaches the provisions of the law",[9] led to a ruling to suspend the group's activities. *Shams* has since filed a complaint against the Tunisian government and, on 23 February 2016, the group won the lawsuit against the state and is now free to pursue its activities legally.

Shams' victory is one example of the perseverance of CSOs in challenging legal and societal intolerance and instilling pluralism and equality. Other CSOs such as *Mawjoudin*, *Damj*, and *Chouf* also work towards improving human rights standards in Tunisia. *Mnemty*, a CSO that aims to raise awareness about the rampant racial discrimination, began its activities in 2011 in a context where racism was not acknowledged by most as an existing issue. During my interview with *Mnemty* President, Saadia Mosbah, in March 2014, she stated "we asked them [the legislature] to criminalize racism and we carried out the necessary procedures. They totally refused to discuss this topic in the main room of the assembly because according to them, the issue does not exist." Two years later, *Mnemty* was making important strides towards publicising race and racism issues in Tunisia: the CSO launched the Tunisian Movement for the Elimination of Racial Discrimination, starting with a march against racism on 21 March 2016 in the main streets of Tunis and seeking "to establish a law that criminalizes all forms of racial discrimination" (Tarfa, 2016). In tandem, an ad hoc CSO coalition led by FTDES presented a draft law criminalising racial discrimination to the parliament.[10] While the parliament has yet to vote on the law, the issue of racism in Tunisia is gaining traction internationally thanks to civil society efforts, with outlets such as Al Jazeera English running featured reportages on the issue.[11]

By looking at the political culture of CSOs, it is evident that the process of democracy learning and the embedding of democratic culture is ongoing. The progress made by the cases of LGBT and anti-racism CSOs is a testament to this. Conducting large-scale, broad studies of civil society that produce evidence of general trends remains valuable for formulating an overview. However, this book has demonstrated that the small stories in addition to the single case observations of CSOs' internal operations, provide micro-level, non-essentialist evidence that the processes of embedding civil political cultures, required for the long-term success of the democratic transition, is occurring. To further Michael C. Hudson's (1995) work on MENA political culture, the case for bringing it back in, carefully, is to ensure that small-scale observation and individual cases are included.

Notes

1 The Nobel peace prize 2015: press release. *Nobelprize.org*. Available at www.nobelprize.org/nobel_prizes/peace/laureates/2015/press.html [Accessed 7 December 2015].
2 Al Jazeera (2016). Tunisia unemployment protests spread to capital. Available at www.aljazeera.com/news/2016/01/clashes-spreading-tunisia-unemployment-protests-160121190816218.html [Accessed 3 February 2016].
3 Human Rights Watch (2015). Tunisia: flaws in revised counterterrorism bill. Available at www.hrw.org/news/2015/04/08/tunisia-flaws-revised-counterterrorism-bill [Accessed 31 March 2016].
4 Réalités (2016). Béji Caied Essebsi: Voilà le résultat de «Winou el pétrole». Available at www.realites.com.tn/2015/06/beji-caied-essebsi-voila-le-resultat-de-winou-el-petrole/ [Accessed 3 February 2016].
5 Human Rights Watch (2014). Tunisia: suspension of associations arbitrary. Available at www.hrw.org/news/2014/08/13/tunisia-suspension-associations-arbitrary [Accessed 11 September 2014].
6 Law No. 75-52 of 13 June 1975, establishing the powers of senior managers of the regional administration. Available at https://legislation-securite.tn/fr/node/41753 [Accessed 15 February 2016].
7 Human Rights Watch (2014). Tunisia: suspension of associations arbitrary. Available at www.hrw.org/news/2014/08/13/tunisia-suspension-associations-arbitrary [Accessed 11 September 2014].
8 Frontline Defenders (2016). Tunisia: court annuls the suspension of LGBTI organisation Shams. Available at www.frontlinedefenders.org/es/node/1750 [Accessed 17 February 2016].
9 Ibid.
10 Mosaique FM (2016). Le FTDES propose une loi pour criminaliser le racisme. Available at www.mosaiquefm.net/fr/actualite-national-tunisie/8368/le-ftdes-propose-une-loi-pour-criminaliser-le-racisme.html [Accessed 17 February 2016].
11 Al Jazeera (2016). Tunisia's dirty secret. Available at www.aljazeera.com/programmes/peopleandpower/2016/03/tunisia-dirty-secret-160316153815980.html [Accessed 16 February 2016].

Appendix

Table A.1.1 Attitude survey results

Section 1: About you

1. What is your gender?

1	Male:		51.0%	52
2	Female:		49.0%	50

2. What is your current age?

1	Under 18 years:		1.0%	1
2	18–25:		49.0%	50
3	26–35:		25.5%	26
4	36–45:		8.8%	9
5	46–55:		14.7%	15
6	More than 55:		1.0%	1

3. What is your educational level?

1	Primary education:		0.0%	0
2	Secondary education:		7.8%	8
3	Vocational training:		2.9%	3
4	High education – professorship/vacation:		49.0%	50
5	Master:		40.2%	41

4. What is your monthly income in Tunisian dinar?

1	Less than 200:		33.3%	34
2	200–399:		9.8%	10

3	400–599:	7.8%	8
4	600–799:	10.8%	11
5	800–999:	9.8%	10
6	1000–1199:	6.9%	7
7	1200–1399:	2.0%	2
8	1400–1599:	2.0%	2
9	1600–1799:	2.0%	2
10	1800–1999:	1.0%	1
11	More than 2000:	14.7%	15

5. Which region in Tunisia are you originally from?

1	Greater Tunis – Ariana, Tunisia, Ben Arous, Manouba:	36.3%	37
2	North – Bizerte:	6.9%	7
3	North-west – Kef, Zaghwan, Jendouba, Beja:	2.0%	2
4	Coast – Nabeul, Sousse, Monastir, Mahdia, Sfax:	29.4%	30
5	Centre – Kairouan, Kasserine, Siliana:	4.9%	5
6	South-central – Gafsa, Sidi Bouzid:	6.9%	7
7	South – Tozeur, Gabes, Medenine, Tataouine:	13.7%	14

6. How would you describe the religious belief?

1	Muslim practitioner:	38.2%	39
2	Non-practising Muslim:	40.2%	41
3	Agnosticism – belief in the existence of God cannot be proved or denied:	12.7%	13
4	Atheist – faith that there is no god:	2.9%	3
5	Other:	3.9%	4
6	Not sure:	2.0%	2

Section 2: Tolerance

7. CSOs with common goals can work together.

1	Strongly disagree:	1.0%	1
2	I do not agree:	2.0%	2
3	I do not know:	0.0%	0
4	I agree:	54.9%	56
5	Strongly agree:	42.2%	43

8. CSOs with different goals can work together on projects of mutual interest.

1	Strongly disagree:	1.0%	1
2	I do not agree:	3.9%	4
3	I do not know:	7.8%	8
4	I agree:	65.7%	67
5	Strongly agree:	21.6%	22

9. Each CSO the right to achieve their goals peacefully.

1	Strongly disagree:	1.0%	1
2	I do not agree:	1.0%	1
3	I do not know:	2.9%	3
4	I agree:	34.3%	35
5	Strongly agree:	60.8%	62

Section 3: Equality

10. Groups with an explicitly religious agenda should be allowed to participate in civil society.

1	Strongly disagree:	13.7%	14
2	I do not agree:	25.5%	26
3	I do not know:	14.7%	15
4	I agree:	36.3%	37
5	Strongly agree:	9.8%	10

11. Groups with a specifically secular agenda clear should be allowed to participate in civil society.

1	Strongly disagree:	4.9%	5
2	I do not agree:	20.6%	21

3	I do not know:	11.8%	12
4	I agree:	47.1%	48
5	Strongly agree:	15.7%	16

12. Members of the former Constitutional Democratic Rally should be allowed to participate in civil society.

1	Strongly disagree:	22.5%	23
2	I do not agree:	20.6%	21
3	I do not know:	16.7%	17
4	I agree:	34.3%	35
5	Strongly agree:	5.9%	6

13. Women should be able to participate as fully and freely as men in civil society.

1	Strongly disagree:	1.0%	1
2	I do not agree:	0.0%	0
3	I do not know:	1.0%	1
4	I agree:	14.7%	15
5	Strongly agree:	83.3%	85

14. Civil society groups should have equal access to the media: newspapers, TV, radio, and other.

1	Strongly disagree:	1.0%	1
2	I do not agree:	0.0%	0
3	I do not know:	2.0%	2
4	I agree:	23.5%	24
5	Strongly agree:	73.5%	75

15. Every citizen has the right to pursue their own cultural preference.

1	Strongly disagree:	1.0%	1
2	I do not agree:	0.0%	0
3	I do not know:	0.0%	0
4	I agree:	26.5%	27
5	Strongly agree:	72.5%	74

156 Appendix

16. Non-Muslim Tunisians are entitled to the same rights as Muslim Tunisians.

1	Strongly disagree:	2.0%	2
2	I do not agree:	1.0%	1
3	I do not know:	3.9%	4
4	I agree:	27.5%	28
5	Strongly agree:	65.7%	67

Section 4: Freedom

17. CSOs should be allowed to pursue any goals, as long as their means and methods are non-violent.

1	Strongly disagree:	3.9%	4
2	I do not agree:	23.5%	24
3	I do not know:	12.7%	13
4	I agree:	39.2%	40
5	Strongly agree:	20.6%	21

18. The government should allow CSOs to operate freely.

1	Strongly disagree:	1.0%	1
2	I do not agree:	6.9%	7
3	I do not know:	4.9%	5
4	I agree:	49.0%	50
5	Strongly agree:	38.2%	39

19. Freedom of expression is essential in civil society.

1	Strongly disagree:	1.0%	1
2	I do not agree:	1.0%	1
3	I do not know:	0.0%	0
4	I agree:	29.4%	30
5	Strongly agree:	68.6%	70

20. Racially offensive views should be silenced.

1	Strongly disagree:	2.0%	2
2	I do not agree:	2.0%	2
3	I do not know:	0.0%	0
4	I agree:	15.7%	16
5	Strongly agree:	80.4%	82

Appendix 157

21. Religiously offensive views should be silenced.

1	Strongly disagree:	2.9%	3
2	I do not agree:	10.8%	11
3	I do not know:	5.9%	6
4	I agree:	36.3%	37
5	Strongly agree:	44.1%	45

22. Some groups represent a threat to the public interest and should not be allowed to practise their activities.

1	Strongly disagree:	2.9%	3
2	I do not agree:	4.9%	5
3	I do not know:	10.8%	11
4	I agree:	48.0%	49
5	Strongly agree:	33.3%	34

23. Freedom of association laws in Tunisia provide sufficient protection for CSOs.

1	Strongly disagree:	2.0%	2
2	I do not agree:	30.4%	31
3	I do not know:	37.3%	38
4	I agree:	23.5%	24
5	Strongly agree:	6.9%	7

24. The government has the responsibility to protect society from offensive opinions.

1	Strongly disagree:	1.0%	1
2	I do not agree:	7.8%	8
3	I do not know:	18.6%	19
4	I agree:	52.0%	53
5	Strongly agree:	20.6%	21

25. The government interferes in civil society.

1	Strongly disagree:	23.5%	24
2	I do not agree:	44.1%	45
3	I do not know:	14.7%	15
4	I agree:	16.7%	17
5	Strongly agree:	1.0%	1

158   *Appendix*

26. The state determines what is considered offensive and improper.

1	Strongly disagree:		8.8%	9
2	I do not agree:		27.5%	28
3	I do not know:		29.4%	30
4	I agree:		32.4%	33
5	Strongly agree:		2.0%	2

27. To what extent do you agree with the universal concept of human rights?

1	Strongly disagree:		1.0%	1
2	I do not agree:		4.9%	5
3	I do not know:		9.8%	10
4	I agree:		35.3%	36
5	Strongly agree:		49.0%	50

Section 5: Pluralism

28. Decisions made by individuals are usually of higher quality than decisions made by groups.

1	Strongly disagree:		10.8%	11
2	I do not agree:		61.8%	63
3	I do not know:		11.8%	12
4	I agree:		12.7%	13
5	Strongly agree:		2.9%	3

29. I respect viewpoints that differ from my own views.

1	Strongly disagree:		1.0%	1
2	I do not agree:		0.0%	0
3	I do not know:		1.0%	1
4	I agree:		52.9%	54
5	Strongly agree:		45.1%	46

30. I often change my mind when I hear other people's arguments.

1	Strongly disagree:		2.0%	2
2	I do not agree:		32.4%	33
3	I do not know:		23.5%	24
4	I agree:		39.2%	40
5	Strongly agree:		2.9%	3

Appendix 159

31. Disagreement is inevitable.

1	Strongly disagree:	2.0%	2
2	I do not agree:	7.8%	8
3	I do not know:	2.9%	3
4	I agree:	47.1%	48
5	Strongly agree:	40.2%	41

32. Alternative opinions should be respected.

1	Strongly disagree:	1.0%	1
2	I do not agree:	0.0%	0
3	I do not know:	0.0%	0
4	I agree:	38.2%	39
5	Strongly agree:	60.8%	62

Section 6: Trust

33. I trust the other members of the organisation that I work within.

1	Strongly disagree:	1.0%	1
2	I do not agree:	7.8%	8
3	I do not know:	6.9%	7
4	I agree:	56.9%	58
5	Strongly agree:	27.5%	28

34. I trust the leadership of the organisation that I work within.

1	Strongly disagree:	1.0%	1
2	I do not agree:	6.9%	7
3	I do not know:	11.8%	12
4	I agree:	53.9%	55
5	Strongly agree:	26.5%	27

35. I trust members of other organisations.

1	Strongly disagree:	2.9%	3
2	I do not agree:	17.6%	18
3	I do not know:	40.2%	41
4	I agree:	35.3%	36
5	Strongly agree:	3.9%	4

160   *Appendix*

Section 7: Democratic practices

36. CSO members should be allowed to express disagreement with the leaders and managers of their organisation.

1	Strongly disagree:	1.0%	1
2	I do not agree:	2.0%	2
3	I do not know:	4.9%	5
4	I agree:	55.9%	57
5	Strongly agree:	36.3%	37

37. The hierarchy in my CSO is a well-defined organisational structure, where members are required to complete their work by going through the proper procedures and persons, and where authority is respected.

1	Strongly disagree:	2.9%	3
2	I do not agree:	12.7%	13
3	I do not know:	10.8%	11
4	I agree:	52.9%	54
5	Strongly agree:	20.6%	21

38. In my organisation job descriptions are flexible and authority is questioned.

1	Strongly disagree:	2.9%	3
2	I do not agree:	17.6%	18
3	I do not know:	22.5%	23
4	I agree:	47.1%	48
5	Strongly agree:	9.8%	10

Section 8: Financial transparency

39. I know who funds the CSO I work for.

1	True:	85.3%	87
2	Error:	4.9%	5
3	I do not know:	9.8%	10

40. The members of the CSOs should know who finances their organisation.

1	Strongly disagree:	1.0%	1
2	I do not agree:	0.0%	0
3	I do not know:	2.0%	2

4	I agree:	22.5%	23
5	Strongly agree:	74.5%	76

41. CSOs should publish their financial accounts.

1	Strongly disagree:	1.0%	1
2	I do not agree:	5.9%	6
3	I do not know:	3.9%	4
4	I agree:	28.4%	29
5	Strongly agree:	60.8%	62

42. The sources of funding that CSOs receive should be made public.

1	Strongly disagree:	1.0%	1
2	I do not agree:	8.8%	9
3	I do not know:	9.8%	10
4	I agree:	35.3%	36
5	Strongly agree:	45.1%	46

Section 9: Your civil society organisation

43. For how long have you been active with CSOs?

1	Less than 3 months:	8.8%	9
2	3–6 months:	5.9%	6
3	7–12 months:	10.8%	11
4	More than 1 year:	16.7%	17
5	More than 2 years:	32.4%	33
6	More than 5 years:	17.6%	18
7	More than 10 years:	7.8%	8

44. Are you paid by the organisation you work for or do you work voluntarily?

1	Volunteers:	93.1%	95
2	Paid:	6.9%	7

45. How often do the organisation members meet?

1	Monthly:	30.4%	31
2	Weekly:	64.7%	66
3	Daily:	4.9%	5

162   *Appendix*

46. Describe your working environment.

1	Very formal:	4.9%	5
2	Formal:	53.9%	55
3	Informal:	34.3%	35
4	Very informal:	6.9%	7

47. Describe the process of decision making in your organisation.

1	Consultation at all levels:	75.5%	77
2	Middle management has authority:	15.7%	16
3	Commands issued by senior management:	8.8%	9

48. How do you determine positions in the organisation?

1	Elections:	60.8%	62
2	Consensus after the debate:	27.5%	28
3	Appointment by the administration:	7.8%	8
4	Appointment by family members:	0.0%	0
5	Friends preference:	2.0%	2
6	Another way: Please detail:	2.0%	2

48.a. another way: Please detail
- After applying allowances and interview.
- EVERY category and discipline and values/e.g. young underground had their place and their leading ships

49. Describe the philosophy and culture of work within your organisation.

| 1 | Power is held by a small group or a central figure. There are few rules and little bureaucracy but decisions are often made quickly: | 10.8% | 11 |
| 2 | Highly defined structure, clear roles, and hierarchical bureaucracy: | 18.6% | 19 |

3	Skilled and specialised people form small teams to solve problems:		22.5%	23
4	All individuals believe themselves superior to the organisation but each partner brings a particular expertise:		44.1%	45
5	Positions in the organisation are secured by outperforming others:		2.9%	3
6	Members are put under pressure which makes them compromise in order to be effective:		1.0%	1

49a. Other: Please state

I do not have a lot of experience in making the right decisions

50. Does your organisation have an internal law or constitution?

1	Yes:		92.2%	94
2	Does not:		7.8%	8

51. Describe your manager's leadership style.

1	Makes decisions which reflect their opinions and personality:		14.7%	15
2	Ensures procedures are followed:		9.8%	10
3	Gives responsibility to staff to make decisions themselves:		26.5%	27
4	Acts as a member of the team:		45.1%	46
5	Less controlling and acts more like a mentor:		3.9%	4

Section 10: Attitude questions: what is desirable?

52. CSOs should be independent of the state institutions.

1	Strongly disagree:		1.0%	1
2	I do not agree:		3.9%	4
3	I do not know:		3.9%	4
4	I agree:		34.3%	35
5	Strongly agree:		56.9%	58

53. CSOs should respect the objectives of other organisations.

1	Strongly disagree:	1.0%	1
2	I do not agree:	0.0%	0
3	I do not know:	2.9%	3
4	I agree:	46.1%	47
5	Strongly agree:	50.0%	51

54. CSOs should be obedient to their government.

1	Strongly disagree:	32.4%	33
2	I do not agree:	34.3%	35
3	I do not know:	20.6%	21
4	I agree:	11.8%	12
5	Strongly agree:	1.0%	1

55. CSOs should operate with internal democratic practices.

1	Strongly disagree:	2.0%	2
2	I do not agree:	0.0%	0
3	I do not know:	2.0%	2
4	I agree:	32.4%	33
5	Strongly agree:	63.7%	65

56. CSOs' activities and campaigns should be limited.

1	Strongly disagree:	11.8%	12
2	I do not agree:	24.5%	25
3	I do not know:	17.6%	18
4	I agree:	41.2%	42
5	Strongly agree:	4.9%	5

T-Test and ANOVA results

T-Test results – demonstrations of association

1. Youth/Non-Youth vs Tolerance Index (Q7–9) = No association
2. Youth/Non-Youth vs Equality Index (Q10–16) = No association
3. Youth/Non-Youth vs Pluralism Index (Q28–32) = No association
4. Youth/Non-Youth vs Trust Index (Q33–35) = Non-Youth > Youth
5. Youth/Non-Youth vs Financial Transparency Index (Q40–42) = No association
   = Non-Youth respondents demonstrate greater Trust values than Youth.

6 Gender vs Tolerance Index (Q7–9) = Women > Men
7 Gender vs Equality Index (Q10–16) = No association
8 Gender vs Pluralism Index (Q28–32) = Women > Men
9 Gender vs Trust Index (Q33–35) = No association
10 Gender vs Financial Transparency Index (Q40–42) = No association = Women respondents demonstrate greater Tolerance, and Pluralism values than Men.

ANOVA tests

1 Region vs Tolerance Index (Q7–9) = No significant difference
2 Region vs Equality Index (Q10–16) = No significant difference
3 Region vs Pluralism Index (Q28–32) = No significant difference
4 Region vs Transparency Index (Q40–42) = No significant difference
5 Region vs Trust Index (Q33–35) = Notable difference between Interior and Capital

Structured interview questions

Structured Interview questions for Tunisian CSO leader

1 Can you tell me about your organisation? What are your objectives/goals, and how you operate?
2 How effective is the informal politics/non-governmental sector in Tunisia?
3 Is your CSO independent or is it affiliated with any other state or non-state body?
4 How collaborative is the work within your CSO? (Prompt: Do you instruct and delegate? Or does a consultative process take place?)
5 How do you think the staff would describe the leadership and management of your CSO?
6 Do you collaborate with other CSOs? Have you worked with CSOs who have differing aims/differing objectives from yours?
7 Can CSOs with different objectives work together for a common purpose?

Democratic practices

8 What do you think motivates people to engage with and participate in civil society activism? (Prompts – For the good of Tunisian society and development of democracy? For personal gain? To fulfil/implement their own ideology?)
9 In business and politics all over the world, sometimes favours are granted to relatives regardless of their abilities. Do you think this practice is also common among Tunisian CSOs?
10 How did you get this position/get your job?

Relations with the government

11 How would you describe civil society's relationship with the government?
12 How have CSOs been contributing to debates over the constitution? How have CSOs been contributing to laws over freedom of association and freedom of expression?
13 Does your CSO work with the government?
14 To what extent do you feel free to operate in Tunisian society?
15 Have you ever felt the pressure from governmental departments/religious institutions/other CSOs to modify your course of action?

Funding

16 Does the Tunisian civil society sector receive sufficient funding?
17 How does your CSO fund its activities? How financially open is your CSO? (Prompt – Are CSOs in Tunisia expected to reveal their sources of funding?)
18 Do you receive a salary for your work with this CSO?

Table A.1.2 Completed interviews

No.	Organisation name	Interviewee name	Location	Organisation type	Organisation goals	Interview date
1	I-Watch	Mouheb Garoui	Tunis	Watchdog	Anti-corruption and transparency	5 February 2014
2	Edupartage	Amel Cheikhrouhou	Tunis	Advocacy – professional	Education reform	7 February 2014
3	Velorution	Adel Beznine	Tunis	Sport	Encourage cycling culture	13 February 2014
4	Union des Jeunes Democrates Tunisiens	Riadh Werghi	Tunis	Youth network	Human rights and citizenship, sustainable development and agriculture	13 February 2014
5	WeYouth	Amir Ben Ameur	Sfax	Youth	Youth development, training	17 February 2014
6	Aljil	Ahmed Missaoui	Sfax	Youth	Cultural revolution	17 February 2014
7	Sfax Outdoor Sports & Sfax Mzyehna	Zaher Kamoun	Sfax	Sport	Sport, ecology, tourism	19 February 2014
8	Inara	Sami Chaherli	Tunis	Welfare	Humanitarian	25 February 2014
9	Forum Tunisien pour les Droits Economiques et Sociaux (FTDES)	Messaoud Romdhani	Tunis	Economic	Social and economic problems	26 February 2014
10	Esslam	Rosaline Matheau	Tunis	Welfare	Encourage production of artisan products from women in the south	28 February 2014
11	Alwen Tounes	Amel Chaherli	Tunis	Women	Charity network	3 March 2014
12	Association pour le Paix et Properity	Iskender Rekik	Tunis	Welfare	Economic development, training	4 March 2014
13	Jeunes Independent Democrates	Zied Boussen	Tunis	Youth	Raising awareness	5 March 2014
14	Association Tunisiennes Femmes Democrates (ATFD)	Sonya Ben Yahmed	Tunis	Women	Gender equality	11 March 2014

continued

Table A.1.2 continued

No.	Organisation name	Interviewee name	Location	Organisation type	Organisation goals	Interview date
15	Reseau d'Observation de la Justice Tunisienne en Transition (ROJ)	Lotfi Ezedine	Tunis	Legal	Improvements in the Justice System Watchdog	12 March 2014
16	Union des Tunisiens Indépendants pour la Liberté(UTIL)	Moez Ali	Tunis	Humanitarian	Gender equality, rule of law and real democracy, citizenship awareness, and human rights	13 March 2014
17	Tunisian Association for Management and Social Stability (TAMSS)	Fahima Askri and Houriya Ben Hassine	Tunis	Development	Social and economic integration of people in vulnerable situations.	17 March 2014
18	Notre Sante D'abord	Yasssine Jabloui	Tunis	Health	Provide specialist health care to interior and neglected regions	17 March 2014
19	Police Reform	Bouthayna Ben Kridis, Bassem Bougerra	Tunis	Watchdog	Improve police anti-corruption	17 March 2014
20	M'nemty (My Dream)	Saadia Mosbah	Tunis	Anti-racism	Raising awareness human rights, education, and development	18 March 2014
21	Centre for the study of Islam and Democracy (CSID)	Radwan Masmoudi	Tunis	Pro-democracy	Think Tank: promotes interparty cooperation and tolerance	19 March 2014
22	Al-Bawsala	Amira Yahyaoui	Tunis	Watchdog	Transparency and visibility	2 April 2014
23	Tunisian Institute of Human Rights Studies	Mohammed Ashraf Ayadi	Tunis	Human rights	Educational reform and anti-nuclear weapons	5 April 2014
24	United Colleges Association	Wafa Garbout	Tunis	Youth	Youth empowerment, English language, human rights	12 April 2014
25	Ofiya Centre	Samir Kilani	Tunis	Network campaigner	Democratic awareness, women's rights	15 April 2014
26	Mourakiboun	Rafik Halouani	Tunis	Election observers	Establish democracy in Tunisia, witness electoral process, enhance democracy, work with youth	15 April 2014
27	Ordre National Advocats Tunisiene (ONAT)	Boubaker Bethabet	Tunis	Lawyers' syndicate	Representing lawyers	16 April 2014

No.	Organisation name	Interviewee name	Location	Organisation type	Organisation goals	Interview date
28	Cultivons la Paix	Marwa Mansouri	Tunis	Democracy promotion	Human rights, political culture	17 April 2014
29	Destourna	Jawher Ben Mbarek	Tunis	Civic engagement	Democracy promoting	18 April 2014
30	We Love Sousse	Anis Boufrika	Sousse (in Tunis)	Local promotion	Culture (art, heritage, cinema) environment, citizenship	23 April 2014
31	Association Tunisienne Droits Constitutionnelle (ATDC)	Chawki Gaddes	Tunis	Legal reform	Consult, advise, guide the government	25 April 2014
32	Association Tunisienne des Jeunes Avocates (ATJS)	Imen Bejaoui	Tunis	Lawyers' syndicate	Represent lawyers	25 April 2014
33	Association Vigilance	Qais Lahmar	Sousse	Civic engagement	Cultural restoration in Sousse	26 April 2014
34	Sousse Demain	Faycal Labayed	Sousse	Reform	Local pressure, advocacy for infrastructural improvement	26 April 2014
35	Associo-Med	Khalid Ouazzani and Nizar Abdessaied	Sousse	Medical students	Medical awareness	26 April 2014
36	Association of Knowledge Forum	Ra'ba Roubia	Sousse	Educative	Cultural, rights, women's rights	27 April 2014
37	Sajin 52	Amal Amraoui	Tunis	Social movement	Against the oppressive Tunisian law on cannabis	28 April 2014
38	Kolna Tunis	Emna Menif	Tunis	Civic engagement	Political, government pressure, lobbyists	1 May 2014
39	Journalists Association of Kairouan	Adel Nagati	Kairouan	Journalists	Representing rights of journalists in the region	2 May 2014
40	Association of Kairouan for a culture of citizenship (Qairawanioun)	Amira Achouri	Kairouan	Culture of citizenship	Citizenship awareness	2 May 2014
41	Open Gov	Souhail Alouini	Kairouan	Transparency	Promote transparency at national and regional government levels	3 May 2014
42	FTDS – Kairouan	Radwan Fatnassi	Kairouan	Economic	Employment and economic rights	3 May 2014

continued

Table A.1.2 continued

No.	Organisation name	Interviewee name	Location	Organisation type	Organisation goals	Interview date
43	Governance Participative	Zouhayer Hammoudi	Kairouan	Advocacy	Promote participative government, democratic culture	3 May 2014
44	Association Tunisienne pour la Promotion du Droit à la Différence (ATPDD)	Saloua Ghrissa	Bizerte	Human rights	Freedom of expression, freedom gender gquality	6 May 2014
45	Association Tunisienne pour la cityonnete (ATPC)	Kamel Abid	Bizerte	Awareness raising on citizenship	Citizenship, political participation	6 May 2014
46	Zaghouan Center for Development and Democracy	Houda Khelil	Zaghouan	Democracy promotion	Human rights, political, culture	14 May 2014
47	Araa pour la Civilisation et la Citoyenneté	Dr. Mohsen Mhadhbi	Zaghouan	Civic engagement	Spreading values of citizenship and democracy, and public political involvement	14 May 2014
48	Jasmine Foundation	Intisar Kherigi	Tunis	Think tank	CSO, academics, and policy makers cooperation and improve CSOs	15 May 2014
49	Network of Sidi Bouzid Associations	Mohammad Masri	Sidi Bouzid	Network	Economic development, environment, women, and culture	21 May 2014
50	Toupat Sidi Bouzid	Aida Daly	Sidi Bouzid	Cultural	Regional heritage protection	21 May 2014
51	I-Lead	Ghada Chokri	Sidi Bouzid	Youth	Culture of dialogue and promote peaceful resolution of conflict	21 May 2014
52	Association of Cultural Citizenship	Hachem Aydi	Regueb	Awareness raising on citizenship	Citizenship political participation	22 May 2014
53	Association of the Friends of the Miner's Basin for the Environment	Adel Hechimi	Gafsa	Environmental Pressure group	Encourage the government to solve environmental issues	23 May 2014
54	Association of Human Development in Gafsa	Nejib Nasra	Gafsa	Employment	Social cohesion and finding employment for people in Gafsa	23 May 2014

No.	Organisation name	Interviewee name	Location	Organisation type	Organisation goals	Interview date
55	Association Cepsa	Yassin Nasr	Gafsa	Local issues	Helping schools and hospitals, anti-corruption	23 May 2014
56	Gabes Action	Abderrahamane Hadj Belgacem	Gabes	Local issues	Regional development, citizenship awareness	24 May 2014
57	Association of Initiative and Reform	Mohammed Ghris	Gabes	Youth	Training youth	24 May 2014
58	Organisation Volonté et Citoyenneté (OVC)	Myriam Belhaj	Gabes	Civic goals	Election observing, citizenship and voter awareness, women and youth	24 May 2014
59	Oxygen Association	Wissem Ksiksi	Medenine	Environmental	Development and employment in environment context	25 May 2014
60	Voix d'enfant rural	Anis Saada	Medenine	Youth	Education and youth employment and development	25 May 2014
61	Association Djerba Ulysse	Chedly Ben Messaoud	Djerba	Environmental and tolerance	Water access, protect minorities, combat hatred	26 May 2014
62	L'Union tunisienne de l'industrie, du commerce et de l'artisanat (UTICA)	Khalil Ghariyani	Tunis	Business syndicate	Defending business and entrepreneurs' rights	4 June 2014
63	Ligue Tunisienne pour la Défense des Droits de l'Homme (LTHD)	Abdurahmane Hdhili	Tunis	Human rights	Defender human rights, politically involved national organisation	6 June 2014
64	L'Union générale tunisienne du travail (UGTT)	Sami Tahri	Tunis	Labour union	Defender workers' rights, politically involved national organisation	07 June 2014
65	Sawty/Sawt Chabab	Ghazoua Ltaief	Tunis	Youth	Democracy promotion and regional development.	20 July 2014
66	Association Tounesa	Selima Abbou	Tunis		Democratic values	23 July 2014

Appendix

Table A.1.3 Additional data verification interviews

	Name	Job title	Date
1	Badreddine Abdelkefi,	Member of the National Constituent Assembly in charge of Relations with Civil Society	5 June 2014
2	Asma Smahdi	Journalist at Tunisia Live	10 June 2014
3	Geoffery Weichselbaum and Rim Dhaoudi	Director and Legal Officer Democracy Reporting International	10 June 2014
4	Lucy Kamoun	Energy Sector INGO	21 June 2014
5	Selim Kharrat	Consultant	11 July 2014
6	Moheddine Abdellaoui	International Republican Institute	13 July 2014
7	Ghada Louhici	Al-Bawsala	14 July 2014
8	Farah Samti	Freelance Journalist	22 July 2014
9	Moujib Errahmen Khaldi	Consultant	25 July 2014

Bibliography

Abaza, Mona (2011). Academic tourists sight-seeing the Arab Spring. *Ahram*. Available at http://english.ahram.org.eg/News/22373.aspx [Accessed 14 July 2015].

Ajmi, Sana (2012). Fact-finding commission counts 338 deaths and 2147 wounded in Tunisian revolution. *Tunisia Live*. Available at www.tunisia-live.net/2012/05/05/fact-finding-commission-counts-338-deaths-and-2147-wounded-in-tunisian-revolution/ [Accessed 11 July 2012].

Al Jazeera (2011a, 23 January). Liberation caravan reaches Tunis. Available at www.aljazeera.com/news/africa/2011/01/2011123124352723753.html [Accessed 12 March 2015].

Al Jazeera (2011b, 23 January). Police join protests in Tunisia. Available at www.aljazeera.com/news/africa/2011/01/2011122133816146515.html [Accessed 12 March 2015].

Al Jazeera (2011c, 6 January). Thousands of Tunisia lawyers strike. Available at www.aljazeera.com/news/africa/2011/01/201116193136690227.html [Accessed 12 May 2013].

Al Jazeera (2013, 16 February). Mass rallies in Tunisia for Ennahda party. Available at www.aljazeera.com/news/africa/2013/02/2013216143220471317.html [Accessed 13 February 2015].

Al Jazeera (2015, 6 February). Tunisia parliament approves unity government. Available at www.aljazeera.com/news/2015/02/tunisia-approves-coalition-government-150205123748042.html [Accessed 7 September 2015].

Al Yafai, Faisal (2018). Tunisia's leading woman politician who found a second act after the revolution. *National*. Available at www.thenational.ae/world/mena/tunisia-s-leading-woman-politician-who-found-a-second-act-after-the-revolution-1.734116 [Accessed 16 April 2019]].

Alexander, Christopher (1997). Authoritarianism and civil society in Tunisia. *Middle East Report* 205 (Winter). Available at https://merip.org/1997/12/authoritarianism-and-civil-society-in-tunisia/ [Accessed 20 August 2013].

Alexander, Christopher (2000). Opportunities, organizations, and ideas: Islamists and workers in Tunisia and Algeria. *International Journal of Middle Eastern Studies*. 32(4), pp. 465–490.

Alexander, Christopher (2010). *Tunisia: stability and reform in the modern Maghreb*. New York: Routledge.

Aleya-Sghaier, Amira (2012). The Tunisian revolution: the revolution of dignity. *Journal of the Middle East and Africa*. 3(1), pp. 18–45.

174 Bibliography

Almond, Gabriel A. (1956). Comparative political systems. *Journal of Politics.* 18, 391–409.

Almond, Gabriel (1989). The intellectual history of the civic culture concept. In *The civic culture revisited*, eds G.A. Almond and S. Verba. Newbury Park, CA and London: Sage, pp. 1–36

Almond, Gabriel and Verba, Sidney (1963). *The civic culture: political attitudes and democracy in five nations.* Princeton, NJ: Princeton University Press.

Almond, Gabriel and Verba, Sidney (1989). *The civic culture revisited.* Newbury Park, CA and London: Sage.

Amara, Tarek (2015). Tunisian PM-designate proposes new coalition cabinet. *Reuters.* Available at www.reuters.com/article/us-tunisia-politics-government/tunisian-pm-designate-proposes-new-coalition-cabinet-idUSKBN0L60ZP20150202 [Accessed 7 August 2015].

Amnesty International (1994). UA 69/94 TUNISIA: health concern/torture: Hamma Hammami. Available at www.amnesty.org/en/documents/mde30/006/1994/en/ [Accessed 15 March 2015].

Anderson, Lisa (1986). *The state and social transformation in Tunisia and Libya, 1830–1980.* Princeton, NJ: Princeton University Press.

Anderson, Lisa (1995). Democracy in the Arab world: a critique of the political culture approach. In *Political liberalization and democratization in the Arab world: comparative experiences*, eds Rex Brynen, Baghat Korany, and Paul Noble. Boulder, CO: Lynne Rienner, pp. 77–92.

Anderson, Lisa (2006). Searching where the light shines. *Annual Review of Political Science.* 9, pp. 189–214.

Anheier, Helmut K. (2001). How to measure civil society. *London School of Economics.* Available at http://fathom.lse.ac.uk/features/122552/ [Accessed 19 June 2012].

Applebaum, Anna (2007). A good place to have aided democracy. *Washington Post.* Available at www.washingtonpost.com/wpyn/content/article/2007/02/12/AR2007021 201063.html [Accessed 12 June 2015].

Arab Barometer (2013). Tunisia, survey report II. Available at www.arabbarometer.org/content/arab-barometer-ii-tunisia [Accessed 9 December 2013].

Armstrong, David, Bello, Sidney, Gilson, Julie, and Spini, Debora (2011). *Civil society and international governance: the role of non-state actors in global and regional regulatory frameworks.* Abingdon: Routledge.

Association Tunisien pour l'Integrité et la democratie des elections (ATIDE) (2014, 31 October). Elections legislatives 2014: Entre l'affirmation de la citoyennete et la faiblesse de l'ISIE. Tunis. Available at www.ATIDE.org [Accessed 10 December 2014].

Atkinson, Paul (1988). Ethnomethodology: a critical review. *Annual Review of Sociology.* 14, pp. 441–465.

Ayubi, Nazih N. (1995). *Overstating the Arab state: politics and society in the Middle East.* London: IB Tauris.

Bakchich (2008, 28 April). Gafsa la rebelle est en ébullition Émeutes | lundi, 28 avril 2008 | par La princesse enchantée. This article was censored on its original website but is available at http://tunisie.tumblr.com/post/33088735/gafsa-la-rebelle-est-en-%C3%A9bullition [Accessed 28 January 2016].

Barrington, Lowell (2009). *Comparative politics: structures and choices.* Boston, MA: Wadsworth Publishing.

BBC Media Action (2013). Audience survey, Tunisia. Available at www.bbc.co.uk/mediaaction/publicationsandpress/research_summary_tunisia_october2013.html [Accessed 11 December 2013].

Bibliography 175

Belghith, Safa and Patel, Ian (2013). Leagues for the protection of the Tunisian revolution. *Open Democracy.* Available at www.opendemocracy.net/en/leagues-for-protection-of-tunisian-revolution/ [Accessed 9 June 2015].

Belhassen, Souhayr (1988). L'opposition introuvable. *Jeune Afrique.* 1454, p. 66.

Belkhodja, Tahar (1998). *Les trois décennies Bourguiba: témoignage.* Paris: Arcante`res.

Bellamine, Yassine (2014). Suspension de 157 associations: quand Mehdi Jomaa préfère les lois liberticides au détriment de la justice. *Nawaat.* Available at http://nawaat.org/portail/2014/08/20/suspension-de-157-associations-quand-mehdi-jomaa-prefere-les-lois-liberticides-au-detriment-de-la-justice/ [Accessed 16 February 2016].

Ben Hamadi, Monia (2015). This is Tunisia's national dialogue Quartet. *HuffPost Tunisia.* Available at www.huffingtonpost.com/2015/10/11/tunisia-national-dialogue_n_8275014.html [Accessed 12 June 2015].

Ben Hassine, Sami (2011, 13 January). Tunisia's youth finally has revolution on its mind. *Guardian.* Available at www.theguardian.com/commentisfree/2011/jan/13/tunisia-youth-revolution [Accessed 21 April 2013].

Ben M'barek, Khaled (2003). L'élan brise´ du mouvement democratique. In *Annuaire de l'Afrique du Nord 2000–2001.* Paris: CNRS Editions, pp. 401–434.

Ben Mhenni, Lina (2010). A Tunisian girl. Available at http://atunisiangirl.blogspot.com/search?updated-max=2011-01-02T09%3A48%3A00%2B01%3A00&max-results=10 [Accessed 20 August 2012].

Ben Said, Safa (2014). Group accused of political violence dissolved by Tunisian court. *Tunisia Live.* Available at www.tunisia-live.net/2014/05/26/group-accused-of-political-violence-dissolved-by-tunisian-court/#sthash.8JaUmiJF.dpuf [Accessed 25 March 2015].

Benkirane, Reda (2012). The alchemy of revolution: the role of social networks and new media in the Arab Spring. GCSP Policy Paper, 7. Geneva: Geneva Centre for Security Policy.

Berman. Sheri (1997). Civil society and the collapse of the Weimar republic. *World Politics.* 49(3) pp. 401–429.

Berque, Jacques (1985). *Aspects de la foi de l'Islam.* Bruxelles: Facultés universitaires Saint-Louis.

Bodenstein, Thilo (2013). High quality political institutions are a precondition for a strong civil society. *LSE blog.* Available at http://blogs.lse.ac.uk/europpblog/2013/06/05/high-quality-political-institutions-are-a-precondition-for-a-strong-civil-society/ [Accessed 7 October 2014].

Boughzala, Mongi and Tlili, Mohamed Hamdi (2014). Promoting inclusive growth in Arab countries: rural and regional development and inequality in Tunisia. Global Economy & Development at Brookings. Working Paper 71.

Bouguerra, Bassem (2014). Reforming Tunisia's troubled security sector. Rafik Hariri Center for the Middle East, Atlantic Council.

Bourdieu, Pierre (1985). The *social space* and the genesis of groups. *Theory and Society.* 14(6), pp. 723–744.

Broecke, Stijn (2012). Tackling graduate unemployment through employment subsidies: an assessment of the SIVP programme in Tunisia. Working Paper Series No. 158. African Development Bank, Tunis.

Brown, L. Carl (2014). The Tunisian exception. Available at www.juancole.com/2014/10/the-tunisian-exception.html [Accessed 23 June 2014].

Brumberg, Daniel (2002). The trap of liberalised autocracy. *Journal of Democracy.* 13(4), pp. 56–68.

Bryman, Alan (2001). *Social research methods.* Oxford: Oxford University Press.

Bibliography

Brynen, Rex, Moore, Pete W., Salloukh, Bassel F., and Zahar, Marie-Joëlle (2012). *Beyond the Arab Spring: authoritarianism & democratisation in the Arab world*. Boulder, CO: Lynne Rienner.

Buckingham, Alan and Saunders, Peter (2004). *The survey methods workbook: from design to analysis*. Cambridge: Polity Press.

Bunbongkarn, Suchit (2004). The role of civil society in democratic consolidation in Asia. In *Growth and governance in Asia*, ed. Yoichiro Sato. Honolulu, HI: Asia-Pacific Center for Security Studies, pp. 137–143.

Carey, John (2013). Electoral formula and the Tunisian Constituent Assembly. Available at http://sites.dartmouth.edu/jcarey/files/2013/02/Tunisia-Electoral-Formula-Carey-May-2013-reduced.pdf [Accessed 12 July 2014].

Carothers, Thomas (1999). Civil society. *Foreign Policy*. 117, pp. 18–29.

Carothers, Thomas (2002). The end of the transition paradigm. *Journal of Democracy*. 13(1), pp. 5–21.

Carter Centre (2011). Carter Center reports peaceful and enthusiastic participation in Tunisia's landmark elections. Available at www.cartercenter.org/news/pr/tunisia-102511.html [Accessed 22 September 2013].

Carter Centre (2014). The Constitution making process in Tunisia: final report 2011–2014. Available at https://cartercenter.org/resources/pdfs/news/peace_publications/democracy/tunisia-constitution-making-process.pdf [Accessed 8 March 2015].

Chekir, Hafedh (2014). The legislative elections in Tunisia: the start of a new phase or continuation of trench warfare? *Arab Reform Initiative: policy alternatives*. Available at www.arab-reform.net/legislative-elections-tunisia-start-new-phase-or-continuation-trench-warfare [Accessed 14 August 2014].

Clarke, Simon and Pringle, Tim (2008). Can party-led trade unions represent their members? *Post-Communist Economies*. 21(1), pp. 85–101.

Cohen, Jean L. and Arato, Andrew (1992). *Civil society and political theory*. Cambridge, MA: MIT Press.

Collier, David and Levitsky, Steven (1997). Democracy with adjectives: conceptual innovation in comparative research. *World Politics*. 49, pp. 430–51.

Collier, Ruth B. and Mahoney, James (1997). Adding collective actors to collective outcomes: labor and recent democratization in South America and Southern Europe. *Comparative Politics*. 29(2), pp. 285–303.

Constitution of Tunisia (1959). World Intellectual Property Organisation. Available at www.wipo.int/wipolex/en/text.jsp?file_id=188948 [Accessed 10 June 2013].

Crapanzano, Vincent (1986). Hermes' dilemma: the masking of subversion in ethnographic description. In *Writing culture: the poetics and politics of ethnography*. A School of American Research Advanced Seminar. eds James Clifford and George Marcus. Berkeley, CA: University of California Press, pp. 51–76.

Dahl, Robert A. (1971). *Polyarchy: participation and opposition*. New Haven, CT: Yale University Press.

Davis, Michael (1996). *The politics of philosophy: a commentary on Aristotle's politics*. Lanham, MD: Rowman & Littlefield Publishers.

Deane, Shelley (2013). Transforming Tunisia: the role of civil society in Tunisia's transition. International Alert, London. Available at eu/publication/tunisia-changes-and-challenges-political-transition [Accessed 16 March 2014].

DeLue, Steven M. and Dale, Timothy (2009). *Political thinking, political theory, and civil society*. London: Routledge.

Diamond, Larry (1999). *Developing democracy: toward consolidation*. Baltimore, MD: Johns Hopkins University Press.
DiMaggio, Paul J. and Powell, Walter W. (1983). The iron cage revisited: institutional isomorphism and collective rationality in organizational fields. *American Sociological Review*. 48(2), pp. 147–160.
Diwan, Ishac (2012). *Understanding the political economy of the Arab uprisings*. London: World Scientific Publishing Co Pte Ltd.
Donker, Teije Hidde (2013). Re-emerging Islamism in Tunisia: repositioning religion in politics and society. *Mediterranean Politics*. 18(2), pp. 207–224.
Doorenspleet, Renske (2005). *Democratic transitions: exploring the structural sources of the fourth wave*. London: Lynne Rienner Publishers Inc.
Dreisbach, Tristan (2014). New Tunisian Constitution adopted. *Tunisia-Live*. Available at www.tunisia-live.net/2014/01/26/new-tunisian-constitution-adopted/#sthash.jPgErbv5.dpuf [Accessed 20 November 2015].
Eckstein, Harry (1996). Culture as a foundation concept for the social sciences. *Journal of Theoretical Politics*. 8(4), pp. 471–497.
Economist, The (2013). Murder most foul. Available at www.economist.com/news/middle-east-and-africa/21571474-assassination-secular-opposition-leader-forcing-islamist-led [Accessed 13 April 2015].
Ekiert, Grzegorz and Kubik, Jan (2014). The legacies of 1989: myths and realities of civil society. *Journal of Democracy*. 25(1), pp. 46–58.
Engel, Andrew (2014). Libya as a failed state: causes, consequences, options. *Washington Institute for Near East Policy*. Available at www.washingtoninstitute.org/policy-analysis/view/libya-as-a-failed-state-causes-consequences-options [Accessed 26 January 2015].
Entelis, John (1996). Civil society and the authoritarian temptation in Algerian politics: Islamic democracy vs. the centralized state. In *Civil society in the Middle East*, Vol. 2, ed. Augustus Richard Norton. Leiden: Brill, pp. 45–86.
Esposito, John L. and Piscatori, James P. (1991). Democratization and Islam. *Middle East Journal*. 45(3), pp. 427–440.
European Union External Action (2011). EU election observation mission to Tunisia in 2011. Available at https://eeas.europa.eu/topics/election-observation-missions-eueoms_en/24404/EU%20election%20observation%20mission%20to%20Tunisia%20in%202011 [Accessed 16 October 2015].
Fisher, Marc (2012). Tunisian court finds broadcaster guilty in showing God's image. *Washington Post*. Available at www.washingtonpost.com/world/africa/tunisian-who-showed-persepolis-on-tv-fined-in-free-speech-case/2012/05/03/gIQA0GpzyT_story.html [Accessed 3 September 2014].
Flyvbjerg, Bent (1998). *Rationality and power: democracy in practice*. Chicago, IL: University of Chicago Press.
Foley, Michael F. and Edwards, Bob (1996). The paradox of civil society. *Journal of Democracy*. 7(3), pp. 38–52.
Foundation for the Future (2013). Study on civil society organisations in Tunisia. Available at https://africanphilanthropy.issuelab.org/resources/20291/20291.pdf [Accessed 25 September 2014].
Frazer, Owen (2014). Mediation perspectives: the Tunisian national dialogue. *International Relations and Security Network*. Available at http://isnblog.ethz.ch/conflict/mediation-perspectives-the-tunisian-national-dialogue [Accessed 18 June 2015].
Freedom House (2009). Tunisia 2009 country report. Available at https://freedomhouse.org/report/freedom-world/2009/tunisia#.Vbn5hEZwaUk [Accessed 12 May 2013].

Bibliography

Freedom House (2012). Countries at the crossroads 2012: Tunisia. Available at https://freedomhouse.org/report/countries-crossroads/2012/tunisia [Accessed 4 July 2013].

Friedman, Elisabeth Jay and Hochstetler, Kathryn (2002). Assessing the third transition in Latin American democratization: representational regimes and civil society in Argentina and Brazil. *Comparative Politics*. 35(1), pp. 21–42.

Gallup Survey (2011). Tunisia: analyzing the dawn of the Arab Spring. Available at www.gallup.com/poll/157049/tunisia-analyzing-dawn-arab-spring.aspx [Accessed 11 December 2013].

Gana, Nouri (2013). *The making of the Tunisian revolution: context, architects, prospects*. Edinburgh: Edinburgh University Press.

Garfinkel, Harold (1967). *Studies in ethnomethodology*. Oxford: Blackwell Publishing.

Geertz, Clifford (1973). *The interpretation of cultures: selected essays*. New York: Basic.

Gellner, Ernest (1996). *Conditions of liberty: civil society and its rivals*. Harmondsworth: Penguin.

Gellner, Ernst (1981). *Muslim society*. Cambridge: Cambridge University Press.

Ghribi, Asma (2014). Tunisian presidential candidate Kennou takes on the patriarchy. *Foreign Policy*. Available at http://foreignpolicy.com/2014/10/10/tunisian-presidential-candidate-kennou-takes-on-the-patriarchy/ [Accessed 20 December 2014].

Gobe, Eric (2010a). The Gafsa mining basin between riots and a social movement: meaning and significance of a protest movement in Ben Ali's Tunisia. *Working Paper*. Available at https://hal.archives-ouvertes.fr/file/index/docid/557826/filename/Tunisia_The_Gafsa_mining_basin_between_Riots_and_Social_Movement.pdf [Accessed 27 July 2012].

Gobe, Eric (2010b). The Tunisian Bar to the test of authoritarianism: professional and political movements in Ben Ali's Tunisia (1990–2007). *Journal of North African Studies*. 15(3), pp. 333–347.

Goldfarb, Jeffery (2011). *Reinventing political culture: the power of culture versus the culture of power*. Cambridge and Malden, MA: Polity Press.

Gramsci, Antonio (1971). *Selections from the prison notebooks of Antonio Gramsci*, ed. and trans. Quintin Hoare and Geoffrey Nowell Smith. London: Lawrence & Wishart.

Guardian (2010, 7 December). U.S. embassy cables: Tunisia – a U.S. foreign policy conundrum. Available at www.guardian.co.uk/world/us-embassy-cables-documents/217138 [Accessed 17 August 2011].

Guardian (2012). Tunisian court fines TV station boss for airing animated film Persepolis. 3 May. Available at www.theguardian.com/world/2012/may/03/tunisian-court-tv-stationpersepolis [Accessed 14 May 2013].

Hall, John. (1995). *Civil society: theory, history, comparison*. Cambridge: Polity Press.

Haouas, Ilham, Sayre, Edward, and Yagoubi, Mahmoud (2012). Youth unemployment in Tunisia: characteristics and policy responses. *Topics in Middle Eastern and African Economies*. 14, September.

Hawthorne, Amy (2004). Is civil society the answer? *Carnegie Papers*. 44, pp. 1–24.

Held, David (1993). *Political theory and the modern state*. Cambridge: Polity Press.

Henry, Clement (2012). Tunisia. In Freedom House: *Countries at the crossroads 2011: an analysis of democratic governance*, eds Jake Dizard, Christopher Walker, and Vanessa Tucker. Oxford: Rowman & Littlefield Publishers, pp. 653–676.

Henry, Clement Moore (1965). *Tunisia since independence: the dynamics of one-party government*. Berkeley, CA: University of California Press.

Henry, Clement Moore (1999). Post-colonial dialectics of civil society. In *North Africa in transition: state, society, and economic transformation in the 1990s*, ed. Yahia H. Zoubir. Gainesville, FL: University Press of Florida, pp. 11–28.

Hermassi, Elbaki (1991). The Islamicist movement and November 7. In *Tunisia: The political economy of reform*, ed. William I. Zartman. Boulder, CO: Lynne Rienner, pp. 193–204.

Hibou, Béatrice (2006). Domination & control in Tunisia: economic levers for the exercise of authoritarian power. *Review of African Political Economy*. 33(108), pp. 185–206.

Hibou, Béatrice (2011). *The force of obedience: the political economy of repression in Tunisia*. Cambridge: Polity Press.

Hofstede, Geert (1991). *Cultures and organizations: software of the mind*. London: McGraw-Hill.

Hourani, Albert (1991). *A history of the Arab peoples*. London: Faber & Faber.

Hudson, Michael C. (1995). The political culture approach to Arab democratization: the case for bringing it back in, carefully. In *Political liberalization and democratization in the Arab world: comparative experiences*, eds Rex Brynen, Baghat Korany, and Paul Noble. Boulder, CO: Lynne Rienner, pp. 61–76.

Human Rights Watch (2013). World report 2013: Tunisia events of 2012. Available at www.hrw.org/world-report/2013/country-chapters/tunisia?page=1 [Accessed 10 June 2013].

Human Rights Watch (2014, 13 August). Tunisia: suspension of associations arbitrary: 157 associations suspended outside the legal process. Available at www.hrw.org/news/2014/08/13/tunisia-suspension-associations-arbitrary [Accessed 7 September 2014].

Huntington, Samuel P. (1991). *The third wave: democratization in the late twentieth century*. Norman, OK: University of Oklahoma Press.

Hussein, Tam (2013). A deep state of mind: Tunisia's deep state could be combated by democratic and social reforms. *Huffington Post*. Available at www.huffingtonpost.co.uk/tam-hussein/tunisia-deep-state_b_3555764.html [Accessed 13 February 2016].

International Centre for Not-for-Profit Law (ICNL) (2011). Decree No. 88 of the year 2011 Pertaining to Regulation of Associations, published 24 September 2011 – Translation by Available at www.icnl.org/research/library/files/Tunisia/88-2011-Eng.pdf [Accessed 19 September 2014].

Ishkanian, Armine (2007). Democracy promotion and civil society. In *Global civil society 2007/8: communicative power and democracy*, eds Martin Albrow, Marlies Glasius, Helmut K. Anheier, and Mary Kaldor. Global Civil Society – Year Books. London: SAGE Publications Ltd, pp. 58–85.

Jamal, Amaney (2007). When is social trust a desirable outcome? Examining levels of trust in the Arab world. *Comparative Political Studies*. 40(11), pp. 1328–1349.

Jankauskas, Algimantas and Gudžinskas, Liutauras (2008). Reconceptualizing transitology: lessons from post-communism. *Lithuanian Annual Strategic Review*. pp. 181–199.

Joffe, George (2009). Political dynamics in North Africa. *International Affairs*. 85(5), pp. 931–949.

Kaldor, Mary (2003). *Global civil society: an answer to war*. Cambridge: Polity Press.

Karam, Patricia (2014). With passage of constitution, Tunisian civil society brings about progress in resource governance. *National Resource Governance Institute*. Available at www.resourcegovernance.org/news/blog/passage-constitution-tunisian-civil-society-brings-about-progress-resource-governance [Accessed 16 November 2015].

Karl, Terry Lynn (1990). Dilemmas of democratisation in Latin America. *Comparative Politics*. 23(1), pp. 1–21.

Keane, John (1988). *Democracy and civil society*. London: Verso.

180 Bibliography

Kedourie, Ellie (1994). *Democracy and Arab political culture.* Abingdon: Routledge.
Keskes, Hanèn (2012). Constituent Assembly members vote in favor of transparency. *Tunisia Live.* Available at www.tunisia-live.net/2012/01/07/constituent-assembly-members-vote-in-favor-of-transparency/#sthash.MRFa8k3c.dpuf [Accessed 7 January 2014].
Keskes, Hanèn (2015). Amidst government response to terror, Tunisia's extractives CSOs struggle to maintain gains in voice and transparency. *National Resource Governance Institute.* Available at www.resourcegovernance.org/blog/amidst-government-response-terrortunisias-extractives-csos-struggle-maintain-gains-voice-and [Accessed 21 February 2016].
Khalil, Andrea (2014). *Crowds and politics in North Africa: Tunisia, Algeria and Libya.* Abingdon: Routledge.
Khlifi, Roua (2013). Universities become ideological battlegrounds. *Tunisia Live.* Available at www.tunisia-live.net/2013/03/11/tunisian-universities-become-literal-and-ideological-battlegrounds/ [Accessed 12 January 2014].
Kilbride, Erin (2016). Tunisia authorizes first LGBT group. *Oximity.* Available at www.oximity.com/article/Tunisia-Authorizes-First-LGBT-Group-Ho-1 [Accessed 19 February 2016].
Krichen, Aziz (1992). *Le syndrome Bourguiba.* Tunis: Cérès Productions.
Kushner, David (2014). The masked avengers. *New Yorker.* Available at www.newyorker.com/magazine/2014/09/08/masked-avengers [Accessed 27 November 2014].
La Presse (2008) Marche populaire de soutien au Président Ben Ali à Gafsa (republished on All Africa). Available at http://fr.allafrica.com/stories/200804110902.html [Accessed 4 June 2014].
Labidi, Kamel (2006). Tunisia: independent but not free. *LeMondeDiplomatique.* Available at https://mondediplo.com/2006/03/04tunisia [Accessed 14 October 2015].
Le Centre pour le Contrôle Démocratique des Forces Armées (DCAF) (2014). Décret-loi n° 2011–6 du 18 Février 2011 portant création de l'instance supérieure pour la réalisation des objectifs de la révolution, de la réforme politique et de la transition démocratique. La législation du secteur de la sécurité en Tunisie. Available at https://legislation-securite.tn/fr/node/43391 [Accessed 15 March 2015].
Lewis, Bernard (1990). The roots of Muslim rage. *Atlantic.* 226(3), pp. 47–60.
Lewis, Bernard (2003). *The crisis of Islam: holy war and unholy terror.* London: Weidenfeld & Nicolson.
Lewis, Charlton Thomas (1879). *A Latin dictionary: founded on Andrew's edition of Freund's Latin dictionary.* Oxford: Clarendon Press.
Lewis, David and Wallace, Tina (2000). *New roles and relevance: development NGOs and the challenge of change.* West Hartford, CT: Kumarian Press.
Lichterman, Paul (2005). Risking inconvenience. States and Societies: Newsletter of the Political Sociology Section of the ASA.
Linz, Juan J. and Stepan, Alfred (1996a). *Problems of democratic transition and consolidation: Southern Europe, South America, and post-communist Europe.* Baltimore, MD: Johns Hopkins University Press.
Linz, Juan J. and Stepan, Alfred (1996b). Toward consolidated democracies. *Journal of Democracy.* 7(2), pp. 14–33.
Lipset, Seymour Martin (1959). Some social requisites of democracy: economic development and political legitimacy. *American Political Science Review.* 53(1), pp. 69–105.
Lipset, Seymour Martin (1994). The social requisites of democracy revisited: 1993 presidential address. *American Sociological Review.* 59(1) pp. 1–22.
Locke, John (1963). *The works of John Locke.* Darmstadt, Germany: Scientia Verlag.

Ltifi, Adel (2014). The Tunisian elections 2014 and societal polarization. *Arab Reform Initiative: Policy Alternatives.* Available at www.arab-reform.net/sites/default/files/Ltifi_Tunisia-Elections-Societal-Polarization.pdf [Accessed 6 March 2015].

Lutterbeck, Derek (2013). Tunisia after Ben Ali: retooling the tools of oppression? Norwegian Peacebuilding Resource Centre. Policy Brief May 2013. Available at www.files.ethz.ch/isn/164193/8a4a01231edc1bc44e19af1182314d46.pdf [Accessed 18 May 2015].

Lynch, Marc (2011). Watching Egypt (but not al-Jazeera) foreign policy. Available at http://foreignpolicy.com/2011/01/25/watching-egypt-but-not-on-al-jazeera/ [Accessed 6 March 2015].

McLaverty, Peter (2002). Civil society and democracy. *Contemporary Politics.* 8(4), pp. 303–318.

McSweeney, Brendan (2002). Hofstede's model of national cultural differences and their consequences: a triumph of faith – a failure of analysis. *Human Relations.* 55(1), pp. 89–118.

Mamelouk, Douja (2012). Scandalous flag incident at Mannouba University: a wake-up call. *Tunisia Live.* Available at www.tunisia-live.net/2012/03/11/scandalous-flag-incident-at-mannouba-university-a-wake-up-call/#sthash.OuXmmrs9.dpuf [Accessed 6 December 2015].

Marouki, Manoubi (1990). Les huit propositions de l'opposition. *Réalités*, 1560.

Martin, Alexander Peter (2014). Islamist party lost Tunisia elections, but it has won the country's trust. *Conversation.* Available at https://theconversation.com/islamist-party-lost-tunisia-elections-but-it-has-won-the-countrys-trust-33697 [Accessed 22 June 2015].

Martin, Alexander Peter (2015). Do Tunisian secular civil society organisations demonstrate a process of democratic learning? *Journal of North African Studies.* 20(5), pp. 797–812.

Martínez-Fuentes, Guadalupe (2010). Divisive electoral policies within authoritarian elections: the Tunisian casuistry (1989–2009). *Journal of North African Studies.* 15(4), pp. 521–534.

Marzouk, Zeineb (2015). Mokhtar Yahyaoui: a tribute to a defender of human rights. *Tunisia Live.* Available at www.tunisia-live.net/2015/09/23/mokhtar-yahyaoui-death/#sthash.XYByfITC.dpuf [Accessed 13 December 2015].

Merone, Fabio and Cavatorta, Francesco (2013). The rise of Salafism and the future of democratisation. In *The making of the Tunisian revolution: context, architects, prospects* ed. Nouri Gana. Edinburgh: Edinburgh University Press, pp. 252–269.

Micaud, Charles A. (1974). Bilingualism in North Africa: cultural and socio-political implications. *Western Political Quarterly.* 27(1) pp. 92–103.

Middle East Online (2012, 8 March). Salafis tear down Tunisia flag: Ennahda blames university dean. Available at www.middle-east-online.com/english/?id=51101 [Accessed 23 October 2013].

Mill, John Stuart (1859). *On liberty.* London: Parker & Son.

Moalla, Asma (2004). *The regency of Tunisia and the Ottoman Porte 1777–1814.* Abingdon: Routledge.

Moore, Clement Henry (1988). Tunisia and Bourguibisme: twenty years of crisis. *Third World Quarterly.* 10(1), pp. 176–190.

Moshiri, Nazanine (2011). Post-uprising Tunisia still struggling. *Al Jazeera.* Available at www.aljazeera.com/video/africa/2011/02/201122564026103476.html [Accessed 7 May 2013].

Murphy, Emma C. (1997). Ten years on: Ben Ali's Tunisia. *Mediterranean Politics.* 2(3), pp. 114–122.

Murphy, Emma C. (1999). *Economic and political change in Tunisia.* Basingstoke: Macmillan.

182 Bibliography

Murphy, Emma C. (2001). The state and the private sector in North Africa: seeking specificity. *Mediterranean Politics*. 6(2), pp. 1–28.

Murphy, Emma C. (2006). The Tunisian mise à niveau programme and the political economy of reform. *New Political Economy*. 11(4), pp. 519–540.

Murphy, Emma C. (2013). The Tunisian elections of October 2011: a democratic consensus. *Journal of North African Studies*. 18(2), pp. 231–247.

National Democratic Institute (2011, 24 October). Project de déclaration préliminaire de NDI sur les élections en Tunisie. *La mission internationale d'observation des élections en Tunisie*. Available at www.ndi.org/sites/default/files/Tunisia%20NCA%20Election%20 Preliminary%20Report%20October%202011%20French.pdf. [Accessed 17 April 2015]

National Democratic Institute (2014). Final report on the 2014 legislative and presidential elections in Tunisia. Available at www.ndi.org/sites/default/files/Tunisia%20 Election%20Report%202014_EN_SOFT%20%281%29.pdf [Accessed 17 April 2015].

Nawaat (2009). Tunisia: behind Tunisia's 'economic miracle': inequality and criminalization of protest. Available at http://nawaat.org/portail/2009/06/18/tunisia-behind-tunisias-economic-miracle-inequality-and-criminalization-of-protest/ [Accessed 12 May 2013].

Newton, Kenneth (2001). Trust, social capital, civil society, and democracy. *International Political Science Review*. 22(2), pp. 201–214.

Norris, Pippa (2012). The impact of social media on the Arab uprisings: the Facebook, Twitter, and YouTube revolutions? Paper presented at Advancing Comparative Political Communication Research: New Frameworks, Designs and Data, European Consortium Joint Workshops, Antwerp, Belgium, April.

Norton, Augustus R. (1995). *Civil society in the Middle East*. Leiden: E.J. Brill.

Nouira, Asma (2011). Obstacles on the path of Tunisia's democratic transformation. *Carnegie Endowment for International Peace*. Available at http://carnegieendowment.org/sada/?fa=43347 [Accessed 15 September 2014].

O'Donnell, Guillermo (1973). *Modernisation and bureaucratic authoritarianism: studies in South American politics*. Berkeley, CA: University of California Press.

O'Donnell, Guillermo (1988). *Bureaucratic-authoritarianism: Argentina in comparative perspective*. Berkeley, CA: University of California Press.

O'Donnell, Guillermo and Schmitter, Philippe (1986). *Transitions from authoritarian rule: tentative conclusions about uncertain democracies*. Baltimore, MD: Johns Hopkins University Press.

Omri, Mohamed-Salah (2013, 11 January). Enshrining idealism: Tunisia's long romance. *Al Jazeera*. Available at www.aljazeera.com/indepth/opinion/2013/01/2013181022963 6675.html [Accessed 9 March 2013].

Paciello, Maria Cristina (2011). Tunisia: changes and challenges of political transition. *MEDPRO Technical Papers, 3*. Available at www.medpro-foresight.eu/system/files/ MEDPRO%20TR%20No%203%20WP2%20Paciello%20on%20Tunisia.pdf. [Accessed 18 May 2012]

Paine, Thomas (1969). *The rights of man*. Harmondsworth: Penguin.

Patai, Raphael (1973). *The Arab mind*. New York: Scribner's.

Perez-Diaz, Victor (1998). The public sphere and a European civil society. In *Real civil societies: dilemmas of institutionalization*, ed. Jeffrey C. Alexander. London: Sage, pp. 211–238.

Perkins, Kenneth (1997). *Historical dictionary of Tunisia*. 2nd edition. London: Scarecrow Press.

Perkins, Kenneth (2014). *A history of modern Tunisia*. Cambridge: Cambridge University Press.

Bibliography

Petkanas, Zoe (2013). From visible to invisible: Tunisia's gendered democracy paradox. *Centre of Governance and Human Rights*. Working Paper #3. Available at www.repository.cam.ac.uk/bitstream/handle/1810/245113/CGHR_WP_3_2013_Petkanas(rev.).pdf?sequence=4 [Accessed 2 May 2015].

Pew Global (2012). Most Muslims want democracy, personal freedoms, and Islam in political life: few believe U.S. backs democracy. Available at www.pewglobal.org/2012/07/10/most-muslims-want-democracy-personal-freedoms-and-islam-in-political-life/ [Accessed 13 December 2013].

Pew Global (2014). Tunisian confidence in democracy wanes. Available at www.pewresearch.org/global/2014/10/15/tunisian-confidence-in-democracy-wanes/ [Accessed 20 February 2015].

Pickard, Duncan (2015). Al-Nahda: moderation and compromise in Tunisia's constitutional bargain. In *Political and constitutional transitions in North Africa: actors and factors*, eds Justin O. Frosini and Francesco Biagi. New York: Routledge, pp. 4–32.

Piot, Oliver (2011). De l'indignation à la revolution. *Le Monde Diplomatique*. Available at www.monde-diplomatique.fr/2011/02/PIOT/20114 [Accessed 6 September 2012].

Pratt, Nicola (2007). *Democracy and authoritarianism in the Arab world*. Boulder, CO: Lynne Rienner.

Pryce-Jones, David (1989). *The closed circle: an interpretation of the Arabs*. New York: Harper & Row.

Putnam, Robert (1993). *Making democracy work: civic traditions in modern Italy*. Princeton, NJ: Princeton University Press.

Pye, Lucian W. and Verba, Sidney (1965). *Political culture and political development*. Princeton, NJ: Princeton University Press.

Ransome, Paul (1992). *Antonio Gramsci: a new introduction*. Hemel Hempstead: Harvester Wheatsheaf.

Reuters (2011, 23 January). Talks under way for body to oversee Tunisia cabinet. Available at http://af.reuters.com/article/idAFTRE70I4P820110124?sp=true [Accessed 13 March 2015].

Reuters (2013, 23 October). Thousands protest before Tunisia crisis talks. Available at http://uk.reuters.com/article/2013/10/23/uk-tunisia-crisis-idUKBRE99M0ML20131023 [Accessed 25 March 2015].

Reuters (2014). Tunisian secular leader Essebsi sworn in as new president. Available at www.reuters.com/article/us-tunisia-politics/tunisian-secular-leader-essebsi-sworn-in-as-new-president-idUSKBN0K90MK20141231 [Accessed 3 March 2015].

Révolution: Journal marxiste (2008). La révolte du bassin minier de Gafsa, en Tunisie Article. Available at www.marxiste.org/international/afrique/tunisie/118-la-revolte-du-bassin-minier-de-gafsa-en-tunisie [Accessed 28 January 2016].

Rifai, Ryan (2011). Timeline: Tunisia's uprising. *Al-Jazeera*. Available at www.aljazeera.com/indepth/spotlight/tunisia/2011/01/201114142223827361.html [Accessed 10 June 2013].

Rishmawi, Mervat (2007). Overview of civil society in the Arab world. *Praxis Paper No. 20*. October. Available at www.intrac.org/data/files/resources/421/Praxis-Paper-20-Overview-of-Civil-Society-in-the-Arab-World.pdf [Accessed 13 July 2013].

Romdhani, Oussama (2014). The Jomaa factor in Tunisia's transition. *Al-Arabiya*. Available at http://english.alarabiya.net/en/views/news/africa/2014/02/11/The-Jomaa-factor-in-Tunisia-s-transition.html [Accessed 20 June 2015].

Rousseau, Jean-Jacques (1998). *The social contract*. Ware: Wordsworth Editions.

184   Bibliography

Roy, Olivier (2012). The transformation of the Arab world. *Journal of Democracy*. 23(3), pp. 5–18.

Rustow, Dankwart A. (1970). Transitions to democracy: toward a dynamic model. *Comparative Politics*. 2(3), pp. 337–363.

Ryan, Yasmine (2010). Another Tunisian protester dies. *Al-Jazeera*. Available at www.aljazeera.com/news/africa/2010/12/201012317536678834.html [Accessed 13 November 2012].

Ryan, Yasmine (2013a). Sniper mystery in Kasserine, the town 'which made Tunisia's revolution'. *Al-Jazeera*. Available at www.thenational.ae/world/middle-east/sniper-mystery-in-kasserine-the-town-which-made-tunisias-revolution [Accessed 11 June 2013].

Ryan, Yasmine (2013b, 20 August). Showdown for Tunisia's fledgling democracy. *Al Jazeera*. Available at www.aljazeera.com/indepth/features/2013/08/201381910165618995.html [Accessed 17 February 2015].

Ryan, Yasmine (2013c, 19 September). Tunisia union says violence is not the answer. *Al Jazeera*. Available at www.aljazeera.com/blogs/africa/2013/08/90781.html [Accessed 2 March 2015].

Sadiki, Larbi (2002). The search for citizenship in Bin Ali's Tunisia: democracy versus unity. *Political Studies*. 50(3), pp. 497–513.

Sadiki, Larbi (2008). Engendering citizenship in Tunisia: prioritising unity over democracy. In *North Africa: politics, region, and the limits of transformation*, eds Yahia H. Zoubir and Haizam Amirah-Fernandez. Abingdon: Routledge, pp. 109–132.

Sadiki, Larbi (2012). Tunisia's illusive concord: A year on from the October 23 elections. *Al Jazeera*. 23 October. Available at www.aljazeera.com/indepth/opinion/2012/10/20121022123255545844.html [Accessed 8 June 2015].

Sadiki, Larbi (2014, 27 January). Tunisia's constitution: A success story? *Al Jazeera*. Available at www.aljazeera.com/indepth/opinion/2014/01/tunisia-constitution-success-s-2014121122929203231.html [Accessed 25 March 2015].

Sadiki, Larbi (2015). Discoursing 'democratic knowledge' & knowledge production in North Africa. *Journal of North African Studies*. 20(5), pp. 688–690.

Said, Edward W. (1978). *Orientalism*. New York: Pantheon.

Salamé, Ghassan (ed.) (1994). *Democracy without democrats: the renewal of politics in the Muslim world*. London: I.B. Tauris.

Samti, Farah (2015). More freedom, more problem. *Foreign Policy*. Available at http://foreignpolicy.com/2015/05/01/more-freedom-more-problems/ [Accessed 11 February 2016].

Schlumberger, Albrecht (2004). Waiting for Godot: regime change without democratization in the Middle East. *International Political Science Review*. 25(4), pp. 371–392.

Scholte, Jan Aart (2002). Civil society and democracy in global governance. *Global Governance*. 8(3), pp. 281–304.

Seligman, Adam B. (1992). *The idea of civil society*. Princeton, NJ: Princeton University Press.

Simon, Roger (1982). *Gramsci's political thought: an introduction*. London: Lawrence & Wishart Ltd.

Sonneveld, Nadia (2015). Introduction: Shari'a in revolution? A comparative overview of pre- and post-revolutionary developments in Shari'a-based family law legislation in Egypt, Indonesia, Iran, and Tunisia. *New Middle Eastern Studies*. 5. Available at www.brismes.ac.uk/nmes/archives/1407 [Accessed 22 May 2015].

Soudan, Francois and Gharbi, Samir (1991). Les Islamists, victimes de la guerre. *Jeune Afrique*. 1578, pp. 48–50.

Stepan, Alfred (2012). Tunisia's transition and the twin tolerations. *Journal of Democracy.* 23(2), pp. 89–103.
Stillman, Peter G. (1980). Hegel's civil society: a locus of freedom. *Polity.* 12(4), pp. 622–646.
Tan, Sor-Hoon and Whalen-Bridge, John (2008). *Democracy as culture: Deweyan pragmatism in a globalizing world.* New York: State University of New York Press.
Tarfa, Inel (2016). The denial of racism: activists call for action on Tunisia's unspoken problem. *Tunisia Live.* Available at www.tunisia-live.net/2016/03/23/the-denial-of-racism-activists-call-for-action-on-tunisias-unspoken-problem/ [Accessed 22 February 2016].
Tocqueville, Alexis de (2003). *Democracy in America: and two essays on America*, trans. Gerald E. Bevan. London: Penguin Books. V.
Torelli, Sefano M. (2012). Al-Nahda's success in Tunisia: a new model of Islamic governance? Conference Paper, Italian Association for African Studies (ASAI).
Torelli, Stefano M., Merone, Fabio, and Cavatorta, Francesco (2012). Salafism in Tunisia: challenges and opportunities for democratization. *Middle East Policy.* 18(4), pp. 140–158.
Touati, Zeineb and Zlitni, Sami (2014). Social networks and women's rights activism in post-revolutionary Tunisia. In *Arab Spring and Arab women: challenges and opportunities*, ed. Muhamad Olimat. Abingdon: Routledge, pp. 162–175.
Tounsi, Bayram (2015). Shams members deserve the same rights and respect as all Tunisians. *Tunisia Live.* Available at www.tunisia-live.net/2015/12/11/opinion-shams-members-deserve-the-same-rights-and-respect-as-all-tunisians/ [Accessed 13 December 2015].
Turner, Bryan S. (1994). *Orientalism, postmodernism, and globalisation.* London: Routledge.
Vatikiotis, Panayiotis J. (1987). *Islam and the state.* London: Croom Helm.
Volpi, Frédéric (2011). Framing civility in the Middle East: alternative perspectives on the state and civil society. *Third World Quarterly.* 32(5), pp. 827–843.
Von Grunebaum, Gustave Edmund (1962). *Modern Islam: the search for cultural identity.* Berkeley, CA: University of California Press.
Voorhoeve, Maaike (2012). Judicial discretion in Tunisian personal status law. In *Family law in Islam: divorce, marriage and women in the Muslim world*, eds Maaike Voorhoeve. London: I.B. Tauris, pp. 199–230.
Waltz, Susan (1995). *Human rights and reform: changing the face of North African politics.* Berkeley, CA: University of California Press.
Walzer, Michael (1998). The idea of civil society: a path to social reconstruction. In *Community works: the revival of civil society in America*, ed. E.J. Dionne. Washington, DC: Brookings Institution Press, pp. 123–143.
Warren, Mark E. (2004). What does corruption mean in a democracy? *American Journal of Political Science.* 48(2), pp. 328–343.
Welch, Stephen (1993). *The concept of political culture.* New York: St. Martin's Press.
Welch, Stephen (2013). *The theory of political culture.* Oxford: Oxford University Press.
White, Stephen (1979). *Political culture and Soviet politics.* London: Macmillan.
Wiktorowicz, Quintan (2000). Civil society as social control: state power in Jordan. *Comparative Politics.* 33(1), pp. 43–61.
Wolf, Anne (2013). An Islamist 'renaissance'? Religion and politics in post-revolutionary Tunisia. *Journal of North African Studies.* 18(4), pp. 560–573.
Wolfsfeld, Gadi, Segev, Elad, and Sheafer, Tamir (2013). Social media and the Arab Spring: politics comes first. *International Journal of Press/Politics.* 18(2), pp. 115–137.

Wood, Pia Christian (2002). French foreign policy and Tunisia: do human rights matter? *Middle East Policy*. 9(2). Available at www.mepc.org/journal/middle-east-policy-archives/french-foreign-policy-and-tunisia-do-human-rights-matter http://othersociologist.com/2012/02/11/egypt-revolution/ [Accessed 27 April 2013].

World Bank (2014). The unfinished revolution bringing opportunity, good jobs and greater wealth to all Tunisians. Development Policy Review, Report No. 86179-TN.

World Values Survey Association (2014) World values survey wave 6 (2010–2014) official aggregate v.20150418. Available at www.worldvaluessurvey.org/WVSDocumentation WV6.jsp [Accessed 13 November 2014].

Yahyaoui, Mukhtar (2001). Open letter to President Ben Ali. *Human Rights First*. Available at www.humanrightsfirst.org/wp-content/uploads/pdf/open_letter.pdf [Accessed 13 December 2015].

Zabas, Hanen (2012). Islamists, leftists clash at Tunisian universities. *Al Monitor*. Available at www.al-monitor.com/pulse/politics/2012/10/tunisia-universities-turn-to-battleground-as-islamists-leftists-clash.html#ixzz2P2Oszijc [Accessed 6 November 2014].

Ziadeh, Nicola A. (1962). *Origins of nationalism in Tunisia*. Beirut: Librairie du Liban.

Zogby Research Services (2013). Tunisia: divided and dissatisfied with Ennahda. Available at https://b.3cdn.net/aai/b8cc8e61b78158d847_8pm6b1oog.pdf [Accessed 11 November 2014].

Index

Page numbers in **bold** denote tables, those in *italics* denote figures.

Abaza, Mona 123
accountability 13, 14, 16, 21, 109
Al Bawsala 63–4, 101–2, 108–9, 113–14, 131
Al Jazeera 54
Alexander, Christopher 40–1
Almond, Gabriel 19, 21, 26, 96;
  The Civic Culture 20, 120–1
Anderson, Lisa 29, 46, 120
Anheier, Helmut K. 9, 14
Arab culture 4, 22–3
Aristotle 8
assassinations 69–70
Associo-Med 95–6
ATFD *see* Tunisian Association of Democratic Women (ATFD)
authoritarianism 1–2, 7, 12, 15, 16, 24, 43, 48, 146
Ayubi, Nazih N. 19

behaviour 3, 20, 23, 26, 59, 93, 120, 134, 145
Ben Ali, Zine El-Abidine 1, 7, 29, 37, 38, 39, 143, 146; downfall of 51–3; false liberalisation 37–9, 44; and human rights 42–4; and Islamists 40–2; superficial stability 48–9
Ben Jaafar, Mustafa 55
Ben Mhenni, Lina 54
Berman, Sheri 13, 15
Bouazizi, Mohamed 51
Bourguiba, Habib 32–4, 36, 37–8, 48, 143
Brazil 16–17
Bryman, Alan 120
Bunbongkarn, Suchit 17
Bus Citoyen project 103

Carothers, Thomas 12–13, 15
Cavatorta, Francesco 66, 67

censorship 20, 44, 50, 67, 142
Chekir, Hafedh 74
citizenship 16, 33, 35, 40, 75, 122, 123
civil political culture (CPC) 1–2, 59, 66, 143–4; and civil society 2–3, 25–7, *26*; six criteria of 4, 5, 20–1, 25, 88, 97, 140, 142, 144, 145
civil society 7–27; addressing social problems 149–51; and civil political culture (CPC) 2–3, 25–7, *26*; and civility 21–2; definition of 8–9; and democracy learning 16–19; and democratic transition 11–15; differing conceptions of 95–6; liberal-associative approach 10, 44, 46, 117, 118, 137, 141, 143, 145; and liberalisation 37–9; National Pact, effects of 39–40; ongoing challenges 148–9; oppositional-resistance role 10, 29, 30, 44, 45, 46, 49, 74, 108, 118, 140–1, 143, 148; relationship with democracy 9–10; role of civil society in democratic transition 15–16
civil society activism: from 1574–2101 28–47; Ben Ali's superficial stability 48–9; civil society before the revolution 44; coalition government 73–4; constitution drafting process and 2011—2014 interregnum period 62–4; European colonialism and the struggle for independence 29–31; human rights and Western support 42–4; by lawyers 53–6; National Pact and the destruction of Islamists 37–9; National Pact and the removal of Islamist political challenge 39–42; nationalist regime in the post-independence era 33–6; Neo-Destour Party (NDP), rise of 31–3;

civil society activism *continued*
  new legal framework for civil society 59–60; opposition political parties 55–6; Ottoman semi-autonomous rule 28–9; political deadlock 69–71; post-Ben Ali era 56–9; religious–secular polarisation 64–9; revolution, events of 51–2, 75; revolution, roots of 49–51; from revolution to transition 48–76; state institutions, role in early transition 60–1; strikes and Ben Ali's departure 52–3; technocratic government and the new constitution 71–3
civil society organisations (CSOs) 1–3, 8, 14–15, 37, 40–1, 44, 46, 48, 142; analysis of attitudes survey results 82–8, 90–1, **152–64**, 164–5; attitudes survey 77–92; completed leader interviews, details of **167–72**; CSO leader interviews 93–119; decision-making processes and democratic practices 107–8, 144–5; and democracy 114–17, 117–18, **160**; demographics 82; equality 82, 84, 106–10, 110–12, **154–6**; executive bureaux 106–7; financial transparency 87, 90–1, **160–1**; freedom 84, 90, 104–6, **156–8**; funding 109–10; independence and effectiveness 112–17; isomorphism 108, 110; language used in the members' survey 78–9; leader interview questions 165–6; leader interview results and findings 97–117; legal status of 59; management style 108–9; members' survey overview 77–8; methodological limitations of the members' survey 88–9; methodology for interviews with leaders 95–7, 118; organisation **161–3**; overview of leader interviews 93–5; pluralism 84–5, **85**, 106–10, 112–17, **158–9**; political culture 108; potential further research 146–7; power relations 107; results of the members' survey 79–82, **79**, **80**, **81**, *81*; role in democratic transition 15–16, 63, 75, 140; tolerance 82, **83**, **154**; tolerance through trust and transparency 97–104, 117, 145; training 109, 116–17; trust 85–6, **86**, **159**; women and racism 110–12; *see also* ethnographic observation and CSOs
Collier, Ruth B. 16
colonialism 29–31, 45
Confédération Générale des Travailleurs Tunisiens (CGTT) 31

constitution 56–7, 58, 61, 78–9, 110–11; drafting process 62–4, 71; and Islam 65
Constitutional Democratic Rally (RCD) 56–8, 60, 74, 84, 146
corruption 21, 43–4, 49, 62, 146
Crapanzano, Vincent 126, 134
culturalism 23–4, 25

Dahl, Robert A. 12
Deane, Shelley 52, 74
Decree-Law 88 (2011) 59, 62, 75, 87, 95, 102, 105, 106, 110, 112, 143, 144, 149, 150
democracy and democratisation 1, 2, 141; civil society and democratic transition 11–16; consolidated democracy 17–18; and CSOs 114–17, 117–18, 133–4, 137–8, **160**; democracy learning and civil society 16–19; democratic transition, criteria of 61–2; political culture of democracy 19–21; relationship with civil society 9–10; stages of transition 15; and tolerance 97–9
despotism 4, 9, 10
Destour party 31–3, 34
Destourna 98
Diamond, Larry 11, 15, 16, 19, 21, 141
Diwan, Ishac 54
Donker, Teije Hidde 94
Doorenspleet, Renske 12

Eckstein, Harry 26
education 14–15, 30, 35, 68, 78; system 116, 135; for voting 127
Ekiert, Grzegorz 17
elections 41, 56, 58–9, 61–2, 73–4
Entelis, John 11, 15
equality 20, 35, 82, 84, **154–6**; identified in democratic practices, learning processes and institutional culture 106–10; limitations of, in CSOs 110–12
ethnographic observation and CSOs 120–39; case study: *Jeunes Indépendants Démocrates* (JID) 121–3; conducting a participant-observation 124–5; decision-making processes 131–2; expansion and restructuring 129; fieldwork ethics 123–4; internal elections and transition 127–9; interpretation of results 132–7; JID charter 129–31; leadership 136–7, 145–6; meetings, efficiency of 135; observation, reasons for 120–3; one-to-one interviews with JID

members 125–6; professionalisation 134–6; projects 126–7; results and findings 126–37; training 133–4; *see also* civil society organisations (CSOs)

Facebook 50, 107
Foundation for the Future (FFF) 63
freedom 4, 20, 35, 40, 49, 50, 51–2, 59, 62, 64, 69, 75, 81, 84, 90, **156–8**; of information 43, 62; legally established freedom 104–6
"Freedom and Dignity" revolution 1, 7
Friedman, Elizabeth Jay 16
Friends of the Mining Basin 131

Gafsa Phosphate Company (CPG) 49–50
Geertz, Clifford 120, 126
Gellner, Ernst 9
gender equality 61, 65, 110–11, 128
General Union of Tunisian Workers (UGTT) 24, 32, 34–5, 36, 37, 40–1, 44, 45, 50, 51, 56, 71, 93, 111, 132, 143; organisation of strikes 52–3
Ghannouchi, Rashid 36, 56–7, 67
Gobe, Eric 53
Gode, Robert 49
Goldfarb, Jeffery 124
Gramsci, Antonio 10, 21
Grey Zone 12–13, 18, 62
Gudžinskas, Liutauras 18

Hall, John 9
Halouani, Rafik 101, 117
Hammami, Hamma 55–6
Hawthorne, Amy 45
Held, David 8
Henry, Clement 33, 34–5
Hibou, Béatrice 44, 48, 60
Higher Authority for the Realization of Revolutionary Objects, Political Reform and the Democratic Transition 58
Hizb Ennahda (Renaissance Party) 39, 41, 58, 61, 64–5, 66–7, 69–70, 71, 75, 94–5, 98; and women's rights 111; *see also Mouvement de La Tendance Islamique* (MTI)
Hochstetler, Kathryn 16
Hofstede, Geert 25
homophobia 133–4, 147
homosexuality 133–4, 147, 149–50
Hudson, Michael C. 25–6, 96, 120, 142
human rights 42–4, 46, 49, 59–60, 62, 84, 112, 133
Human Rights Watch 59–60

I-Lead 110
I-Watch 101, 112–13, 118
identity 22, 33, 36, 45, 65–6, 67, 68, 74
Inara 110
Independent High Commission for Elections (ISIE) 58–9, 61, 73
information technologies 43
ISIS 149
Islam 22, 32, 35, 36, 46, 48, 94–5; National Pact and the destruction of Islamists 37–9; *niqab* 68; as a part of the constitution 65–6; social expression of 66; and tolerance 97–9, 103–4
isomorphism 108, 110

Jamal, Amaney 105
Jankauskas, Algimantas 18
Jasmine Foundation 96–7
Jeunes Indépendants Démocrates (JID) *see* ethnographic observation and CSOs
Joffe, George 28
Jomaa, Mehdi 72
Jribi, Maya 55

Karl, Terry Lynn 12
Keane, John 9, 15
Kedourie, Ellie 22
Kolna Tounes 98–9
Kubik, Jan 17

La Presse (newspaper) 50
Law 52, 149
Law of Associations 42, 105; *see also* Decree-Law 88 (2011)
Le Parti socialiste destourien (PSD) 36, 37
Le Tunisien 30
Leagues for the Protection of the Tunisian Revolution (LPR) 68, 72, 94–5, 105, 144
legitimacy 14, 16, 30, 37, 54, 59, 62
liberalisation 12, 36, 37–9, 44, 47, 48, 54
Linz, Juan J. 17–18, 61–2, 141
Lipset, Seymour Martin 12
Locke, John 10
LTDH *see* Tunisian League for Human Rights (LTDH)
Ltifi, Adel 74
Lynch, Marc 54

McLaverty, Peter 9, 15
McSweeney, Brendan 25–6
Mahoney, James 16
Mamelouk, Douja 68

Marzouki, Moncef 55
Merone, Fabio 66, 67
Mhadhbi, Mohsen 115
Mill, J.S. 13, 21
Mnemty 112, 130, 150–1
Mouvement de La Tendance Islamique (MTI) 36, 38, 39; *see also Hizb Ennahda* (Renaissance Party)
Murphy, Emma C. 29, 59

National Action Plans 72
National Democratic Institute 73
national organisations (NOs) 34–5
National Pact: and the destruction of Islamists 37–9; and the removal of Islamist political challenge 39–42
National Solidarity Fund 43
nationalism 29, 33–6, 38, 45, 46
Neo-Destour Party (NDP) 31–3, 34
Newton, Kenneth 13
Nidaa Tounes 73
non-violence 20, 67
Norris, Pippa 54–5

O'Donnell, Guillermo 12, 16
Open Government Partnership (OGP) initiative 72
OpenGovTN 62–3, 94, 116
opinion polls 72
Ordre National des Avocats (ONAT) 53–6
orientalism 23, 24

Paciello, Maria Cristina 58
Perez-Diaz, Victor 9
Perkins, Kenneth 29
Persepolis (film) 67
Personal Status Code 36
Philippines 17
Pickard, Duncan 71
pluralism 20–1, 24, 35, 37, 38, 46, 62, 64, 66, 75, 84–5, **85**, 130, 131, 150, **158–9**; identified in democratic practices, learning processes and institutional culture 106–10; independence and effectiveness of CSOs 112–17
police 50–1, 54, 58
political culture 59; in CSOs 108; definition of 19; of democracy 19–21; as discourse and practice 141–2; dualistic conceptualisation of 22; and historical experience 45–6; studies conducted in the Middle East and North Africa (MENA) region 22–5; theory of 3, 7

privatisation 29, 43–4
Pryce-Jones, David 22
Putnam, Robert 11, 15, 16, 85

Quartet 70, 71, 93, 148

racism 112, 150–1
RCD *see* Constitutional Democratic Rally (RCD)
religion 2, 22, 35, 36, 41, 46, 65, 94–5; and the CSO members' survey 88–9; Islam as a part of the constitution 65–6; National Pact and the destruction of Islamists 37–9; *niqab* 68; religious–secular polarisation of civil society 64–9; Salafism 66–7, 105; social expression of Islam 66; tolerance and Islam 97–9, 103–4; twin tolerations relationship with politics 65–6
research 22; argument summary 2; historical summary 142–4; interpretivist method 23–4, 26; methodological summary 141–2; methodology 3, 25–7, *26*; positivist approach to 23, 26; potential further research 146–7; questions and aims 1–2; structuralist approach 24; theoretical summary 140–1
revolution: events of 51–2; roots of 49–51
Rousseau, Jean-Jacques 20
Roy, Olivier 86
rule of law 9, 17
Rustow, Dankwart A. 11–12

Sadiki, Larbi 18–19, 33, 46, 64, 71, 132–3
Said, Edward W. 24, 120; *Orientalism* 23, 120
Salafism 66–7, 68, 69, 105
Salamé, Ghassan 46
Sawty 102, 108, 109, 131
Schmitter, Philippe 12, 16
Scholte, Jan Aart 8–9, 13, 14–15, 21
secularism 32, 40, 44, 46, 97; religious–secular polarisation of civil society 64–9
security issues 148–9
Seligman, Adam B. 9
Shams 150
social media 50, 54–5, 107
South Korea 17
state-building 18, 45, 75
state institutions 15, 45, 60–1, 143
Stepan, Alfred 17–18, 29, 61–2, 65, 141

terrorism 43, 149
Thailand 17

Tocqueville, Alexis de 10, 11, 13, 15, 16, 21, 96, 116–17; *Democracy in America* 20
tolerance 21, 50, 64, 68, **154**; CSO members' survey 82, **83**; tolerance through trust and transparency 97–104, 117, 145; twin tolerations relationship between religion and politics 65–6
transitional justice 62, 63
transitology 11–12, 15, 18, 56
transparency 21, 43, 63, 87, 90–1, 138, **160–1**; tolerance through trust and transparency 97–104, 117, 145
trust 21, 50, 85–6, **86**, **159**; tolerance through trust and transparency 97–104, 117, 145
Tunisia, map 6
Tunisian Association of Democratic Women (ATFD) 39
Tunisian Islamic Front (TIF) 67
Tunisian League for Human Rights (LTDH) 37, 38, 39, 40, 42, 50, 111

UGTT *see* General Union of Tunisian Workers (UGTT)
unemployment 49, 51, 54, 148
Union des Tunisiens Indépendants pour la Liberté (UTIL) 103, 114

Union Générale des Étudiants de Tunisie (UGET) 34, 35, 38, 40
Union Générale Tunisienne des Étudiants (UGTE) 38, 40, 41, 42, 68
universities 68

Verba, Sidney 21, 26, 96; *The Civic Culture* 20, 120–1
violence 68; government violence 50–1, 54

Walzer, Michael 8
Welch, Stephen 3, 7, 22, 23, 26, 92, 118, 141
White, Stephen 23, 25–6
Wolfsfeld, Gadi 54
women 35–6, 38–9, 42, 58, 61, 63, 65; and CSOs 106; equality issues 110–12; and tolerance 82, **83**, 103
Wood, Pia 42–3

young people 54, 63, 74; and trust 86, 91; unemployment 49; *see also* ethnographic observation and CSOs
Young Tunisians 29–30

Ziadeh, Nicola A. 31

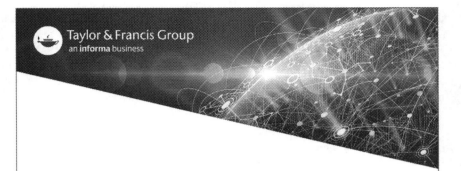